Data Processors' Survival Guide to Accounting

DATA PROCESSORS' SURVIVAL GUIDE TO ACCOUNTING

William E. Perry, CPA

A Ronald Press Publication

JOHN WILEY & SONS

New York • Chichester • Brisbane • Toronto • Singapore

This publication is designed to provide accurate and authoritative information in regard to the subject matter covered. It is sold with the understanding that the publisher is not engaged in rendering legal, accounting, or other professional service. If legal advice or other expert assistance is required, the services of a competent professional person should be sought. *From a Declaration of Principles jointly adopted by a Committee of the American Bar Association and a Committee of Publishers.*

Library of Congress Cataloging in Publication Data:

Perry, William E.
Data processors' survival guide to accounting.

"A Ronald Press publication."
Includes index.
1. Managerial accounting. 2. Electronic data processing departments—Accounting. I. Title.

HF5657.P42 1985 657'.458 84-21024
ISBN 0-471-88178-3

Printed in the United States of America

10 9 8 7 6 5 4 3 2 1

This book is dedicated to the one common language of the world—money—and to the accounting process used to record revenues and expenses

Preface

The world is getting more complex, and the need for specialists is increasing. Even within the data processing function, it now takes a team of individuals to make an application operational. Each group of specialists develops a language of technical jargon which distinguishes that group of specialists from all other specialists.

The ability to communicate diminishes as technology progresses. However, senior management uses a common language to address all aspects of their organization. This common language is accounting, and individuals are not welcomed into the senior management ranks until they have mastered the principles of the language of accounting.

This book is written to assist data processing management in bridging the gap between computer technology and managerial accounting. The book is not designed to teach data processing managers how to become accountants or even how to prepare financial accounting statements. The book is designed to help data processing management survive in a managerial environment in which technological issues must be expressed in accounting concepts.

Accounting as practiced by accountants is a highly structured process that is subject to rigid accounting standards and principles. The accounting described in this book is internal accounting, such as budgets, project justification, and return on investment. To many people, the principles described in this book may be called creative accounting. They are designed to help data processing management present data processing issues in a favorable manner to senior management.

The principles work. Data processing managers who master the practical accounting concepts presented in this book should increase their probability of personal success and at the same time improve the credibility and acceptance of the data processing function.

WILLIAM E. PERRY

Orlando, Florida
January 1985

Contents

Part One

ACCOUNTING— THE COMMON LANGUAGE OF MANAGEMENT

The objective of Part 1 is to explain why the lack of accounting skills has had a negative impact on the credibility of the data processing function and data processing personnel. The chapters explain accounting principles, why they are important, and how to use accounting to create a positive image of the data processing function.

Chapter One

Accounting— It Can Be the Friend or Foe of the Data Processing Manager

As one advances to more lofty positions, the need to converse in the language of accounting increases. Surveys of data processing managers show the need to improve accounting skills. It almost appears that there are two types of managers—those who know accounting and those who don't. The "don't know accounting" types rarely advance, and many fail as managers.

Because of its project nature, data processing has been closely linked to accounting from the early days of computing. Accounting phrases such as chargeout, return on investment, and budget variances are well known in principle to many data processing professionals, but not necessarily well understood. The objective of this book is to help the data processing manager speak "accountingese." This language of management can be used to convert any activity, event, or project into dollar units of measurement.

This chapter is designed to open the door to the world of accounting. The pitfalls and promises of accounting are explored. The chapter concludes with some recommendations designed to put accounting at the service of the data processing manager, and not vice versa.

WHAT IS ACCOUNTING?

In the beginning, there were no accountants. Craftsmen did work, bartered their product with other craftsmen, and all seemed well. However, as the craftsmen became more proficient and their needs and desires expanded, barter did not always work. For example, a diamond merchant might not want 1,000 pairs of shoes.

Evil crept into the world with the introduction of money. The Bible says that money is the root of all evil. With money came the need to store it, loan it, invest it, and tax it. These required records of money to be maintained.

Accounting is the science of maintaining records about money. It is, in fact, an information-gathering and -processing system. The information processed is economic in character; in other words, it involves money.

Accounting primarily involves processing economic transactions. It is, as data processing managers know, a system that gathers information, processes it, maintains files of economic activity, and produces reports about the information processed.

Understanding the accounting process is similar to understanding any automated information processing system. Let's examine the accounting information system as an information system. The components of this system are user and professional requirements, journals, ledgers, chart of accounts, and financial statements.

Accounting Requirements

The requirements for an accounting information system originate from two sources. First, as with any system, are the requirements of the user. In organizations, the comptroller is the primary user of accounting applications. The requirements for accounting systems are normally specified in the accounting procedures written and maintained by the comptroller. Second, the requirements come from a body of practice normally referred to as generally accepted accounting procedures (GAAP). When auditing the accounting process, an organization's public accountant (CPA/CA) must attest to the fact that the financial statements of the organization were processed in accordance with generally accepted accounting procedures. Many of these procedures are discussed in this and the following chapters.

Accounting Journals

Journals are the source transactions for the accounting process. Accountants may refer to a sales journal, which is merely a listing of the sales made by the organization during the day. With electronic cash registers, the sales journal has become automated. In data processing terms, the journal is a transaction file, and journal entries are records in the transaction file.

Accounting Ledgers

Ledgers are the repository of financial transactions. Accountants refer to two types of ledgers. The first are specific ledgers such as customers' accounts receivable. The data processing professional calls this specific ledger a computer file. What is an accounts receivable ledger to an accountant would be an accounts receivable file to someone in data processing. The general ledger contains the totality of financial information about the organization. To a data processing professional, it is just another file, but to the accountant it is "the" file for accounting purposes. It is from this file that the financial statements of the organization are prepared.

Chart of Accounts

The chart of accounts represents the "buckets" into which financial information can be prepared. It is a master list of the accounts into which financial information can be recorded. It is the equivalent in accounting to the list of customers in an accounts receivable ledger, or the number of items in an inventory ledger. While there are many common accounts between corporations, the chart of accounts can be customized for a specific organization. In later chapters we discuss some of the constraints placed on the data processing function by the accountants' selection of the organization's chart of accounts.

Financial Statements

These are the outputs from the accounting information systems. The two major financial statements are the statement of income and expenses and the balance sheet. These are discussed and explained in Chapter 2. However, there are no practical limits to the number of reports that can be produced from an accounting information system. They are generally divided into two categories. One consists of statements or outputs that are required by accountants to report the financial status of the organization to stockholders, government, and other interested parties. The second category of statements are prepared for internal use within the organization. These are prepared to assist managers in their internal operations. An example of an internal statement is a budget.

If one scrutinizes the above attributes of an accounting system, one can see the requirements, design, and implementation needs of an accounting information system. As mentioned, these needs are specified by generally accepted accounting procedures and standards that have been established within the accounting profession. Data processing management should understand these basic accounting concepts.

To assist data processing management in "surviving" in a senior management world dominated by accounting, a series of "recommended accounting and auditing principles" (RAAPs) for the data processing professional are presented throughout this book. Accountants have their GAAP, so this book will counter with RAAPs that are designed to highlight the key points within this book.

RECOMMENDED ACCOUNTING AND AUDITING PRINCIPLE FOR THE DATA PROCESSING MANAGER
Data processing managers should understand accounting terms and concepts in the same manner that they expect users of their services to understand data processing terms and concepts.

THE ONGOING BATTLE BETWEEN ACCOUNTANTS AND THE DATA PROCESSING FUNCTION

The roots of the data processing profession in business go back to the late 1950s. At that time, business organizations began acquiring computers to process their business applications. Many of the early applications processed were accounting systems, for example, payroll, billing, accounts receivable, and inventory control.

The early data processing professionals plotted a course for themselves that led to the presidential suite. These pioneers envisioned the computer as the heart of business. From the central computer center, they envisioned controlling and directing all major business operations. In such an environment, data processing professionals would have to be dominant, because it would be those individuals who would develop and understand how the business functioned. They also visualized minimal dependence on other areas of the organization, and as a result of specifying outside managers viewed many of the systems with suspicion.

The results of the early years were phenomenal in many organizations. The return on investment, the new methods of operation, and the speed of operation heralded the rapid growth of data processing in many organizations. The accountants began tracking this growth; at that time one corporation projected that within 10 years at the current rate of growth the data processing budget would exceed the annual sales for the organization. Senior management recognized a need to control data processing, but did not know how. As in many corporations, management turned to the comptroller for control guidance.

Accounting is the primary control of senior management. Through accounting, senior management is able to evaluate and control any operations, because accounting is a concept common to all activities within an organization. Because it would be impractical for senior management to attempt to control data processing technically, their only visible tool is accounting.

Senior management quickly selected out of their control basket the accounting control methods of budgets, chargeouts, and return on investment. These control mechanisms were applied to the data processing function in order to slow the growth of those functions. Many argue that it is a poor way to manage, but it is the most common way and one that data processing managers need to understand so they can utilize it to their own advantage.

The accounting controls worked very effectively in controlling what appeared to be runaway growth in the data processing function. In that same process, the accountant became dominant in many organizations. While very few data processing managers have moved into senior positions within organizations, the accountants have been very successful in getting promoted into senior positions.

The lessons in this historical scenario should be quite clear. Lesson one is that accounting is the major control used by senior management. Lesson two is that the less senior management knows about an area, the more they are inclined to use accounting to control that area. The third lesson is that those that use accounting will rise to the top.

Some years ago, the Peter Principle of managerial cream rising until it sours explained a phenomenon of individuals rising rapidly and then petering out. The principle also talked about people being promoted to their level of incompetence. What was missing from this principle was:

What makes the cream sour?

What is one's level of incompetence?

The answer to both of those questions is: One's knowledge of accounting. Individuals who do not understand accounting and accounting principles are deemed "incompetent" by senior managers. This accounting deficiency causes senior management to "sour" on prospective budding managers. Perhaps so few data processing managers have moved into senior management because few data processing managers understand and believe in accounting as the language of management and the major control tool of management.

ACCOUNTING AS A MANAGERIAL CONTROL

Visualize for a moment parents attempting to control the activities of their teenage children. Once the children leave the house, the control options available to parents become extremely limited. All of the "don't dos" by parents may be ignored by the teenage children while away from the parents. In addition, parents do not understand or appreciate many of the activities in which the teenager is engaged, because those activities, such as video arcades, did not exist when the parents were teenagers.

When it is difficult for parents to control the teenager's activity because parents do not understand those activities and cannot be present when the activities occur, then new methods of control must be introduced. The methods of control that parents can exercise are those over which they have authority. In general, these relate to economic and scheduling controls. For example, parents can tell the child to be home by 9 P.M., can limit the amount of funds the child has, or can threaten economic consequences, such as withholding allowance or not permitting the child to use the family car.

Let's switch the scenario to that of the president of the corporation and the data processing manager. The president does not understand what the data processing manager does because of the technical complexity of the data processing tasks, and in many instances has difficulty relating to a computerized environment. Many of the decisions made in the data processing department, for example, whether to utilize data base technology, are decisions that would be extremely difficult for the president to effectively second guess. However, just as the parent, the president wants to stay in charge of the data processing function. In fact, a couple of years ago the IBM Corporation developed a small brochure for senior management entitled "Staying in Charge."

The two major controls that the president can exercise over the data processing function are the same that parents have over their teenage child. These are economic and scheduling controls. For example, the president can say that X application should be installed by December 1, or the data processing department can only have Y dollars for operations. In addition, the president can use economic threats as a control. While the president cannot take away the data processing manager's car, the president can put a "cap" on the data processing budget or threaten to withhold certain funds unless a particular goal or objective is achieved within a stated time span or dollar amount.

There are four basic accounting controls: schedule, budgets, chargeout, and return on investment.

Schedule (Tied to Funding)

Accounting and scheduling go hand in hand. Accounting is a time-oriented discipline. Tying funding and reporting to accounting controls is a common practice. For example, invoices have due dates, payroll occurs under certain schedules, contractual payments are tied to dates and performance, etc. Schedules are particularly helpful when the one establishing the schedule does not understand the technical complexity of the task. This means that the individual cannot assess the goodness or badness of the work, only completed tasks or deliverables tied to specific dates.

Budgets

Budgeting is an internal accounting system. It requires activities to enable one to estimate the amount of revenue that they will generate and/or the expenditures required to operate for a budgeting period. It is closely associated with planning, and establishes the amount of funds required to accomplish specific plans. The growth or activities on which data processing can be performed can be directly linked to the budget approved by senior management. Management usually reserves the right to set budget limits, and to veto, approve, or expand specific line items of the budget. For example, senior management may determine the size of the budget and also limit the amount of funds within that budget that can be utilized for travel.

Chargeout

Chargeout is an accounting control that shifts responsibility from the area expending the money to the area using the services. Chargeout is normally associated with a service-oriented activity, such as data processing. It is widely used in data processing because senior management is uncertain how to control specific items within the data processing budget. Under a chargeout system, data processing is given a budget, but not necessarily the right to expend that budget. This is because the expenditure will be charged against another activity within the organization. The activity being charged now has the right to accept or reject the charged service. If data processing is on a full-chargeout basis, meaning that all their costs must be charged to users, then they must find users willing to accept those charges. If the users will not accept the charges, then the data processing function will have an unfavorable chargeout variance, and most likely it will be cut during or at the end of the budgetary period.

Return on Investment

Return on investment is an accounting method used for decision-making purposes. For example, if senior management is uncertain whether or not to install an application system or acquire computer hardware, it can require a return on investment calculation. This requires data processing to estimate the benefits to be derived from the project and the costs associated with the project. Using the return on investment rules, a calculation is made that shows an internal percent of profit, or return on investment, generated from undertaking an activity. Note that while the numbers are precise, much of the return on investment process is subjective in nature.

Much of the remainder of the book covers these four uses of accounting. These controls affect the growth, direction, credibility, and performance of the data processing function. If the accounting is improper, the decisions may be improper. For example, the return on investment calculation may or may not include unfunded costs such as depreciation. This subjective decision in developing the return on investment algorithm may affect whether or not a specific project is undertaken. It is important for data processing management to understand how accounting is used, and the options available in using accounting in organizations.

RECOMMENDED ACCOUNTING AND AUDITING PRINCIPLE FOR THE DATA PROCESSING MANAGER

There is more than one way to perform accounting, just as there is more than one way to develop any other system. Data processing management should understand the options and select options that are advantageous to the data processing function.

ACCOUNTING AS AN INFORMATION SYSTEM

The accounting system is an integral part of the functioning of an organization. Accounting is designed to assist in decision making, quantify the resources associated with decision making, and then measure actual performance against expected or desired results.

Accounting is an information system. It serves the same purpose in managing a function within an organization as an inventory information system performs in managing the inventory of an organization. Just as it would be difficult to run an inventory control system without good information, it is difficult to manage an economic unit such as data processing without good accounting information.

The relationship between accomplishing the data processing mission and the accounting system is illustrated in Figure 1. The objective of data processing is to accomplish its mission. The mission is normally expressed in the following two documents:

1. *Annual Data Processing Plan.* Explains what is to be done and when it is to be accomplished. Also, the plan normally states who will be responsible for accomplishing the items within the plan. Note that some of the items are repetitive, such as operating computers.
2. *Annual Data Processing Budget.* This document identifies the resources allocated to accomplish the annual data processing plan. The plan and budget are closely related documents, and may in fact be incorporated into a single document even though they are two separate items.

   The return on investment concept (ROI) is an input to the annual data processing plan. This return on investment rate is used to determine what items to put in the plan. The plan must also provide schedules as to when items are to be completed. The plan and the mission are the input to the preparation of the annual budget.

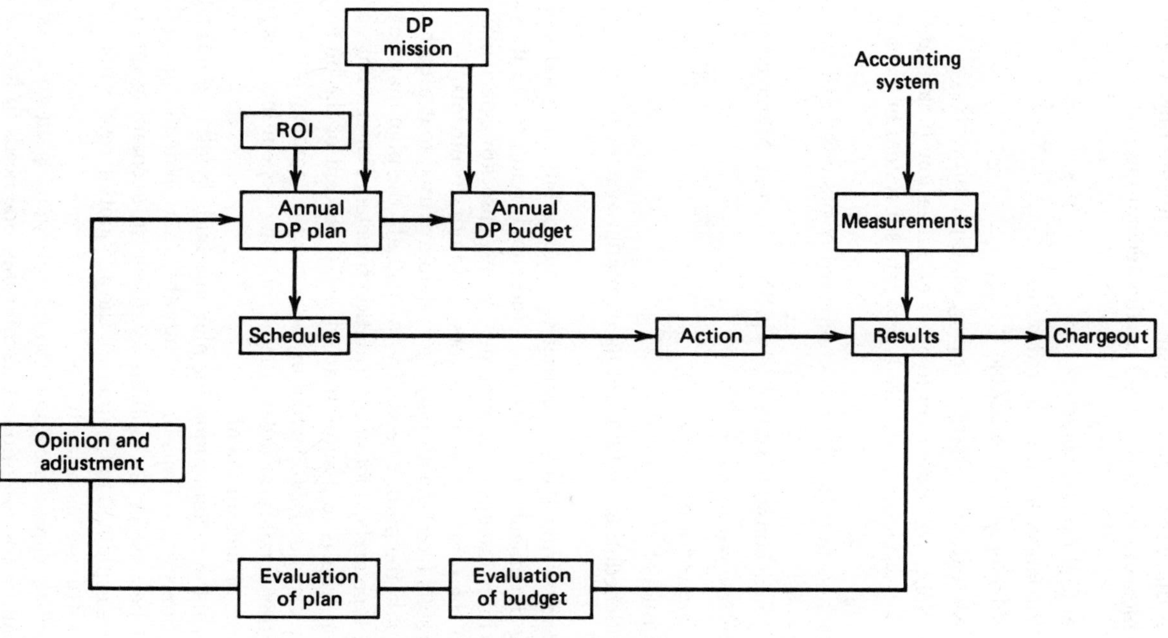

Figure 1. The DP Mission and Accounting Systems.

Once the plan and budget are approved, action can commence within the planning and budgeting period. The action produces results that are partially measured by the accounting system. The type of measurements provided by the accounting system are:

Actual expenditures
Variances from budgeted items
Variances from schedule
Allocation of charges among multiple projects
Chargeout of services to other organizations (note that the chargeout system is normally a separate subsystem unto itself)

The accounting system is comprised of many subsystems including:

Job accounting system (e.g., IBM's Systems Management Facility)
Time reporting
Project status reporting
Budget reporting
Scheduling and budgeting computer systems

The results from the accounting system are both internal and external reporting documents. As previously indicated, budgets are internal documents, while statements of income and expense are external documents. Note that the same information goes into both documents.

The results from the accounting system are used to evaluate the budget and evaluate the plan. The ability to evaluate the plan may be dependent upon the type and extent of information selected. For example, a common evaluation trap is to assume that when 50 percent of the budgeted items have been expended, 50 percent of the project is completed. It is unrealistic to draw this conclusion unless the accounting system includes the appropriate basis of measurement.

Based on these evaluations, the plan and budget will be adjusted. In most organizations, this is done briefly monthly, and in-depth quarterly. Again, note that because of the options available in accounting (many of these options are explained in Chapter 2), the accounting results may or may not reflect the true status of activities.

Accounting can be used and abused in managing an area. As a basis of understanding the intention of accounting, one needs to look at the principles on which accounting is based. Data processing management needs to understand these principles in order to understand how to interpret accounting results.

THE PRINCIPLES ON WHICH ACCOUNTING IS BASED

Financial statements to an accountant are like blueprints to a builder. The accountant reads financial information like others read a novel. The reports containing accounting information tell a story about the organization they represent.

To the casual observer, financial data is a factual presentation of past history. To the accountant, this financial information explains the strengths and weaknesses of an organization. It is similar to looking at an X ray in order to identify whether there any broken or troublesome spots. However, just as it takes a trained medical doctor to read an X ray, so does it take a trained accountant to read and interpret financial statements.

A common error made by nonaccountants is in the assumption that the accounting reports are finite statements of fact. For example, when an organization states that its profit is X dollars, the nonaccountant believes that is the organization's profit. However, one cannot assume that X dollars means anything until the basis by which that X dollars was produced is understood. Some of this understanding is an understanding of accounting, but much of it is understanding how accounting was used in the organization that produced X dollars profit.

Stating that a corporation made X dollars profit is similar to stating that a programmer can write one COBOL statement per hour. Obviously, an individual can physically write more than one statement in an hour. What needs to be known is what does writing one statement mean? Does it mean defining requirements, does it mean developing designs, does it mean testing, does it mean documenting the statement, does it mean interacting with users, etc., etc.? When talking about a corporation making X dollars profit, we need to know the answers to questions like:

How is the inventory valued? There are many different methods for valuing inventory.

What depreciation method is used to depreciate capital assets? Again, there are many methods and the amount of depreciation varies.

Are pension costs funded or unfunded?

Is there any potential litigation against the corporation?

What type of guarantees has the organization made on its products?

The above are but a few of the characteristics that can change the stated profit significantly. One must understand these options and which were selected in order to understand profit. For example, two corporations could have made X dollars profit. One of these could be very conservatively stated because of the accounting decisions made, and another be a very optimistic profit picture.

It is important to understand both the principles on which accounting is based and the options available within those principles. Second, it is important to know how accounting is implemented at a specific organization. Once we know this, the financial results produced by the accounting information system will be meaningful.

The Four Basic Principles of Accounting

Accounting is based on four broad principles.

An Economic Measurement System

The primary objective of accounting is to measure the operating results of an organization. The measurement is expressed in economic terms. These economic terms are the currency used by the organization. For example, in the United States this would be dollars, and in Germany, marks.

The need for measurement is to evaluate performance and compare performance against other like units. In achieving this objective, there needs to be consistency in the application of the measurement system. The statements normally made by accountants when they issue an opinion on the adequacy of financial statements addresses the consistency of measurement from accounting period to accounting period.

If the means of measurement changes, then the accountant must state that change. For example, if inventory had been valued on first-in, first-out basis, and that valuation was changed to a last-in, first-out basis, that measurement change would have to be publicly stated by the corporation. If not, the profit generated from period to period would not be comparable. For example, a corporation might be able to swing profit significantly if they could change the rules of measurement.

A Going Concern Concept

Accounting is based on the assumption that an organization will stay in business. Thus, accounting need not reflect the actual value of an organization at a point in time. This actual worth of an organization would be important if the organization were going to be liquidated. It would represent the value that someone might pay for an organization on the open market.

The going concern concept is more concerned with the measurement aspect than the valuation aspect of accounting. A major discussion over this point that has been going on for the past few years relates to inflation accounting. The proponents of inflation accounting state that the assets of an organization should reflect the increase in worth of those assets. For example, a corporation may have built a building for $100,000 fifteen years ago that after depreciation is shown on the books of the organization as worth $20,000. However, on the open market the building could easily be sold for $500,000. Under the going concern concept of accounting, it is unimportant what the building or any other asset is worth on the open market. This going concern principle devises methods that record, distribute, and measure costs on a consistent basis. It is not designed to show true costs or true worth but, rather, to measure performance over a period of time.

Fiscal Period Approach

Accounting is designed to present status information at predetermined intervals. Most organizations are on an annual basis for reporting the results of operation. They may also report monthly and quarterly results for status purposes. However, these more frequent reports are sometimes less precise than the ones prepared at the end of an accounting period. This end is frequently referred to as a financial closing.

Because accounting uses fiscal periods, there are elaborate procedures to allocate costs to the appropriate period. For example, if one buys inventory to make products, one does not want to charge that inventory to production until the point it is used in production. If items were charged to expense at the time they were acquired, the measurement results would be distorted.

Generally Accepted Accounting Procedures

Accounting procedures regulate the details of external reporting. The accounting procedures can be determined by government, special accounting boards, or professional associations. If organizations followed these generally accepted accounting procedures, then financial statements prepared using them will be more comparable than those that are not. Therefore, the accountants state in their opinion whether or not the statements were prepared by generally accepted accounting procedures and, if not, they normally have to indicate in their opinion which procedures were not followed.

In the United States, these generally accepted accounting procedures are defined by the following four organizations:

Securities and Exchange Commission
Financial Accounting Standards Board
American Institute of Certified Public Accountants
Cost Accounting Standards Board

In addition, the Internal Revenue Service makes additional rulings regarding taxes. For example, the standards are general in nature regarding certain expenses such as expenses for a personal automobile. Under accounting standards, an organization is free to pay an employee any amount it wants per mile for traveling when using a personal automobile. The Internal Revenue Service can state that only X cents per mile is allowable. In some instances, organizations must maintain a set of records for external financial reporting, and then another set of records for income tax reporting.

ROADMAP THROUGH THE BOOK

This book is designed to help data processing management understand accounting as it is applied to the data processing profession. As such, the standards and regulations regarding external financial reports are only of minimal concern to the data processing manager. Those items of most concern are normally the ones relating to tax accounting.

The materials are directed at the use of accounting within the data processing function. Within data processing, accounting serves to:

Communicate with senior management.
Manage the data processing function.
Measure operational performance.
Justify data processing projects.
Acquire funds to fulfill the data processing mission.

The objective of the book is to help the data processing manager survive in an environment in which accounting is a dominant force, while at the same time to use that knowledge to help accomplish the data processing mission. The book is divided into five parts and 13 chapters, as follows:

Part 1. Accounting—The Common Language of Management

The objective of this part is to explain to data processing managers how a lack of accounting can hurt them, as well as to provide the general principles of accounting. This section includes three chapters:

1. ACCOUNTING—IT CAN BE THE FRIEND OR FOE OF THE DATA PROCESSING MANAGER

This chapter provides background material on the importance of accounting in business and the general principles of accounting.

2. ACCOUNTING PRINCIPLES—USES AND ABUSES

The objective of this chapter is to present a minicourse in accounting as it applies to the data processing professional. It explains how accounting works, what accounting statements are, and then describes how those principles can be effectively used and also how they can be abused.

3. CREATING A POSITIVE DATA PROCESSING IMAGE THROUGH CREATIVE ACCOUNTING

Traditional accounting within data processing accounts primarily for costs. This chapter explains how accounting for benefits can be used to show a positive return on investment utilizing the data processing function.

Part 2. Using Accounting to Justify Data Processing Activities

Data processing is primarily a job shop operation. Most of its activities have to be justified and this part explains how.

4. Justifying Application Systems

This chapter presents a methodology on how to justify new computer systems and the ongoing maintenance function.

5. Justifying Data Processing Support Activities

As the data processing function becomes more specialized, the need for activities to support the application project team increases. This chapter explains how to ensure that each of the support methods is worthwhile.

6. Justifying Computer Operations

The computer center is a group of activities each of which needs to be justified. For example, the inability to justify the disaster recovery activity has led to the inability in some organizations to recoup after disasters.

Part 3. Generating Funds to Operate the Data Processing Function

This part covers accounting for revenue generation. The chapters address the accounting topics that are needed to acquire the funds necessary to accomplish the data processing mission.

7. Budgeting the Data Processing Function

This chapter explains how to develop and use a budget in accomplishing data processing activities and projects.

8. Pricing Strategies

The objective of this chapter is to explain how to use accounting properly in pricing data processing services. It deals with the theory of pricing and not the methods.

9. Building Chargeout Systems

This chapter explains how to create and operate a system that will charge users for the services consumed in accordance with the pricing strategies described in Chapter 8.

Part 4. Accounting as a Managerial Tool

The emphasis in Part 4 is to explain both how senior management controls data processing with accounting, and how data processing management can control their activities through those same accounting control concepts.

10. Accounting for Unrecorded Data Processing Assets

The two major unrecorded assets in most organizations are people and computer applications. This chapter explains how to properly manage a huge unrecorded asset.

11. Using Accounting to Identify Data Processing Problems

Accounting provides the clues needed to identify problems. This chapter explains how to use financial analytical techniques to identify data processing problems.

12. Communicating With Management in the Accounting Language

This chapter presents a plan of action for data processing management to follow in communicating with senior management and for presenting data processing in the most positive light possible.

Part 5. Evaluating the Integrity of Accounting Systems

Senior management has the responsibility to ensure that the accounting systems work. This part of the book is designed to explain how to ensure the integrity of accounting data and how to work with auditors in performing that evaluation.

13. How to Survive an EDP Audit

This chapter explains the objective of auditing and its relationship to accounting systems. It provides a strategy for minimizing negative aspects of audits.

A SIMPLE SOLUTION TO A COMPLEX PROBLEM

Accounting has, is, and will continue to be a complex technical science. Just as data processing is difficult for users to understand, accounting is difficult for nonaccountants to understand. Let us then look for a moment at how users cope with mastering computer technology:

Solution 1. Hire the enemy: In many organizations, users hire data processing professionals to help them better understand computer technology.

Solution 2. Establish an interface point: Many users focus all data processing questions through a formal interface person between data processing and/or a data processing project and user personnel. This interface person can then translate requests and get the appropriate responses.

These same solutions can be applied to the accounting dilemma. This does not substitute for an accounting knowledge by data processing managers. Those individuals must still understand the basic principles and methods of accounting. What it does address is the proper response and interface to corporate accounting systems.

The solution is to appoint or acquire one individual within the data processing function responsible for accounting and accounting systems. The title frequently used for this individual is data processing comptroller. The responsibilities assigned to that individual normally vary depending on the size of the data processing function. A small organization can probably not afford a high-level person and may not even be able to afford a full-time data processing comptroller. On the other hand, a very large organization may have a highly skilled individual who has a staff assisting in fulfilling the accounting function.

RECOMMENDED ACCOUNTING AND AUDITING PRINCIPLE FOR THE DATA PROCESSING MANAGER

One of the rules of accounting is to make someone accountable for each task. Applying this rule to data processing means that someone within the function must be responsible for accounting for the data processing function. This individual should be called the data processing comptroller.

Chapter Two

Accounting Principles—Uses and Abuses

Data processing management cannot play the accounting game until they know the rules of the game. Accounting as used in most organizations is a double-entry bookkeeping method. This provides a check and balance on the entry, as well as documentation of the full use of economic resources.

This chapter has two basic objectives. The first is to explain how financial data is recorded, processed, and presented by accounting systems. The second is to explain how accounting can be misused and abused. A self-evaluation accounting test is provided early in the chapter to help individuals assess their own personal knowledge of accounting, and areas where additional accounting knowledge would be helpful.

ACCOUNTING VERSUS ACCOUNTABILITY

Accounting and accountability are two important but different concepts in organizations. Both are necessary to measure and protect economic resources. The assurance that both occur is normally the responsibility of the organization's comptroller.

Accounting has been previously defined as an information-gathering system. Chapter 1 identified many of the principles and premises of accounting. It is a formal process subject to principles and generally accepted procedures.

Accounting is normally performed by accountants. These individuals are trained in the methods, procedures, and standards prescribed for processing financial information by an accounting process.

Accountability is holding someone responsible for acts and/or activities under their area of responsibility. All employees within an organization should be held accountable for their own work and the activities under their control. To be accountable is to be responsible.

Accountability covers all acts and activities. One can be accountable for an accounting system, or accountable for the accuracy of a production report. Thus, while accounting is an information system, accountability is a control.

The validity and reliability of accounting information will be partially dependent on holding individuals accountable for the information they provide the accounting system, plus the integrity of the accounting process.

Let's look at a brief example that illustrates the difference. An individual reports the number of hours he worked within an accounting period. Let us assume that in a week an individual reported 40 hours of regular work and four hours of overtime. That 44 hours of work would be entered into the payroll accounting system for processing. The economic value of those 44 hours is calculated by a payroll accounting system and then processed to produce payroll records and the other accounting results produced by the payroll system.

The employee who reported 44 hours of work should be held accountable for the accuracy of those 44 hours. If the employee did not work 44 hours, then that individual should be "held accountable" for improper reporting. At a minimum, the individual should be reprimanded for violating a trust, and may be terminated for this act. In addition, the individual's supervisor may be held accountable for the accuracy of time reported by subordinates. This accountability is frequently implemented by requiring supervisors to cosign employee timecards.

The principles of accounting and accountability are closely interrelated as demonstrated in the previous example. An accounting system without accountability may not produce the desired results. A major objective of accounting is to measure, and if the data used to measure is incorrect, the results of measurement will be incorrect.

A SELF-ASSESSMENT EXERCISE ON ACCOUNTING CONCEPTS

A common definition of knowledge used by educators is "know what you don't know." The premise for this statement is that until you know what you don't know you cannot embark upon a course of learning the unknown. Without this knowledge of the unknown, bad decisions can be made. For example, if while driving, one becomes lost, not knowing where one is can lead to driving away rather than toward one's destination. Rather than stopping for directions, many hope a familiar location will be around the next corner. It isn't until one truly recognizes that one is hopelessly lost that stopping and asking directions becomes the obvious solution.

The following accounting self-assessment exercise is designed to identify areas where additional accounting knowledge might prove helpful. The self-assessment exercise is a series of yes–no questions about knowledge of accounting principles. The result of the exercise will be a list of accounting principles known, and a list of accounting principles unknown.

At this point, the self-assessment exercise (Figure 2) should be completed. If the principles are understood, the yes response column should be checked, and if the respondent is unsure or does not understand the principle, the no column should be checked.

	Item	Response: Yes	Response: No
1.	Can you identify the steps in the accounting cycle?		
2.	Do you understand the purpose of double-entry bookkeeping?		
3.	Can you define the meaning of the terms assets, liabilities, and owner's equity?		
4.	Do you understand the difference between a debit and credit entry?		
5.	Do you know when revenue should be recorded as income of an organization?		
6.	Can you state the purpose of a trial balance?		
7.	Can you differentiate between a statement of income and expense and a balance sheet?		
8.	Can you identify two different methods for depreciating an asset?		
9.	Can you explain why computer systems are not recorded as assets on the financial statements of organizations?		
10.	Can you explain the difference between a budget and a statement of income and expense?		
11.	Given a trial balance, could you produce a statement of income and expense?		
12.	Do you use accounting information to control the data processing function?		
13.	Can you identify potential data processing problems from accounting information (including budgetary statements)?		
14.	Can you identify where in your organization's statement of income and expense and balance sheet the specific expenses associated with data processing are located?		
15.	Can you identify how tax law provisions affect the accounting for data processing assets and expenses?		
16.	Do you regularly study and analyze the financial statements of your organization?		
17.	Can you explain the relationship between using accounting to justify data processing projects and accounting to summarize the costs associated with those projects?		

Figure 2. Accounting Principles Self-Assessment Exercise.

Evaluating the Self-Assessment Checklist

After completing the self-assessment exercise, total the number of yes responses. Use the following table to evaluate your mastery of accounting.

Number of Yes Responses	Interpretation of the Response Score
13–17	You have a good comprehension of accounting, and probably do not require any additional study. The major value of this book to you is the application of accounting to data processing.
9–12	There are areas of accounting in which you should undertake additional study. The no response items will help identify those areas. This lack of accounting knowledge may have an impact on your personal credibility with senior management.
5–8	You have a major deficiency in accounting. This deficiency must affect your use of accounting as a science and as a control. You should take accounting courses to improve your skills.
0–4	Your complete lack of accounting knowledge will most likely block any opportunity for personal growth within your organization. It probably affects the credibility of the data processing function, and prohibits you from using an effective control to improve data processing performance. A crash course in accounting may be one of the most effective uses of your time in the near future.

Several surveys in leading data processing publications indicate that one of the most needed skills for data processing management is accounting. For years, data processing management has wanted senior management to gain a better understanding of data processing. Management has fought this and continues to use accounting as the language of communication between senior management and data processing management.

Figure 3 indicates that the data processing (DP) manager's accounting skill level is relatively low within the total body of knowledge in accounting. On the other hand, senior management's mastery of accounting skills is high. The questions to be answered are: Should senior management adjust their managerial style in order to communicate with the data processing manager? Or, must the data processing manager learn the language of management? The figure answers that question, indicating

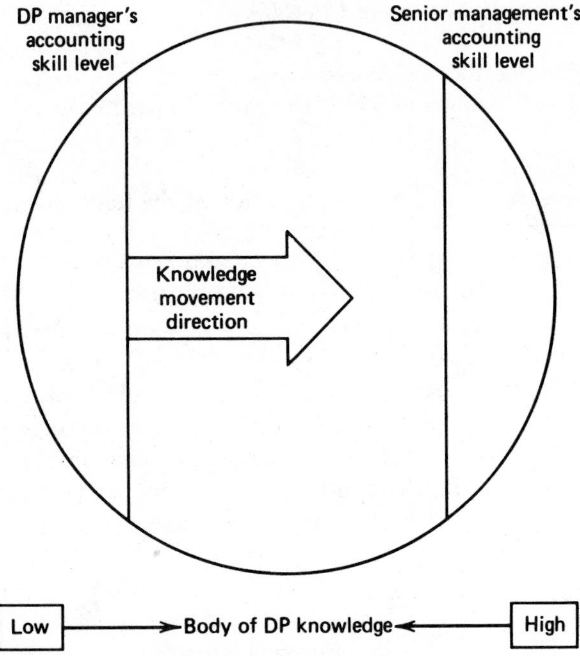

Figure 3. Who Must Move to Understand and Use Accounting.

that it behooves data processing management to increase its accounting skill levels in order to better communicate the needs and plans of data processing in a language readily understandable to senior management.

UNDERSTANDING THE METHODS OF ACCOUNTING

The accounting methods are designed to show the financial activities of the owners of an organization. An accounting system begins when an organization starts. The owners normally invest funds into the organization. These funds are then used to accomplish the mission of the organization and, in the case of profit-making corporations, produce a profit.

The funds invested by the owners are referred to as "owners' equity." Since the owners have invested these funds, the accounting system must maintain records on what funds have been invested and how those funds are utilized.

The funds invested by the owner can be used to acquire assets. For example, they might buy land, buildings, and equipment for use in profit making. Thus, the owner's equity is then expended to buy assets in the hope that those assets will produce profit for the owners.

For many organizations, the funds invested by the owners are inadequate to meet their financial needs. Additional funds can be raised by borrowing from banks or by buying products on credit. The use of other organizations' funds incur liabilities that are described as liabilities in the accounting records.

The accounting records of an organization must then account for the owner's equity, the assets of the organization, and the liabilities incurred by the organization.

In the recording of these three categories of economic events, there is a transfer between the three categories. For example, if the owners invest money in the corporation, the corporation has an asset and it also has owners' equity. If the organization borrows money, it has the cash as an asset, but it also has a liability.

The transfer of resources can be within the same category or between any or all of the three categories. For example, the asset cash can be used to buy the asset inventory. One type of liability can be transferred for another type of liability, or the owners can give some of their equity to pay off liabilities.

The resulting accounting system is a "double-entry" accounting system. This means that each item that is recorded in the accounting system shows these relationships. The assets of the organization are represented by debit entries. Liabilities and owner's equity are recognized by credit entries. In simplistic terms, accounting is an equation as follows: Assets equal liabilities plus owner's equity.

A double-entry accounting system means that the equation is always kept in balance. In other words, the totality of the assets must always equal the totality of the liabilities plus owner equity.

This accounting equation is often expressed as follows:

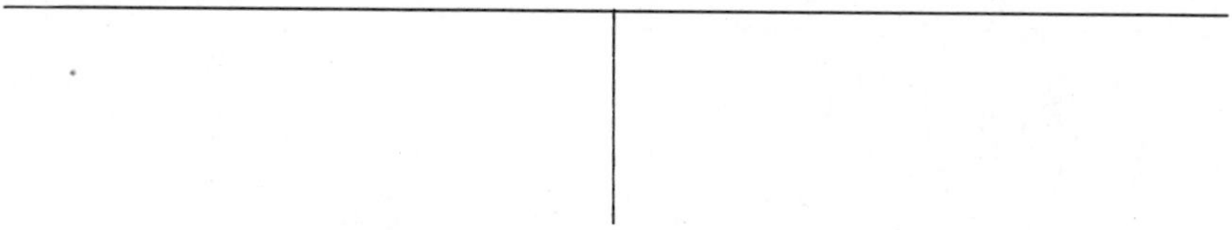

Accountants call this form a "T account" because it is shaped like the letter T. The left side of the T account is referred to as the debit side, and the right side of the T account as the credit side.

Each T account, frequently called a ledger account, represents one asset, one liability, or one type of owner's equity account. Each entry in the accounting system will then be recorded in at least two T accounts. One part of the entry is on the debit side, and another on the credit side. This is important in order to maintain the quality of the accounting equation (assets equal liabilities plus owner's equity).

Generally, debit balances mean asset balances, and credit balances, liabilities or owner's equity balances. However, we can have credit entries to asset accounts and debit entries to liability and owner's equity accounts. These opposite entries are done to reduce asset accounts, and to reduce liability or owner's equity accounts.

Let's look at a brief example of a few accounting entries:

Accounting Entry 1. Owners invest $1,000 cash into a corporation.

Cash	
$1,000	

Owner's Equity	
	$1,000

At the end of this transaction, our double-entry accounting system is in balance: the assets equal $1,000 and the owner's equity equals $1,000.

Accounting Entry 2: The corporation buys $500 of merchandise.

Cash	
$1,000	$500

Merchandise	
$500	

Owner's Equity	
	$1,000

At the end of this transaction, we have reduced cash by $500 (note that the balance has not yet been calculated) and increased our merchandise account by $500. The double-entry accounting equation is still in balance. At this point, the business has $500 in cash, $500 in merchandise, and $1,000 of owner's equity.

Accounting Entry 3: The organization sells merchandise that costs $200 for $400.

Cash	
$500	
$400	

Merchandise	
$500	$200

Retained Earnings	
	$200

Owner's Equity	
	$1,000

At the conclusion of this transaction, the organization has made $200 profit by selling $200 of merchandise for $400. The $400 is recorded in cash, the merchandise is reduced by $200, and retained earnings is recorded as part of owner's equity for $200. At this point, our equation is still in balance, but it has changed from $1,000 to $1,200 because of the profit generated. Note that while in this illustration we have shown the $200 as profit, a few steps have been skipped to simplify the illustration. In actual practice, a sales account would reflect the $400 sale that, through the accounting cycle, would be incorporated into a profit and loss statement that would generate the $200 profit to be recorded in retained earnings.

The processing of accounting information from the recording of a transaction through the production of the balance sheet is called the accounting cycle. We will walk through this accounting cycle to show how information is recorded, accumulated, and presented.

THE ACCOUNTING CYCLE

The accounting cycle represents a series of events that occur during the process of accounting. It also represents the sequence in which the events occur. The accounting cycle can be manual, automated, or part manual and part automated.

The accounting cycle represents the flow of information through the accounting information system. The flow is the totality of steps that occur daily, weekly, monthly, quarterly, and annually. The accounting cycle represents input to the accounting information system, the processing that occurs, and the output produced from the accounting information system.

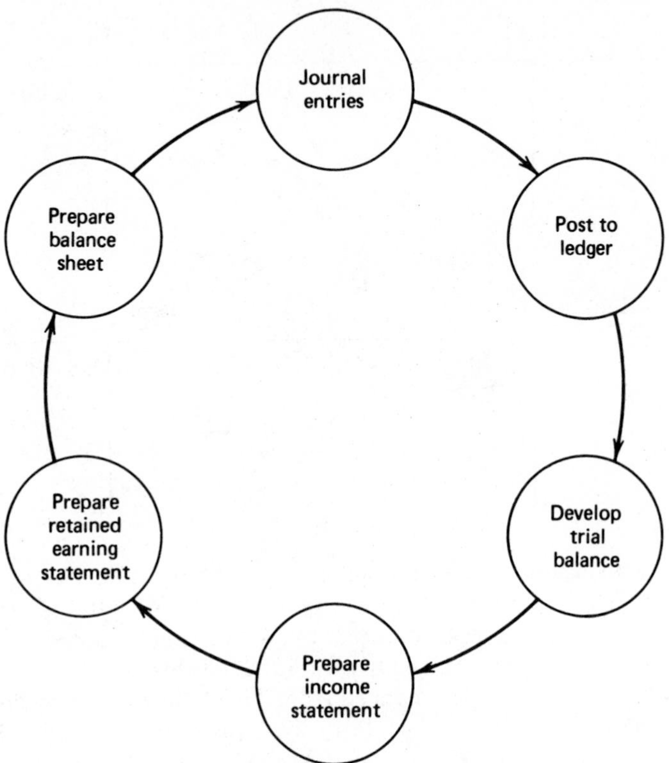

Figure 4. The Accounting Cycle.

The accounting cycle represents the basic parts of the accounting information system. The information system can be expanded to include other specialized information processing needs. For example, budgeting is not an integral part of the accounting cycle, but could be and is added in many organizations.

The accounting cycle is illustrated in Figure 4 and briefly described below:

Journal Entries. The recording of accounting transactions. The journal entry represents the input data to the accounting information system.

Post to Ledger. The posting is the recording of the input transactions (i.e., journal entries) into a file of financial accounts.

Develop Trial Balance. The trial balance is a proof of the integrity of the file of financial accounts (i.e., a proof of the ledger). Accounting is a double-entry system so that the trial balance proves that the accounting equation is in balance (i.e., assets equal liabilities plus owner's equity).

Prepare Income Statement. This statement shows the results of operations. If income exceeds expenses, the organization has a profit, but if expenses exceed income, the organization has a loss.

Prepare Retained Earning Statement. This step in the accounting cycle shows the changes that have occurred in retaining earnings during the financial period. Note that the major change will be the income or loss developed by the statement of income and expense.

Prepare Balance Sheet. This statement represents financial conditions of the organization as expressed through the results of this accounting system.

Each of these steps in the accounting cycle will be individually explained. Included with the explanation will be an example of the actions that occur during that step. The illustrations were used and expanded from the previously illustrated T account examples.

Step 1. Journal Entries

A financial journal entry is the recording of a financial transaction. In accounting terminology, these are represented as a debit(s) and a credit(s). In our previous example, we showed accounting transactions as T accounts. Prior to being expressed in a T account, they would have been recorded as a journal entry. Let's look at two more transaction examples to illustrate journal entries:

TRANSACTION 1. RECORDING A SALE

Event 1

Debit—Cash: $400

Credit—Sales: $400

Event 2

Cost of sales: $200

Credit merchandise: $200

These are the two journal entries that would be needed to properly record a sale that was more simply illustrated above. In this example, we increased cash $400 from the sale, and recorded the sale as a $400 credit. The second event debited cost of sales and credited merchandise that in effect reduced the merchandise by the $200 that represented the cost of the merchandise sold for $400.

TRANSACTION 2. PAYING AN EMPLOYEE

Debit—Payroll expense: $100

Credit—Cash: $85

Federal withholding tax payable: $9

Social security tax payable: $6

This transaction represents the recording of an employee's earnings of $100. The $100 represents gross pay and is charged to payroll expense. The organization must deduct federal withholding taxes of $9 and social security taxes of $6 from the employee's salary. These are because of the federal government and are recorded as liabilities. They will remain liabilities until paid to the federal government. In smaller organizations this may occur monthly. The employee receives net pay of $85, which at the time of payment is a reduction in the cash account.

Journal entries are normally not recorded in the format presented above. The journal entry for sales is usually a combination of two activities. The first is the invoicing of a customer through a billing computer system. This represents the credit side of the transaction. The debit side is recorded through the removal of merchandise from inventory. The creation of an invoice normally creates a shipping order that becomes the debit side of the sales entry. In the payroll system, the journal entry would be the employee's pay stub that shows gross pay, deductions, and net pay. This is produced by the payroll computers.

Step 2: Post to Ledger

The T account illustrations provided earlier represented the posting to the ledger. When the $85 paid to the employee is recorded in the cash T account, we say that the cash expenditure has been posted to the general ledger (note that the general ledger is the main listing of financial accounts).

In automated computer systems, the entry for posting to the general ledger can be produced automatically by the individual accounting system. For example, the results of paying individual employees are first "posted" to individual employee accounts—which is referred to in computer terms as the weekly or monthly payroll master file. This file shows the status of all the accounts relating to specific employees. In accounting terms, this is considered a subsidiary ledger, or a supporting ledger for the major general ledger that is maintained by the organization's accountant.

The summation of the subsidiary ledger, in this example our payroll master file, is posted to the organization's general ledger. This is frequently maintained by a computerized general ledger system. Thus, only the total of all cash payments posted to the cash account, the gross pay posted to the payroll expense account, and the benefits posted to the appropriate benefit accounts are maintained.

Step 3: Develop Trial Balance

The trial balance is a proof that the accounting formula is in balance. It is designed to determine that the totality of the debits equals the totality of the credits. If the two are equal, our trial balance is in balance. See Figure 5 for a trial balance of our illustrative organization.

Financial Account	Trial Balance	
Cash	815	
Sales		400
Cost of sales	200	
Payroll expenses	100	
FWT payable		9
SS tax payable		6
Merchandise	300	
Owner's equity		1,000
	1,415	1,415

Figure 5. Developing a Trial Balance.

The objective of this process in a manual system was to determine that all of the journal entries had been correctly posted. For example, if the debit side of the journal entry had been posted, but not the credit side, that error would have been detected by creating a trial balance.

The objective in an automated general ledger system is the same. However, it is not necessary to physically list the trial balance in the automated system. The step can be performed as desired through a simple program that will total the debits, total the credits, and compare the system. In some general ledger systems, the trial balance record is maintained as part of the file that shows the total of the debits and credits.

Step 4: Prepare Income Statements

This step is performed monthly in most organizations. The starting point for this step is the trial balance. This is the input to the statement of income and expenses. The output is the actual statement.

The tasks performed in developing this statement are specified through generally accepted accounting procedures. Although options are available in determining the amount of income and expenses, the general procedures to be followed are uniform and must be practiced by all organizations if they desire to have their statements certified by an independent public accountant. As stated earlier, one of the tasks of that individual is to verify that the statement of income and expense is prepared in accordance with generally accepted accounting procedures.

The objective of this step is to summarize the income and expense accounts included within the general ledger. An income account represents the generation of revenue, whereas an expense account accumulates the costs associated with generating that revenue.

Expenses fall into two general categories. The first category is cost of sales. This represents the expenses directly associated with a sale, such as merchandise and commissions paid to sales personnel. The second category

Financial Account	Trial Balance		Statement of Income	
Cash	815			
Sales		400		400
Cost of sales	200		200	
Payroll expenses	100		100	
FWT payable		9		
SS tax payable		6		
Merchandise	300			
Owner's equity		1,000		
	1,415	1,415		
Net income			400	400

Figure 6. Preparing an Income Statement.

is administrative expenses. These are the expenses associated with operating the organization and include all of the costs associated with the staff functions of an organization, including the cost of data processing. Note that in a chargeout system the cost charged to the departments and activities that are related to cost of sales are included in cost of sales.

The statement of income is illustrated in Figure 6. This illustration shows that the items included within the trial balance that represent generation of revenue and cost associated with that revenue generation are included in the statement of income. The difference between the revenue and the cost of generating that revenue is shown as net income or loss. In this example, we have $400 in sales and $300 expended to generate that revenue, which resulted in a net income of $100. Also note that the debits in all aspects of accounting must equal credits.

Step 5: Prepare Retained Earning Statement

The retained earnings statement shows all of the activities resulting from operations that affects owner's equity. The $1,000 contributed by the owners represents their contributed equity. They also have equity in earnings that they retained in the organization. If we assume that the $100 earnings will be retained in the organization, then the statement of retained earnings shows that that net income is kept in the business as retained earnings. For purposes of this illustration, that is what we will assume. See Figure 7 for the information recorded in the statement or retained earnings.

If the owners have decided to pay themselves dividends, that would have resulted in a reduction of retained earnings. Let us assume that they wanted to pay themselves a $100 dividend, then cash would be credited to make the payments to the owners and retained earnings debited. The debit to retained earnings would reduce the amount of earnings retained in the organization. This transaction is reflected in the statement of retained earnings.

Financial Accounts	Trial Balance		Statement of Income		Statement of Retained Earnings	
Cash	815					
Sales		400		400		
Cost of sales	200		200			
Payroll expenses	100		100			
FWT payable		9				
SS tax payable		6				
Merchandise	300					
Owner's equity		1,000				
	1,415	1,415				
Net income			100		100	
			400	400		
Retained earnings						100
					100	100

Figure 7. Developing Statement of Retained Earnings.

Step 6: Prepare Balance Sheet

The balance sheet represents the financial position of the organization at the end of an accounting period. The balance sheet includes all of the accounts that were not included in the statement of income. It also reflects any adjustments made during the preparation of the statement of retained earnings.

Financial Accounts	Trial Balance		Statement of Income		Statement of Retained Earnings		Balance Sheet	
Cash	815						815	
Sales		400		400				
Cost of sales	200		200					
Payroll expenses	100		100					
FWT payable		9						9
SS tax payable		6						6
Merchandise	300						300	
Owner's equity		1,000						1,000
	1,415	1,415						
Net income			100		100			
			400	400				
Retained earnings						100		100
					100	100		
							1,115	1,115

Figure 8. Preparing a Balance Sheet.

The balances remaining are used to prepare the trial balance. For our example, these balances are shown in the balance sheet column of Figure 8. Again, note that the debits always equal the credits.

What Do the Statements Look Like?

Figure 9 shows the statement of income and expense and the balance sheet as they would look when formally prepared. These are the more traditional statement formats that one would see as prepared by a general ledger computer system, and printed in any financial statement of an organization. Note that they contain the same accounts and same results as were produced through the cumulative statement preparation process as illustrated in Figures 5 to 8.

CASE ILLUSTRATION CORPORATION
Income Statement
For the Period Ended 12/31/19XX

Sales		$ 400
Less cost of sales		
Merchandise	$ 200	
Payroll	100	300
Net income		$ 100

CASE ILLUSTRATION CORPORATION
Balance Sheet
As of December 31, 19XX

Assets		
Cash		$ 815
Merchandise		300
		$1,115
Equity		
Current liabilities		
FWT payable	$ 9	
SS tax payable	6	$ 15
Stockholder equity		
Investments	$1,000	
Retained earnings	100	$1,100
		$1,115

Figure 9. Financial Statement Forms.

How Accrual Accounting Affects Financial Statements

The case illustration did not show the expenses made in one period whose contribution to revenue occurs over several financial periods. In the merchandise example, the merchandise was physically present and, thus, could be removed from an access account as consumed.

Let's look at two other typical examples:

Example 1: Purchasing Major Assets

Let us assume that the organization decided to buy a computer for $10,000. In the accounting periods in which they acquire the computer, they will reduce cash by $10,000 and record the computer as an asset for $10,000. However, the asset is used to generate revenue, and the asset will wear out over a period of time. This requires two decisions to be made. The first is how long the asset will last, and the second is over that period of time how much money should be charged to cost of sales in each accounting period.

The governmental agency that taxes revenue normally provides lists of the acceptable life of assets for tax purposes. Most organizations follow these taxing guidelines. For example, the life of the computer may be three years for tax purposes.

The second decision is how much of the value of that asset should be charged to cost of sales during each of the three years. If it is divided equally, in this example $333,333 per year would be charged against sales. This amount is called depreciation. However, there are many different methods of depreciation, some of which accelerate the expenditure so that, for example, $5,000 might be charged the first year to cost of sales, $3,333.33 the second year, and $1,666.67 the last year. Depreciation methods such as this are permitted to encourage organizations to purchase assets.

Example 2: Prepaid Expenses

If expenses are prepaid, such as purchasing insurance on the computer center, the charging of that expense against sales should be allocated. For example, let us assume that an insurance policy covering physical damage in a computer center was acquired for a three-year period at a cost of $3,600. As with other expenditures, cash would be credited for the $3,600 to reduce cash, and a prepaid expense account debited for the $3,600. This account would then be reduced by $100 per month over the 36 month life of the insurance policy. The objective of this is to charge the cost of the expense to the period benefiting from that expenditure.

Both the depreciation example and the prepaid example illustrate the going concern concept of accounting. Obviously, the asset has been purchased and may have little or no value on the open market. The insurance has been paid for, and there may or may not be a refund due if the insur-

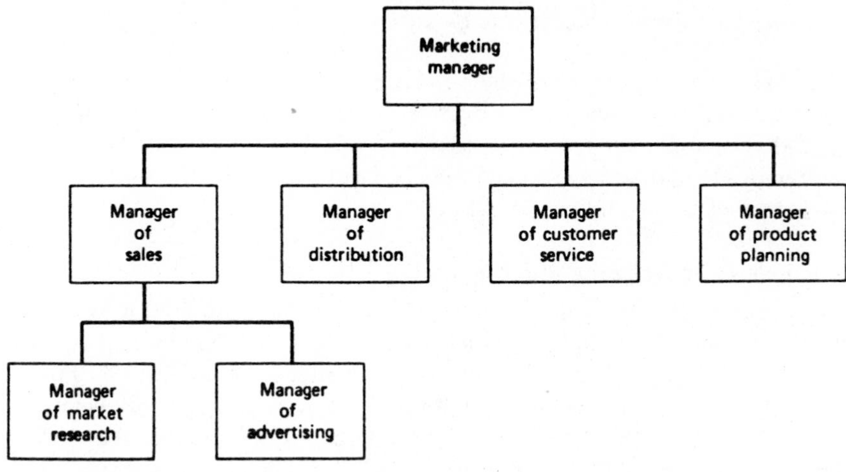

Figure 10. Marketing Function Organization Chart.

ance is cancelled. Thus, after one month, showing a $3,500 asset for prepaid insurance on the books makes little sense from a liquidation perspective, but a lot of sense from a going concern perspective.

THE IMPACT OF THE COMPUTER ON ACCOUNTING SYSTEMS[1]

This section illustrates how an automated marketing system affects corporate accounting. To understand marketing, it is important to understand the major sections of marketing and the responsibilities of each section. In large organizations each section of the marketing function is headed by a manager; in smaller organizations one individual may be responsible for two or more sections.

The typical marketing function organization chart is illustrated in Figure 10. All these managers work together to produce revenue for the organization. Their functions and responsibilities are tied together in a series of related links, or steps, that we call the marketing system chain.

The marketing system chain has the responsibility for satisfying customer needs. This is accomplished by a chain of events composed of many links; it begins when the customer initiates a purchase order and continues through the warranty, repair, and replacement procedures. The chain also includes the replenishment of inventory. Figure 11 illustrates a marketing system chain for an organization that is selling a product. The chain comprises many links, or steps, such as credit approval, billing, and

[1]Most of the material in this section is taken from William E. Perry, *Accountants' Guide to Computer Systems*, (New York: John Wiley & Sons, 1982). Reprinted with permission.

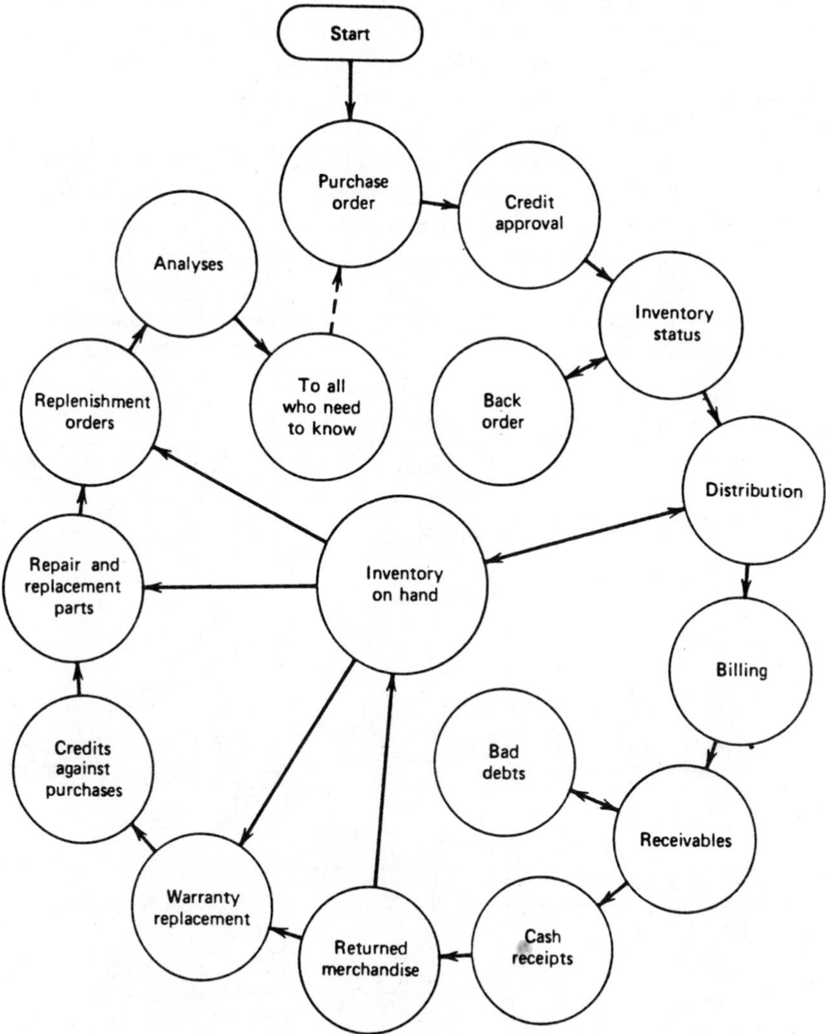

Figure 11. Marketing Systems Chain.

so on. If the organization deals in services, the same general framework would apply. However, in a service organization the steps relating to inventory would be replaced with service-oriented links.

All the links in the marketing system revolve around the sale and movement of the company product or service. The marketing systems chain produces numerous documents. Some are documents to be used later as input documents and others are solely output reports—all produced from the data within the system. As systems become more complex, there are fewer hard-copy documents generated from the system. On-line marketing systems operate with minimal input documents. The expression "a paperless society" reflects the small number of system documents, and the low volume of paper produced by systems. In many instances, the system functions without any paper output.

The purchase order, product return, and cash receipts are the documents that initiate action in the marketing systems chain. All other documents can be generated from data contained within the computerized application. Figure 12 shows the links in the chain and which links utilize those documents.

Figure 13 shows the marketing system and its relationship to paperwork, the organization, and the system rules. As with any system, the initiation of

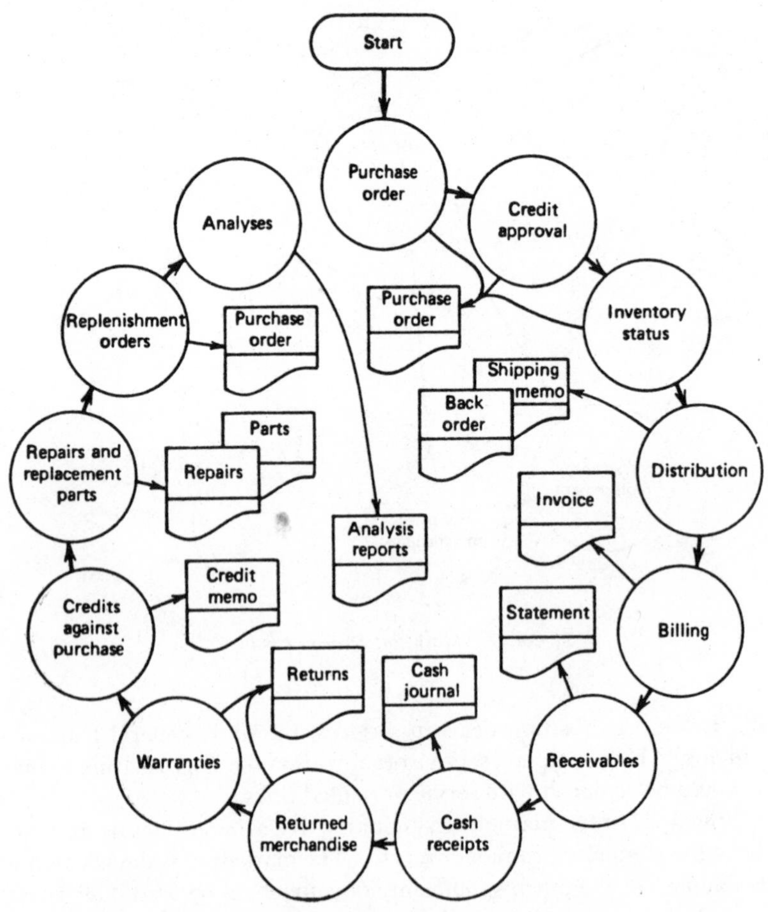

Figure 12. Paperwork Marketig Systems Chain.

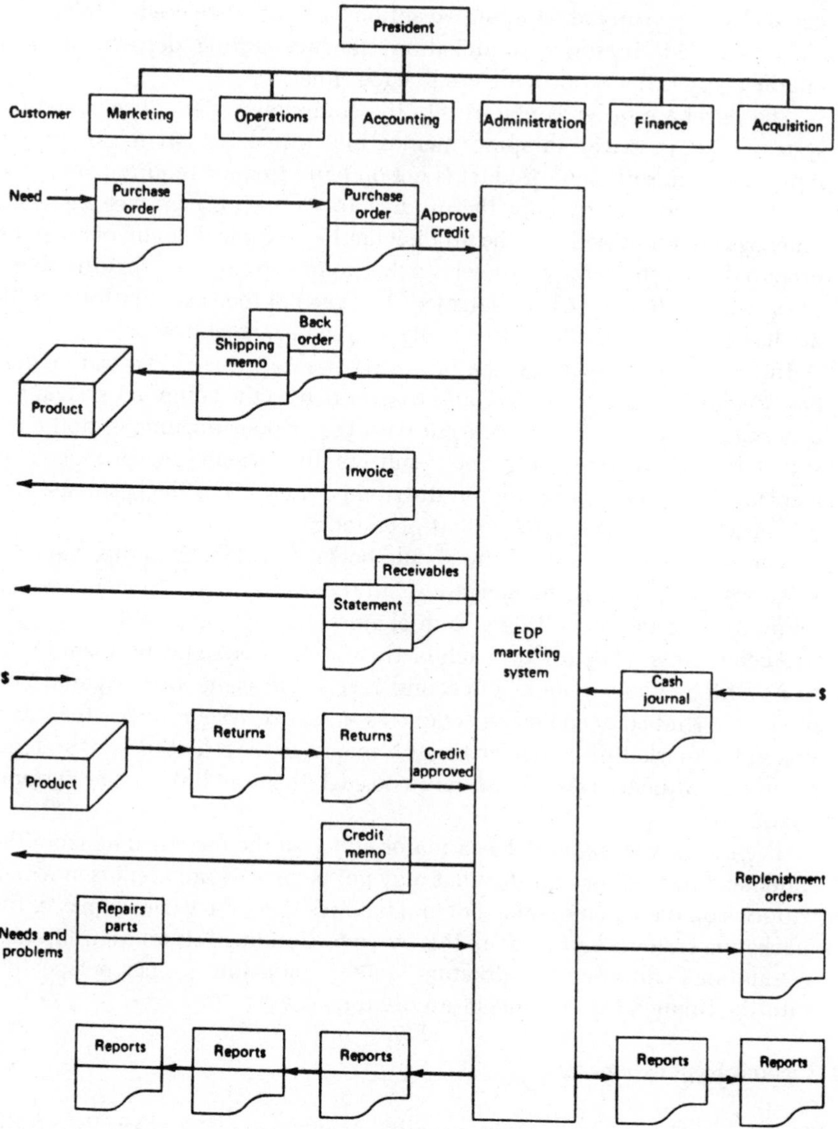

Figure 13. Systems Flow—Marketing Systems Chain.

transaction (a need to be satisfied) begins with the customer of the system. In the marketing system, this is the customer's purchase order. The marketing department authorizes the transaction and requests approval of credit, if requested by the customer, from the accounting department. As previously stated, this credit approval can be built into the system, with the accounting department handling exceptions such as when credit limits have been exceeded. In some organizations the accounting department will handle every order, approving credit each time.

The purchase order is placed into the computer system. The computer system then prepares shipping memos and any back order documents required when sufficient product is not on hand to meet requirements. The operations department ships the product to the customer. Once the computer system is notified that the product has been shipped, an invoice can be prepared and sent to the customer. At this point, we can state that the objectives of the system have been satisfied. The need of the customer for a product has resulted in the product's being shipped to the customer.

In terms of system steps, the following has happened. The transaction has been *authorized*, *recorded*, and *transmitted* to the computer system for processing. *Processing* has occurred with the various documents and data *stored* for future reference. The results of the system (the product and associated paperwork) have been distributed (*output*) to the customer and the customer will make use of that product.

The concept of systems chains should become evident from this example. It has taken many links to accomplish all the steps. However, there are still many links of the marketing system chain yet to be completed.

Accountants tend to view each of these links as systems by themselves. For example, you can look at accounts receivable as an entire system. You may have studied accounts receivable as an entire system rather than as a link in the marketing system chain. It is incorrect to look at these as systems complete in themselves. We should consider them as links in the systems chain.

The marketing function has a major effect on the income data from the statement and balance sheet. What may not be readily apparent is in which captions on the income statement and balance sheet the various links of the marketing system chain end up. It is by understanding this relationship that accountants can put the marketing system chain into proper perspective with the financial statements of an organization.

Income Implications

The marketing system chain usually encompasses the majority of the income and expense dollars of an organization. Figure 14 shows this relationship. The income statement shown is simplified. The objective of the figure is to show how the various captions relate to the links in the marketing system chain. This is not to imply that the total amount in the caption comes from the data in one link in the marketing system chain. For example, "bad debts" goes in selling expense but it is only a part—and, one hopes, a very small part—of selling expense.

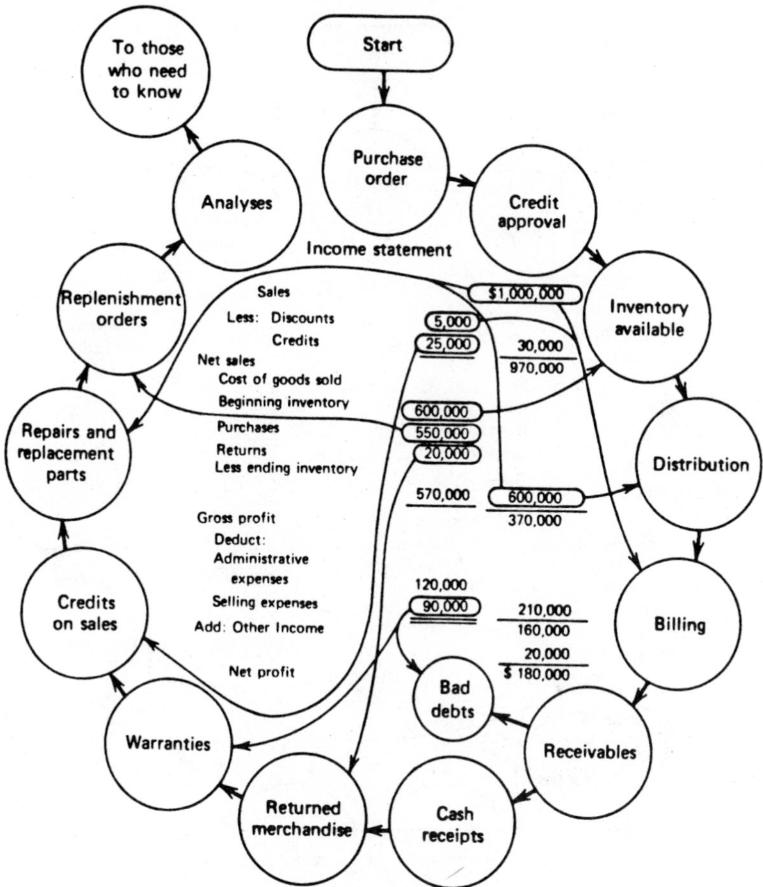

Figure 14. Income Implications—Marketing Systems Chain.

Many of the items on the income statement come from two or more links in the marketing system chain. For example, the sales figures come both from regular sales and from selling repair work and replacement parts.

Balance Sheet Implications

The marketing system's major impact on the balance sheet is the contribution to profit and loss. The total income/loss is reflected in retained earnings on the balance sheet. Since profit is a reflection of all the links in the total marketing system chain, it cannot be readily illustrated in Figure 15. However, Figure 15 does illustrate which balance sheet captions are individually affected by the various links in the marketing system chain. For example, cash receipts will be reflected in the balance sheet cash caption at

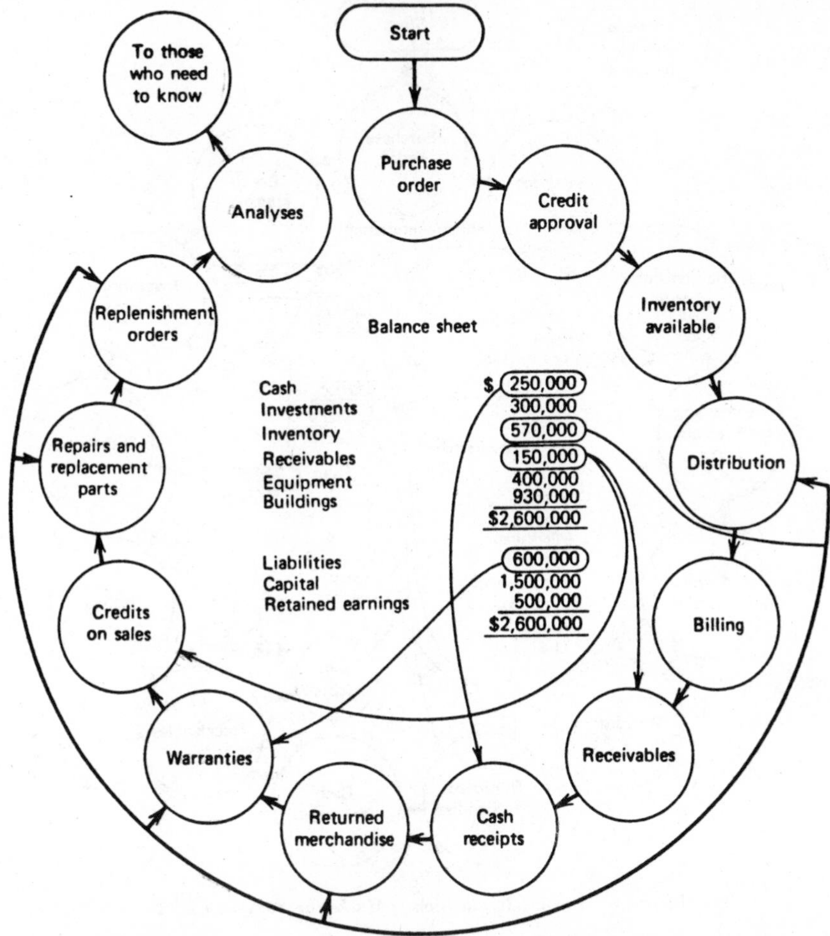

Figure 15. Balance Sheet Implications—Marketing Systems Chain.

the end of an accounting period. Reserves for warranties would be reflected in the liabilities caption. Inventory and receivables are affected by many links in the marketing system chain. This is because a sale and the accompanying reduction in inventory affect receivables, returns, warranties, repairs, and all inventory-related links.

Importance of Accounting Implications

In actual practice, information from two or more computer system chains feeds into the same financial statement caption. For example, there may be several marketing system chains in an organization. This is especially true in a corporation with subsidiaries or special product lines. In addition, some parts of the marketing system chain may be manual while others are computerized. For instance, some organizations will sell advertising promotional material to customers on a special request basis. Because this is not a routine function of the organization, it is handled manually when it occurs. At other times sales to employees are specially handled because of special prices or other considerations.

The net result is that only a few people in an organization understand how the amount listed for a specific financial statement caption is accumulated. Dollar amounts can come from a variety of divisions of an organization, and the original figures are lost as they are accumulated at various levels of an organization.

Accountants who wish to understand the development of financial statements need to have a good understanding of systems. The implications of a change in one system must be reflected in other systems to maintain continuity in a double-entry accounting system. Occasionally, a change will occur that affects only half of an accounting entry. For example, if returned merchandise is reflected only in a dollar credit to the customer and a reduction of sales, the inventory will be out of balance.

Few have the knowledge and skill to understand how accounting information from many different computer systems is consolidated into the financial statements of the organization. Figures 14 and 15 should prove helpful in illustrating that relationship. Accountants studying systems should try to develop charts such as these as a basis for understanding the relationship between systems and financial records. But because so few understand the control implications of computerized systems, problems can occur and go undetected.

THE ABUSES OF ACCOUNTING

The uses of accounting have been illustrated in the previous material in this chapter. It is used to record transactions, to process that information, and to produce financial statements. Those statements are used in evaluating and operating the business.

The accounting process can also be abused. Much of the abuse is related to a lack of understanding of accounting and how it works. Let's look at five of the more common abuses about accounting.

Abuse 1. Implied Precision

The financial statements can be prepared to the nearest penny. In other words, income could be expressed as $52,387.29. In our previous discussions we explained how depreciation can vary based upon two decisions. These were the life of the asset and the rate at which the asset would be depreciated. Therefore, it is quite easy to change the amount of profit depending on what decision you make.

Accounting is a measurement tool based on the process established for that measurement. This process is a combination of accounting theory (e.g., the going concern concept), generally accepted accounting procedures, and decisions made by the organization.

The net result of accounting are statements of financial conditions. The key concept of these statements is that they should be prepared on a basis consistent from year to year, and follow some generally accepted principles. The resulting financial statements, therefore, are a measurement system that can be used to compare the results from accounting period to accounting period and between organizations. It is not designed to be representative of a real-world situation, or to present real accuracy. For this reason, many organizations round their financial amount to the nearest thousand dollars to avoid the aura of high precision.

Abuse 2. Incomplete Measurement

The chart of accounts determines what is measured. What is not included in the chart of accounts is not measured. For example, in the data processing department we may measure an employee's salary, but might not measure the expenditure of systems and programming effort on building or maintaining a project.

If something is not measured, it is difficult to manage. For example, if the data processing manager does not know how much time is being spent on projects, it is difficult to control the cost associated with those projects.

A better illustration of this dilemma that is more typical is the failure to record the amount of time expended on testing computer systems. These costs are frequently buried in general project costs. Therefore, data processing management does not know how many resources are allocated for testing and, thus, has great difficulty controlling and improving testing.

RECOMMENDED ACCOUNTING AND AUDITING PRINCIPLE FOR THE DATA PROCESSING MANAGER
You cannot control what you do not measure. The failure to measure an activity like testing makes the control and management of that activity difficult.

Abuse 3. Limitations of Accounting Periods

One of the premises of accounting is to develop statements and record items in specific accounting periods. These periods may be monthly, quarterly, or annually. The segments produced at that time are used by senior management to evaluate performance of activities and functions within their organization.

This arbitrary selection of an accounting period is inconsistent with the operation of most activities within the organization. For example, the cost of developing new systems, acquiring new buildings, or increased salaries to staff represent sharp jumps in expenditures in a single accounting period, with the benefits derived in much later periods. For example, if data processing spends two years building a computer system, there is no benefit to the organization during that development time. However, the costs associated with building the system are charged to the department during that development period.

American management has been accused of putting too much emphasis on the accounting period and not enough emphasis on the long-range goals and missions of the organization. Concepts like quality and improved productivity are long-range activities. As such, it is difficult to provide short-term return on investments for long-term projects.

Abuse 4. Shows Cost, Not Value

Financial statements do not show the actual worth or value of an organization. In many instances, the financial statements are very misleading regarding the value of an organization, or where that value resides. For example, people are a valuable asset of an organization, yet they don't appear on the financial statements. Likewise, computer applications represent a value that would be difficult to replace, but also are not shown on the financial statements.

Abuse 5. Financial Statements Do Not Include Interpretation

The financial statements, like any measure, are only that—a measure. If we calculate the number of statements that a programmer can write in a day, we have a measure of performance. However, that measure must be interpreted to be valid. The fact that programmer A writes eight statements a day, and programmer B writes 16 statements a day does not mean that programmer B is a better programmer. For example, programmer A's statements may be complex statements and, as discussed earlier, might include requirements, documentation, and so on. On the other hand, programmer B's statements may be mostly comment statements and relatively straightforward statements.

It is good practice never to issue financial statements without a commentary. Note that in the financial statements issued to stockholders, there is always a commentary about those statements, usually provided by the chief executive officer. The reason for this is that statements without commentary may be misinterpreted.

RECOMMENDED ACCOUNTING AND AUDITING PRINCIPLE FOR THE DATA PROCESSING MANAGER
The easiest method to overcome accounting abuses is to provide with any financial statement commentary interpreting the results reported in that statement.

Chapter Three

Creating a Positive Data Processing Image Through Creative Accounting

Creative accounting is a term coined for accounting practices employed for one's personal advantage. It is usually associated with accounting that is designed to explain or justify a business situation. The individual preparing the accounting information usually makes assumptions that create an advantageous situation for that individual.

Accounting as described in Chapters 1 and 2 is designed primarily for external use. The outputs are the financial statements given to stockholders, governmental agencies, financial institutions, and the public at large. It is the preparation of these external financial statements that is governed by generally accepted accounting procedures. Accounting statements prepared for internal usage are not governed by any externally imposed generally accepted accounting procedures. It is in the preparation of internal statements that most creative accounting is utilized.

This chapter explains how accounting can be used advantageously by the data processing manager. While the term creative accounting has a devious connotation, the ojective of this chapter is to assist data processing management in presenting the status of data processing in the most positive manner. The chapter explains the difference between internal and external accounting. The uses of internal accounting are explained, recommendations are made regarding what should be measured within data processing, and the chapter concludes with recommendations to the data processing manager on how to use accounting most effectively.

RECOMMENDED ACCOUNTING AND AUDITING PRINCIPLE FOR THE DATA PROCESSING MANAGER

Figures don't lie, but liars can figure. This historical saying warns that management will always be suspicious of the integrity of financial statements.

EXTERNAL VERSUS INTERNAL ACCOUNTING SYSTEMS

External accounting measures the external performance of the organization. External performance is usually expressed in terms of earnings, use of earnings, and the financial status of the organization as presented in the balance sheet.

External accounting was the main topic of Chapter 2. This showed how the results of operation are processed through the accounting cycle. Chapter 1 discussed the various agencies and boards that regulate the procedures used to produce statements for external purposes.

For profit-making corporations, traded through stock exchanges, the external statements can significantly impact stock prices and the desirability of acquiring stock in the corporation. The taxes paid by a corporation are closely tied to the external financial statement. It was previously discussed that there may be some differences between the accounting used by the corporation to prepare its financial statements and tax limitations. In those cases, the financial statements need to be change for tax purposes. Note that on the corporation tax form there is a place to reconcile differences between the corporation's accounting system and the statements of financial condition reporting for tax purposes. For example, the corporation may decide to use straight-line depreciation for its own records, but use accelerated depreciation for tax purposes.

The external financial statements are frequently used as a basis for executive bonuses and stock option plans. Many company benefits are tied to the earnings of the corporation. Some union contracts are now tied to the earnings as presented in the financial statements. We are also seeing more unions evaluating the financial records of an organization and using those analyses as a basis for wage negotiations.

All of these factors put emphasis on the earnings of a corporation. Management is constantly pressured to improve earnings. Frequently, this emphasizes short-term benefits, as opposed to long-term gains.

Quality is a long-term concept. It takes extensive time to train employees, build production processes that are highly effective and productive, and do the type of planning and preparatory work needed to ensure that only high-quality defect-free products are produced. This concept of quality is frequently counter to the short-term profit incentives given to executives. It is interesting to note that more and more corporations are tying executive bonuses to long-term performance rather than short-term profitability.

RECOMMENDED ACCOUNTING AND AUDITING PRINCIPLE FOR THE DATA PROCESSING MANAGER
Quality operations are normally front-end-loaded with costs. The long-term payback for investments in quality (e.g., investments in new equipment and processes) may negatively impact short-term profits. Thus, some internal accounting may be needed to demonstrate long-term benefits.

Internal accounting are segments of the organization's accounting system specifically designed for internal usage. The information collected, processed, and outputted from the internal accounting aspects of accounting information systems are for use by management in managing the organization.

The most widely known internal accounting system is budgeting. This accounting system requires managers to plan and estimate the resources required to accomplish those plans. The budget provides the resources needed to operate a function like data processing, and then issues regular status reports on the use of those budgeted funds.

The budget illustrates the interaction between internal and external accounting systems. The budgeted amount in budget reports is an internal accounting system process. The actual expenditures recorded against that budget are produced by the external reporting system.

The only restrictions imposed on internal accounting are those posed by the organization. The procedures for internal accounting are normally developed and enforced by the organization's comptroller. These are frequently called comptroller procedures.

Internal accounting is used for many purposes within the organization. Because accounting is a language of management, it is important to translate discussions and proposals to management into accounting. For example, when acquiring a computer, management is not overly concerned with the speed of the equipment, the type of hardware devices that can be attached, the problems of building networks, and so on. What management is concerned with are the accounting aspects of the acquisition.

Let's look at the type of questions that management normally asks about the acquisition of a new computer:

What is the purchase price of the computer?

What is the lease price of the computer?

What will it cost to maintain the computer?

Will we get any trade-in or resale value for our existing computer?

What is the expected life of the computer?

What are the tax laws related to depreciating or expensing the computer?

What will it cost to operate the computer?

Will there be any changes in cost of operation between the current and the new computer?

How will the new computer affect the cost per unit of work?

The answers to these questions are expressed using internal accounting information systems. It is in the development of answers to questions like these that internal accounting can be used creatively to present data processing in the most positive manner. It is important that data processing management learn how to use accounting to effectively present their cases.

The remaining chapters in this book describe the methods that data processing can use in communications with management. Accounting can be used to justify projects, new facilities, and technical support. Accounting can be used to show the benefits of data processing to the organization and the results of alternate methods of processing and edicts imposed on data processing by regulatory agencies, users, and senior management.

COST OF QUALITY ACCOUNTING

One recommended use of accounting is to measure the internal performance of organizations and activities within an organization. We stated earlier that net profit is a measure of external performance, and we described the many uses of this performance measure. However, net profit is not necessarily a good measure of internal performance, particularly of individual activities.

The cost of quality accounting is used to measure internal performance. The difficulty with external measures is that they do not indicate the quality, productivity, and performance of functions like data processing. The internal costs are merely accumulated to produce an external result—net profit.

Let's reexamine the attributes of the statement of income and expense. Here is a simplified income statement:

XYZ CORPORATION
Statement of Income and Expense
For the Year Ended December 31, 19XX

Income from sales	$1,000,000
Less cost of sales	800,000
Net profit	200,000

In this illustration, all of the costs associated with data processing are buried within the cost of sales. The costs associated with poor quality work or poor performance are not recorded. The data processing department may have done an outstanding job or a terrible job, but that performance is not reflected through the accounting system.

Accounting cannot measure internal performance at present because the cost of quality is not measured. Let's first look at the components of the cost of quality, then why we would want to measure them, and then how they can be used in the measure of internal performance.

Cost of Quality Components

Quality means compliance with standards or requirements. In data processing, this is interpreted as following procedures and meeting user needs. The costs of "doing it right the first time" are identified as the costs of quality.

The costs of quality are the costs associated with ensuring that the products produced are defect free. If defects are encountered in the product, then those defects must be fixed, and this increases the cost of quality. It is a cost associated with not doing it right the first time.

There are three components to the cost of quality. These components are illustrated in Figure 16 and described on page 52:

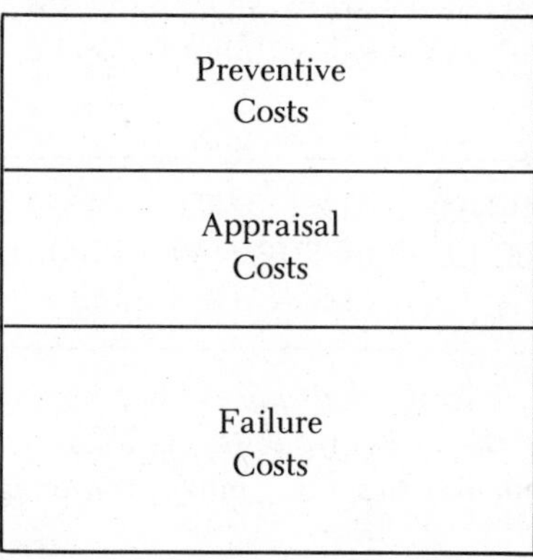

Figure 16. Cost of Quality Components.

Preventive Costs. The costs associated with preventing projects and tasks from being improperly performed. Preventive costs include training of staff, development of procedures and standards, development of acquisition of system development life cycles, and staff meetings to explain procedures.

Appraisal Costs. These are the costs associated with evaluating the quality of the product throughout its developmental cycle. The appraisal can be performed by the individual responsible for the task, such as the computer operator, or it can be performed by a review group or independent function, such as EDP quality assurance. The appraisal costs include project reviews, checkpoint documentation, operation checklists, and input/output control procedures.

Failure Costs. Failure costs include all of the costs associated with not doing it right the first time. For the data processing function, these include costs associated with the data processing function as well as costs incurred by users of incomplete or inaccurate information. The costs of failure include software repair maintenance, computer reruns, removal of syntax errors, time expended in explaining why it was not right, user time expended to correct errors, lost business due to ineffective procedures, inaccurate information, and loss of data processing credibility.

The objective of cost of quality is to produce defect-free products. In striving for this objective, we encounter tradeoffs between preventive, appraisal, and failure costs. Note that failure is only acceptable during development and is not acceptable in the final product. For example, making compiler errors, which is a failure cost requiring a recompilation, may be cheaper than paying the appraisal costs to desk debug (manually search for problems) that computer program.

Generally, the costs of quality are not recorded through the normal accounting system. For example, there are no accounting buckets for repair maintenance, peer reviews of software systems, lost business due to computer goofs, and costs associated with not following standards.

RECOMMENDED ACCOUNTING AND AUDITING PRINCIPLE FOR THE DATA PROCESSING MANAGER
You cannot control what you cannot measure. If you do not measure the cost of quality, you cannot control the cost components that go into producing defect-free products.

Why Measure the Cost of Quality?

Quality is the key to improving data processing productivity and credibility. Users and management base much of their assessment of the data processing function on the quality of the products produced by that function. Quality by definition is compliance with standards and requirements. If these standards and requirements are not defined, people will judge the quality of data processing products by their own quality yardstick.

Dr. W. Edwards Deming, the individual responsible for much of the turnaround in Japanese industry after the Second World War, has stated that it can take up to 20 years to change a managerial philosophy from profit and productivity to one of quality. The time span is due to both the difficulty in making attitudinal changes and the problem of improving processes to the point where they regularly produce high-quality products.

Quality principles are not applicable to an art form. With the introduction of system development methodologies, standardized data definitions, operating and programming standards, and the like, the processes are being developed to develop quality systems. However, it is difficult to build processes that produce high-quality data processing products quickly.

The first step has taken place in the data processing profession. Analysts, programmers, and operators are being given processes to follow that will enable them to build data processing products. The second step is to identify and improve those processes. To perform this step, data processing functions are establishing EDP quality assurance groups. The objective of quality assurance is to measure, evaluate, and improve the process. To do this, these groups need information on the defects or failures associated with the data processing process.

Current accounting systems cannot provide the type of information needed to evaluate processes. The measurement associated with most accounting systems is either an external measurement for profit, or an internal measure of financial controls. The accounts and items measured are not the ones that are related to the preventive, appraisal, and failure costs associated with cost of quality accounting.

The problems that plague data processing management from a quality and productivity perspective are:

What are the costs and benefits associated with issuing new standards?

Where do defects occur in the developmental process?

If I introduce a new tool, such as a testing tool, what effect will it have on the number of defects and the productivity of the systems and programming staff?

Where is it most effective to conduct tests?

What is the dollar benefit of the building system and program documentation?

What is the value associated with training data processing professionals?

The reason these questions cannot be answered is that the needed cost-of-quality information is unavailable. Data processing managers should be demanding accounting systems that provide this type of information. This attitude puts data processing management on the offensive to get the type of information needed to run their operation. Too many data processing managers are "slaves" to the corporate accounting system. This means that they give much more than they get.

Using Cost of Quality Information to Measure Internal Performance

The external measurement of performance is net profit. If an organization makes 12 percent net profit, it means that 12 cents of each dollar received for sales is not consumed by the expenses associated with making that sale. In other words, the organization spends 88 cents to take in one dollar.

An internal measure of performance is similar. If the cost of quality in a data processing function was 12 percent, that would mean that for every dollar given to the data processing department, 88 cents was expended to directly satisfy the data processing mission. Twelve cents of that dollar was spent either to prevent defective products from being made, appraising or reviewing the products to ensure they are what was requested, or building something that was not needed or building it incorrectly.

Quality control experts state that in a very well-run organization the cost of quality should be about 15 percent. In actual practice, it is averaging 50 percent for the entire data processing profession.[1] This means that for every dollar given the average data processing organization, 50 cents is spent on the cost of quality. Much of this is expended on failure. Much of the failure is represented by repair maintenance costs, and maintenance associated with failure to get the specifications right the first time.

Few data processing managers know the cost of quality. Once they can identify the cost categories, they need to collect accounting information about those costs. The concept of your not being able to control what you cannot measure comes into play in cost of quality.

In most organizations, data processing management has lost control of its costs. This has been primarily responsible for much of the loss of credibility of data processing and for failure of data processing managers to be promoted into senior management.

In the factory, there is much better information available about the cost

[1]Leon W. Ellsworth and Claude W. Burrill, *Quality Data Processing: Profit Potential for the 1980s.* (Tenafly, N.J., Burrill-Ellsworth, 1982).

of quality. This is provided by cost accounting, a branch of accounting that is designed to break costs into their component pieces as a means of determining the costs of products. While the actual cost of failure may not be measured completely, an understanding of the theoretical costs for a part versus the actual costs gives good insight into the cost of quality. In addition, the industrial engineers are continually evaluating and measuring the process, looking for process deficiencies and making recommendations on how to improve them.

RECOMMENDED ACCOUNTING AND AUDITING PRINCIPLE FOR THE DATA PROCESSING MANAGER
The cost of quality for the data processing profession is estimated to be 50 percent. This means that 50 cents out of every data processing dollar is expended for purposes other than performing the mission of the function. This 50 percent cost of quality is excessive, but it can only be reduced by installing new accounting measurement processes.

MEASURE WHAT YOU WANT TO CONTROL

Measurement of any type is a two-edged sword. One data processing manager became enamored with the widely discussed programming standard of the 1970s, which was programmers producing one line of code per hour. The manager decided to use this as a measure of performance and, as a means of improving performance, established an incentive bonus for programmers who significantly surpassed the standard.

The self-fulfilling prophecy of measurement came into play, and the manager got more statements produced per hour than the standard. The programs were not necessarily any better, because rather than developing sophisticated statements the programmers opted for simple, straightforward statements in order to produce more per hour.

This same fallacy can be observed in most measurement systems. People do what the system measures. For example, if you measure data processing projects on their ability to meet schedules and budgets, they will meet schedules and budgets. The product developed may be terrible, and the cost of quality horrendous, but the measurements will be achieved. It is always interesting to note how many accounting budgetary accounts and quotas are fulfilled. One frequently wonders what shenanigans need to take place in order to make the numbers work out correctly.

Data processing management should be very leery of any measurement system. The challenge should be both with measures placed on them, and measures they place on subordinates.

The questions that need to be asked for every measurement system are:

What is the objective of measuring, and does this measure measure the intended variable? For example, when analysts are requested to make an estimate for a new project, are we really measuring their ability to make a good estimate, or are we measuring their ability to complete the project within the estimate?

Can reliable information be collected for the measure? For example, if we asked staff to report hours worked on each project, how reliable is the information collected? If reliable information cannot be collected, which is the case in many accounting systems, then we are not really providing valuable information to management.

Can the measurement information be collected within a time span that will make it useful to management? Some information is interesting, but is of little value. For example, it is nice to know information regarding the status of a project, but if that information is not available in time to make adjustments, for example, adding extra staff, then the status or measurement information is of little value.

Any measure must meet the following three criteria:

1. It should be easy to collect. The cost of collecting measurement information should never exceed the benefits from collecting it.
2. The measurement information must be reliable and valid. In other words, the information must be reproducible, given the same variables, and must be a proper measure to accomplish the objective of measurement.
3. The information must be available on a timely basis. The information collected must be reported back to the decision maker in time for use in making decisions.

DATA PROCESSING AS A PROFIT CENTER

Senior management can view organizations in one of two ways. There are activities that are cost centers and activities that are profit centers. Profit centers are always the favored activities because they generate the revenue that keeps the organization in business.

By all standard measures, data processing is a cost center. Generally, it contributes nothing to the revenue of the organization and, in fact, detracts from that revenue by adding to the cost of sales. This is not to say that it isn't an important cost, a worthwhile cost, and a necessary cost but, rather, that it is a cost.

The important difference between a cost center and a profit center is the attitude of management when economic times get tough. It is the rare organization that attempts to cut revenue, instead, management cuts costs. One always looks at cost centers for cost cutting, as opposed to cutting the costs associated with profit centers.

It is important to note that profits can be increased in either of the following two ways:

1. Increase revenues received by the organization.
2. Reduce the cost of sales.

The profit formula is:

Revenue minus cost of sales equals profit.

Either of the two variables affect the profit. Therefore, if an activity or function within the organization contributes to the profitability of the organization, it should be dubbed a "profit center."

Data processing can be called a profit center when its activities contribute directly to reducing the cost of sales, or enable revenue to be increased. This change in name is not a sleight-of-hand technique but, rather, a philosophy and attitude change.

When data processing is viewed as a cost center, there is difficulty in determining and evaluating the contribution to the organization. On the other hand, when data processing becomes a profit center the individuals within the data processing function become entrepreneurs. This entrepreneurial approach to business has proven extremely successful in many organizations. Some organizations even permit their employees to share in the entrepreneurial profits as a bonus or profit-sharing plan.

Profit centers have the following attributes:

1. Identifiable products.
2. Methods to associate costs of building and maintaining those products.
3. Methods for pricing or associating benefits with the products.

Many data processing functions already possess the above three attributes. Although many of the products have not been identified for accounting purposes, they are identified products. Among the data processing products are:

Computer runs or outputs

Consulting services
Application systems or programs
Software maintenance
Training
Data storage
Data recovery procedures

The above list of products illustrates a potential need for the "unbundling" of data processing services. For example, many users pay for services they do not want. For example, users may pay for developing recovery procedures or extensive system documentation. When the costs are "bundled" into a single cost package, the elements of the free market place are not allowed to work.

The premise of the profit center is that all of the activities must be installed on a pay-as-you-go basis. If the data processing department cannot find customers for services, then those services should be deleted. Note that this does not include overhead for activities that the data processing function perceives as essential to the success of the operation. For example, it would be impractical to attempt to market to users the value of training to the data processing professional. Training is the responsibility of the data processing department and, thus, it benefits all users equally. What should be unbundled are those services that may or may not be of benefit to users, but are not necessary for the integrity of data processing operations.

We will explore this profit center concept in Part 3 of this book. In the justification of applications, technical services, and operations, the profit center concept is an important justification strategy. Using accounting as a means for justifying data processing activities presents a positive image to senior management, and at the same time helps to create an incentive and an entrepreneurial attitude among the data processing staff.

RECOMMENDED ACCOUNTING AND AUDITING PRINCIPLE FOR THE DATA PROCESSING MANAGER
When data processing is a profit center, all of the activities within that function must pay their own way. This philosophy not only creates a positive image with management, but helps eliminate unwanted and unneeded services.

RECOMMENDATIONS ON USING ACCOUNTING EFFECTIVELY

A good data processing manager should be able to turn the accounting tide in favor of the data processing function. It is the way in which accounting is used that determines whether it will be the friend or foe of the data processing manager. Let's review the five creative uses of accounting for fostering the data processing function.

Creative Use 1. Referring to Data Processing as a Profit Center

Things become what people believe they are. If the data processing manager does not believe the data processing function is a profit center, neither subordinates nor superiors will. It will be a new concept to many, and opposed by some. The arguments earlier in this chapter will explain the concepts. The problem is in going from a concept to a reality. The latter chapters in this book help to implement the profit center concept.

Creative Use 2. Calculating the Cost of Quality

This is a new and important concept in accounting. It is particularly applicable to data processing. Currently, GUIDE International has a very extensive project on how to calculate the cost of quality. (Note: GUIDE International is an IBM users group for large mainframe computer users.) This emphasis on internal performance should help to improve the credibility of the data processing function with senior management.

Creative Use 3. Justifying All New Projects by Showing Benefits

Return on investment is a powerful presentation concept. It is difficult for senior management to turn down projects that project a high return on investment. It is far superior to use accounting as the basis for justifying new data processing projects as opposed to oral and narrative presentations of elusive and poorly defined benefits.

Creative Use 4. Using Accounting to Identify Data Processing Vulnerabilities

Accounting presents a picture of performance for those willing to spend the time doing the analysis of the financial statements. Data processing management should request and scrutinize the details of the data processing accounting systems. Discrepancies in cost or benefit normally represent problems with systems. Data processing personnel are optimistic by nature, and believe they can overcome most obstacles. Accounting figures represent the hard truth and in the confines of a private office speak a reality that most project leaders and supervisors would be reluctant to express. Managers should rely on accounting to guide them to the necessary decisions.

Creative Use 5. Establishing Objectives Before Building Accounting Systems

Accounting systems are not different than any other system. If the requirements are well stated, the system will perform well. On the other hand, if the system is designed with sketchy requirements, the results will probably not satisfy the user. In creative accounting it is important to know the objective of accounting and measurement before determining what to measure and how to accomplish it.

RECOMMENDED ACCOUNTING AND AUDITING PRINCIPLE FOR THE DATA PROCESSING MANAGER
Accounting is a tool for management. Management should run accounting, and not let accounting run management.

Part Two

USING ACCOUNTING TO JUSTIFY DATA PROCESSING ACTIVITIES

Accounting can be used by data processing management as a basis for communicating to management the desirability of performing a project. Part 2 explains how to use accounting to justify application systems, data processing support activities, and computer operations. While accounting alone will not justify the project, it is a powerful adjunct to communicate the benefits in economic terms.

Chapter Four

Justifying Application Systems

Application systems are the primary product of the data processing function. Most other activities are supportive of acquiring, developing, installing, and maintaining application systems.

Each application that is built represents an expenditure of resources and thus that expenditure needs to be justified. The objective of this chapter is to present a process for presenting the accounting information needed to make a decision on whether or not to install, enhance, or extend the life of applications through maintenance.

The chapter presents a six-step process for justifying application systems. In addition, the process is supplemented by material to help justify the system maintenance function, when that maintenance consists of small changes and repair maintenance as opposed to major enhancements. The chapter addresses the make and buy decision for application software, as well as purchase versus lease.

THE NEED TO JUSTIFY APPLICATION SYSTEMS

The obvious reason that one justifies the development of acquisition of an application system is to get approval to do the work. The justification is as simple or as complex as conditions warrant to acquire the needed approval. However, important as this is, it is only one of many reasons why data processing management should want application systems justified using accounting principles.

Justification using accounting principles demonstrates the dollar value of installing the application system to management. The benefits of doing this include:

Benefit 1. Providing a Basis for Evaluating the Value of an Application System

What one thinks is valuable and what the economics show to be valuable may be different. Performing an economic evaluation of an application system forces the proposers to identify and quantify benefits as well as costs. Once the value of the benefits are quantified a more logical decision can be made regarding the merits of creating or acquiring a new application system.

Benefit 2. Assisting Users in Making Application Decisions

Before users can determine the systems and/or alternatives within that system that they want, an economic evaluation helps determine the appropriate decision. Frequently, users have choices to make such as build or buy; install quickly or wait; modify an existing system or build a new one. Economics help make these decisions.

Benefit 3. Prioritizing Work

IBM states that the average data processing function has a three-year backlog of work, and that that backlog is growing. It would be unfortunate to pick work from that backlog with a low return on investment, while other work with a high return on investment went unimplemented. Knowing the economic advantages of installing various application systems helps to establish priorities in work from a corporate perspective versus satisfying the user that manages to get attention by making a lot of noise.

Benefit 4. Assisting Data Processing Management in Rejecting Uneconomic Work

Data processing management has the responsibility to oversee the use of computers in the organization. Part of this responsibility is to ensure that the resources are only used when it is advantageous to use those resources. An economic assessment of projects helps data processing management fulfill the responsibilities as guardian of the organization's computer resources.

Benefit 5. A Measure of Performance

Calculating the economic expectations of an application system provides a basis for measuring the effectiveness of the use of computer resources. Unless measurable objectives are defined, the value of operational applications may be difficult to determine. However, if a project is projected to provide a 30 percent return on investment, the performance of the operational application system can be measured against that return on investment performance standard.

THE CHALLENGE OF JUSTIFYING APPLICATION SYSTEMS

The benefits of justifying application systems are countered by arguments that the concept is good in theory, but may be unnecessary or impractical in practice. Let's look at the five major arguments against justifying projects and then discuss a proposed solution:

Counterargument 1. It Is Unnecessary If the Projects Need To Be Installed

In many instances, application projects are mandated by management or edicted by regulatory agencies. If the project is implemented regardless of the economic analysis, the argument states that the time spent on the economic analysis would be better expended on developing the project.

Counterargument 2. The Benefits Are Hard To Quantify

Many project benefits are intangible in nature, which makes them hard to quantify. For example, if it is believed that a project will improve customer goodwill, increase opportunity in the marketplace, or reduce processing errors, these are hard benefits to quantify. The argument states that because it is difficult, it should not be done.

Counterargument 3. Data Processing Personnel Lack Training in Economic Evaluation

This argument states that individuals should not be asked to do tasks for which they lack the necessary qualifications. The argument states that if the accountants want economic evaluation, let them do it and leave the tasks to the data processing personnel for which they are best qualified.

Counterargument 4. The Implied Precision of Economic Evaluation May Not Exist

One of the problems of measurement is that if the measurement is no good, it should not be used. If economic evaluation is to be used as the basis of measurement, then it should be a reliable and valid calculation. This argument states that to propose a return on investment that implies a precision that is not there may be more misleading than to not provide that evaluation.

Counterargument 5. The Calculated Economic Return May Not Be Accepted

In many organizations economic evaluations are not regularly performed. When provided, they may be viewed suspiciously and not relied upon by the individuals with whom the economic evaluations are given. If they will not be accepted, the counterarguments state they should not be prepared.

The underlying fallacy in all of these arguments is that the lack of measurement is associated with the lack of control. It is highly probable that the early attempts at justification will produce unreliable evaluations. This may be due to the fact that there is no process for performing these evaluations, and lacking a process it is difficult to improve deficiencies.

The solution to the arguments against determining the economic justification of projects is to adopt a process for performing those economic calculations. In many organizations such a process already exists. Where it exists the process has usually been developed by the organization's accountant, as opposed to the data processing function. This means that the economic evaluation provides what the accountants want, but may not provide what data processing management needs to manage and evaluate application systems.

If no process exists for developing economic evaluations, data processing management should develop such a process. If one does exist and it was not developed by the data processing management, it should be heavily scrutinized to determine that it provides the information needed by data processing management. It is unwise to place one's destiny in the hands of another function.

RECOMMENDED ACCOUNTING AND AUDITING PRINCIPLE FOR THE DATA PROCESSING MANAGER
The value of any accounting process is the ability of that process to produce consistent and comparable results. It is more important that the results be consistent and comparable than for the results to be representative of real-world economics.

A SIX-STEP APPLICATION JUSTIFICATION PROCESS

The data processing function initiates and implements a large number of application systems in the course of the year. If each of these projects is justified, the process will be repeated as frequently as projects are proposed. Any process repeated frequently should be formalized and practiced in the same way by all involved parties.

A six-step estimation process is listed below with the steps individually explained afterward:

Step 1. Define application requirements.
Step 2. Determine application benefits.
Step 3. Develop application implementation alternatives.

Step 4. Develop the cost to implement each alternative.

Step 5. Calculate the return on investment for each alternative.

Step 6. Make an application decision.

The responsibility to perform these steps is normally given to the project leader. However, the project leader may want to work closely with the user responsible for the application. In addition, the project leader may want to take counsel with the organization's accountants regarding the correct use of the justification process.

Step 1. Define Application Requirements

Projects cannot be justified until the requirements have been defined. The level of definition will vary based on the type of project and the technical complexity. The level and format of requirements will also be dependent upon the organization's developmental process, which in most instances specifies the requirements deliverables.

Step 2. Determine Application Benefits

The benefits associated with an application system commence as soon as the application goes into operation. Thus, while costs begin accumulating from the point that a project is proposed, the benefits do not start accruing until many months later. The point at which benefits start to occur is an important factor in determining the return on investment from that application.

There are three categories of potential benefits from installing an application system:

Cost reductions

Cost avoidance

Intangible benefits

Cost reduction benefits are normally the most favorably received of the three categories of benefits. These are also the benefits that are the most easily substantiated. Many of the early computer systems produced significant cost reductions due to reductions in force in the area automated. However, these benefits are getting harder to obtain as many of the new systems are decision support systems as opposed to mainline accounting systems.

The types of costs that can be reduced through the installation of a new application system include:

Reduction of people

Reduction in the use of supplies

Elimination of space

Reduction in administrative support
Reduction in computer time
Reduction in supplies/equipment
Reduction in contractual support

The second benefit area is cost avoidance. This category of benefits eliminates the need to acquire additional people, space, support, and so on because the new application system can fulfill that need. For example, let us assume that an organization had to hire a new individual for every additional 1,000 customers that dealt with the organization. If the installation of a new computer system could stabilize the work force, then a benefit of cost avoidance could be calculated based upon the expected growth in customers.

The cost avoidance areas are approximately the same as the cost reduction areas. The difference is that in reduction the organization will experience an actual lessening of costs. With cost avoidance, they will stabilize, which makes the results of cost avoidance more difficult to positively demonstrate.

The third and most difficult area to estimate are intangible benefits. Some organizations follow the practice of calculating cost reduction and cost avoidance benefits, but only list intangible benefits. For example, after calculating the direct benefits, they will list additional benefits such as improved customer goodwill, but not put a price on it.

The pricing of cost reduction and cost avoidance is relatively straightforward. In these instances, the item of cost can be identified, and the accountants and accounting system can normally provide sufficient accounting information from the current system to use to project benefits.

The calculation of intangible benefits is much more difficult. Examples of intangible benefits include:

Improved resources utilization
Improved administrative and operational effectiveness
Reduced error rates
Improved service
Reduced risk of incorrect processing
Improved information handling
Enhanced organizational image
Less loss and fraud
Improved goodwill
Improved morale
Improved work effectiveness

A suggested method to estimate intangible benefits is to use the annual loss expectation formula. Loss expectation is an actuarial tool for calculating the potential effect of the occurrence of an event. The loss expectation formula is:

> Frequency of occurrence times loss per occurrence equals annual loss expectation

Let's look at an example of how this might be used in the calculation of the intangible benefit goodwill. Goodwill is only a valuable benefit if it can be translated into some positive act. If the organization sells products, then the favorable act from improved goodwill will be additional or new purchases by customers. Using the annual loss expectation formula, one must determine the quantity of products that customers will purchase in the course of the year due to improved goodwill (the frequency of occurrence part of the formula); and then estimate the average profit associated with those purchases (the loss per occurrence variable of the formula). If we assumed that 1,000 customers would buy one more product each per year, and the profit associated with that product was $100, then the benefit (i.e., annual loss expectation) for the intangible goodwill benefit is $100,000 (i.e., 1,000 purchases with each purchase generating $100 profit equals $100,000 benefit).

The last part of the benefit calculation is the determination of the number of years the benefits will be derived, and which benefits will be derived during which of those years. A benefit calculation worksheet is provided as Figure 17. At the conclusion of this step, the worksheet will have been completed and the benefits accumulated for each year of expected useful life of the application project.

RECOMMENDED ACCOUNTING AND AUDITING PRINCIPLE FOR THE DATA PROCESSING MANAGER
An effective rule of thumb to follow in selecting applications for implementation is: If the benefits cannot be calculated, there may not be any.

Step 3. Develop Application Implementation Alternatives

Benefits can be calculated once the business requirements for the application are known. However, the costs for implementing the system cannot be determined until the method of implementation has been developed. It is

	YEAR						
	0	1	2	3	4	5	TOTAL
Nonrecurring Benefits							
Cost Reduction:							
Reduction of resource requirements							
Improved operating efficiency							
Improved data entry, storage and retrieval techniques							
System performance monitoring							
Software conversion and optimization							
Data compression techniques							
Centralized/decentralized processing							
Value Enhancement:							
Improved resources utilization							
Improved administrative and operational effectiveness							
Reduced error rates							
Subtotal							
Recurring Benefits							
Cost Reduction:							
Equipment lease, rental, and in-house maintenance							
Software lease, rental, and in-house maintenance							
Data communications lease, rental, and in-house maintenance							
Personnel salaries and fringe benefits							
Direct support services							
Travel and training							
Space occupancy							
Supplies and utilities							
Security and privacy							
Contractual services, such as EDP services, data communications, software, technical and other support							
Overhead							
Cost Avoidance:							
Equipment lease, rentals, and in-house maintenance							

Figure 17. Benefit Calculation Worksheet.

	YEAR						
	0	1	2	3	4	5	TOTAL
Software lease, rental, and in-house maintenance Data communications lease, rental, and in-house maintenance Personnel salaries and fringe benefits Direct support services Travel and training Space occupancy Supplies and utilities Security and privacy Contractual services, such as EDP services, data communications, software, technical, and other support Overhead							
Subtotal							
Total Benefits							
Present Value Benefit							

Figure 17. Benefit Calculation Worksheet (continued).

frequently easier to state general requirements than it is to state meaningful general design specifications.

In determining costs, one needs to evaluate various alternatives. Cost justification is not a concept of a solution looking for a project. It is a process that attempts to determine the best of the possible alternatives through the use of economic analysis.

The determination of the alternatives available is a responsibility of the project team. At a minimun, the alternatives that should be considered include:

Do nothing.

Modify, extend, or enhance the existing system.

Purchase the application if the needed application is commercially available.

Lease the application if the needed application is commercially available.

Develop the application in house.

Contract the development of the application to a software house.

Each of the alternatives should be examined to determine if it is practical and, if so, it should be explored to the point where it can be determined whether or not that alternative is a viable alternative. For example, if the needed application is not available commercially, there is no need to explore that alternative. On the other hand, if a commercially available software package would come close to meeting the application requirements, the acquisition of that software package should be investigated.

Step 4. Develop the Cost to Implement Each Alternative

Two categories of cost must be developed in pricing each alternative:

One-time development costs

Operational costs (these are continuous costs throughout the life of the application after it is placed into production)

Three general methods are available for estimating the cost of developing an application system:

Experience and Judgment. The estimator calculates the cost of the various alternatives using personal experience and judgment. In most instances, the process equates the existing system with one with which the estimator has had experience. This process is sometimes referred to as breadboarding.

Attribute Estimating. Under this process, the various attributes of the application system are identified. This can be done in many ways. It can be done by estimating the number of lines of code to be written, the number of inputs and outputs, or the functions to be developed. Once the attributes have been determined, an estimate can be made as to the amount of time required to develop each attribute, and then those individual costs totaled to obtain an estimate for developing the application.

Risk Estimating. Many new estimating processes are based upon risk. These estimating methods state that the degree of risk in an application is a much better estimating factor than the individual components. Risk can normally be related to the size and structure of the application being developed, plus an assessment of the complexity and newness of the technology on which the application will be installed.

The type of risk questions that need to be answered are provided in Figure 18. These factors are weighted and scored, and then used to calculate the amount of resources required to build an application system possessing those characteristics and risk.

If the alternative being considered is purchased or leased, those costs should be obtainable from the vendor. It is important to get all of the costs, because frequently vendors neglect to describe some of the costs associated with acquiring application software such as:

Question	Answer
1. How many user organizations must sign off on requirements definition?	________
2. Identify the number of company locations that require travel for information gathering.	________
3. Identify the number of hundreds of people in each organization identified in Question 1.	________
4. How familiar is the development group with this business application?	________
5. What is the level of user management agreement on system objectives?	________
6. How significant will be commuting to the project site?	________
7. Will staffing be by developer, or developer and user?	________
8. How many people might conceivably be relocated for this effort?	________
9. How many major business functions are being implemented?	________
10. How many unique logical business inputs will the system process?	________
11. How many unique logical business outputs will the system generate?	________
12. How many logical files (views) will the system access?	________
13. How many major types of on-line inquiry are envisioned?	________
14. Will the user's knowledge of data processing aid the application effort?	________
15. What percent of proposed business functions does the user already perform?	________
16. What percent of these are already automatic?	________
17. Is a system of this type in operation anywhere?	________
18. Will the operational environment be distributed, on-line, or batch?	________
19. Is this a critical business system?	________
20. Is a backup system being developed?	________
21. Will the system require any special disaster-recovery mechanisms?	________
22. Will performance or load levels be specified as explicit design criteria?	________
23. Is the proposed system primarily batch, on-line, or real-time?	________
24. Does the processing logic seem to be simple, average, or complex?	________
25. Will automated error detection and correction be required?	________

Figure 18. Risk Estimating Questions.

Training data processing personnel

Training users in the use of the acquired software

Modifying the software to meet specific user requirements not handled by the commercial package

Modifying the package to conform to the organization's operational procedures (e.g., using standardized job control language statements)

Rewriting operation documentation

Cost of updates to keep it technologically current

The second category of costs are operational costs. These are the costs associated with operating the software in the computer center. While the development or acquisition costs are one-time costs, the operational costs are continuous. The operational costs normally include:

Input preparation

Input and output control function

Computer charges

Supplies and media charges

Rerun and failure costs

Technical support costs

Software maintenance costs (for purchased applications this may be under a maintenance contract)

Enhancement costs to keep the application current with changing business conditions

Enhancement costs to keep the application technologically current (e.g., changes required when moving to a new version of the operating system or data base management system)

Costs are generally calculated using historical experience. The data processing comptroller should collect and have available the costs associated with developing and operating application systems. These costs include such items as hourly rate for programming, computer time costs, compilation costs and test costs.

The last piece of information that the estimator will need is the estimated length of time to develop the project, and then the estimated life of the project. The estimated life and the point at which the system is needed in production should be available from the Step 2 benefit calculation. However, the operational costs may have to be adjusted based on anticipated volume of work. (*Note*: In this calculation and in the benefit calculation it is unnecessary to consider inflation in these steps.)

A worksheet for recording the one-time development costs and operational costs is provided in Figure 19. One worksheet should be completed

Cost Categories	Amount
NONRECURRING COSTS	
Capital Investment Costs	
Include costs for acquiring, developing, and installing:	
(a) Site and facility	$ ________
(b) EDP equipment	________
(c) Data communication equipment	________
(d) Environmental conditioning equipment	________
(e) Security and privacy equipment	________
(f) EDP operations, multipurpose, and applications software	________
(g) Purchased software	________
Other Nonrecurring Costs	
Include costs for:	
(a) Studies (requirement and design studies)	________
(b) Procurement planning and benchmarking	________
(c) System design, programming, and testing	________
(d) EDP software conversion	________
(e) Reviews and other technical management overhead	________
(f) Training, travel, and other personnel-related costs of development and installation (except salaries and fringe benefits)	________
(g) Involuntary retirement, serverence and relocation costs for personnel	________
(h) Contractual or other direct support services	________
(i) Incremental or additional overhead costs	________
TOTAL NONRECURRING COSTS	$ ________

Cost Categories	Amount
RECURRING COSTS	
Operating and maintaining costs over the system life, including:	
(a) Equipment lease, rentals, and in-house maintenance	$ ________
(b) Software lease, rental, and in-house maintenance	________
(c) Data communications lease, rental, and in-house maintenance	________
(d) Personnel salaries and fringe benefits	________
(e) Direct support services	________
(f) Travel and training	________

Figure 19. Worksheet for Recording Costs.

(g) Space occupancy	________
(h) Supplies and utilities	________
(i) Security and privacy	________
(j) Contractual services, such as EDP services, data communications, software, technical, and other support	________
(k) Overhead	________
TOTAL RECURRING COSTS	$ ________

Figure 19. Worksheet for Recording Costs (continued).

for each alternative evaluated. Also, at the completion of this step, Figure 19 should again be completed, and the costs totaled for each alternative.

Step 5. Calculate the Return on Investment for Each Alternative

The return on investment calculation is a mathematical calculation that takes into account the following variables:

Start and stop points for application benefits
Time span and cost to build the system
Start and stop points and value of operational costs
Value of money
Expected inflation rates

The expected inflation rates can be obtained from any of the economic projection institutes. Federal governments also predict the expected inflation rates. Given these, the costs and benefits in future years can be adjusted accordingly to reflect the effect of inflation. (Note that some organizations ignore inflation costs for the purposes of return on investment calculation.)

The basis for the calculation is the expected worth of money during the life of the project. Many organizations use the expected prime rate for the value of money. This is needed so that future dollars can be compared to present dollars. In other words, the present value of benefits two years hence are not worth the dollar benefits that will be received two years later. Those dollars must be discounted to represent their worth today (i.e., present value of money) in order to compare it to the development costs being expended at today's dollars.

The basic concept of return on investment is to convert all benefits to their present value, and all costs to their present value. It is now possible to compare benefits and costs in order to make a return on investment calculation.

A present value of money table is illustrated in Figure 20. If money is worth 16 percent, we can see in the 16 percent column of the table that a dollar benefit two years hence is worth .743 in today's dollars.

Rate	.10	.12	.14	.16	.18	.20	.22	.24	.26	.28	.30
Year											
1	.909	.893	.877	.862	.847	.833	.820	.806	.794	.781	.769
2	.826	.797	.769	.743	.718	.694	.672	.650	.630	.610	.592
3	.751	.712	.675	.641	.609	.579	.551	.524	.500	.477	.455
4	.683	.636	.592	.552	.516	.482	.451	.423	.397	.373	.350
5	.621	.567	.519	.476	.437	.402	.370	.341	.315	.291	.269
6	.564	.507	.456	.410	.370	.335	.303	.275	.250	.227	.207
7	.513	.452	.400	.354	.314	.279	.249	.222	.198	.178	.159
8	.467	.404	.351	.305	.266	.233	.204	.179	.157	.139	.123
9	.424	.361	.308	.263	.225	.194	.167	.144	.125	.108	.094
10	.386	.322	.270	.227	.191	.162	.137	.116	.099	.085	.073
11	.350	.287	.237	.195	.162	.135	.112	.094	.079	.066	.056
12	.319	.257	.208	.168	.137	.112	.092	.076	.062	.052	.043
13	.290	.229	.182	.145	.116	.093	.075	.061	.050	.040	.033
14	.263	.205	.160	.125	.099	.078	.062	.049	.039	.032	.025
15	.239	.183	.140	.108	.084	.065	.051	.040	.031	.025	.020

Figure 20. Present Value of Money Table.

It is recommended that the return on investment calculation be performed on a microcomputer. This software is readily available in most accounting packages and is far easier to perform than attempting to do it manually.

Step 6. Make an Application Decision

At this point, the individual(s) responsible for making a go–no go decision on the application has the following information:

Application requirements
Benefits to be derived from installing the application
The alternatives being considered
The cost of each alternative
The return on investment for each alternative

This information primarily provides the cost factor associated with decision making. However, there are normally other factors than cost that come into play in application decision making, such as:

Make/Buy Policy. If it is the organization's policy to acquire commercial software packages rather than build it in-house, those alternatives will receive favored treatment assuming there are no significant cost differences.

Attitudes Regarding Make or Buy. Many data processing professionals suffer from the "not invented here" syndrome. This syndrome basically states that unless the software is built in-house, it will not be worth anything. When this idea comes into play, there would have to be a major advantage to acquisition for it to win out over in-house development.

Time Available to Install. The date on which the software is needed may prohibit in-house development and because of time constraints require that the package be commercially obtained.

Skill Level of In-House Personnel. A decision needs to be made on whether individuals of sufficient skills to develop the application successfully are available in-house. If not, then either commercial acquisition or outside contracting becomes a more viable alternative.

Staff Availability. Projects cannot be developed unless a staff is available to develop them. If the in-house staff is committed to other projects, a decision will need to be made whether to delay this project, acquire a commercial software package if available, or contract the work to a software house.

Confidentiality of Applications. Many software packages process proprietary information. In some instances the process itself is proprietary. In these instances, it may not show good business sense to permit the work to be contracted outside and, thus, alternatives developed in-house would be favored unless there were significant cost differences.

The final decision on which alternative to select, and whether or not to install an application is based on managerial judgment. The objective of this process is to provide information to managers to assist them in making a good business decision. Accounting information should be one of the key variables that is plugged into the decision-making process.

JUSTIFYING SOFTWARE MAINTENANCE

Maintenance poses two dilemmas in attempting to justify these activities. First, there are many maintenance projects, and many of them are very small in size. For example, some maintenance changes can be completed in less than eight hours of effort. Therefore, it becomes questionable whether it is worth attempting to justify a task that may take almost as long to justify as it does to perform.

The second dilemma in justifying maintenance is that the benefits are less clear-cut than in a new development. Many of the benefits have existed prior to the maintenance change and exist afterwards. While there may be some impact on the benefits, it can be very difficult to measure. The maintenance becomes necessary to keep the system operational as opposed to providing new benefits.

Some organizations differentiate maintenance from enhancements by the cost of making the change. The two concepts are differentiated by an economic dollar limit as opposed to the objective of the change. For example, any change over $5,000 might be considered an enhancement, and under $5,000 a maintenance.

The enhancement would be subjected to the six-step justification process previously described. The alternatives would be evaluated and priced, and a decision made based on an economic return on investment. Maintenance, being under $5,000, would not be subjected to the return on investment calculation.

When these arbitrary guidelines are provided, ingenious systems analysts will find ways to install five $4,000 maintenance changes, rather than one $20,000 enhancement. Remember, whatever you measure is what you get.

A reasonable premise is that if maintenance is not beneficial, it should not be performed. The rule of thumb previously described stated that if the benefit for a project could not be determined, it would be good practice not to implement that item. In other words, why do something for which there is no benefit. If it is worthwhile, somebody will come up with a benefit.

There are four primary benefits associated with maintenance:

Increase the Useful Life of the Application. Many of the maintenance projects are designed to increase the life of the project. For example, maintenance that incorporates new standards, adopts new technological processes, improves the structure or documentation, or eliminates complex logic contributes to extending the life of the software. The original justification assumed a project life of five years, and if maintenance can extend that life seven, ten, or even more years, the benefits may be huge. Once the development costs have been recouped, the return on investment should grow significantly as the life of the project is extended.

Increase Existing Benefits. One of the current benefits may be increased or extended because of maintenance. For example, if a major benefit was cost avoidance, and a new feature may help avoid additional costs, the existing benefit increases.

Improved Operational Productivity. Many of the changes make the system more efficient to use. This benefit should be reflected in an improved cost of quality percentage. Reducing failure, even though not measured, has a positive impact on the profitability of the organization.

Generate a New Benefit. Maintenance, even though it is small in scope, may produce a new benefit.

The real question that management faces is: Does it want its staff to spend the time to justify maintenance? The answer to that question should be yes, but the process for arriving at the answer should be consistent with the maintenance effort. In other words, if there is a four-hour change, the calculation of return on investment should not take eight hours, or even two hours. What is important is that people think through whether or not there is a benefit. This challenging exercise, even if it only consists of a few questions, forces people to evaluate the value of the work they are doing or being asked to do.

A valuable accounting concept can be applied to software maintenance. This concept is called "zero-based budgeting." The concept says that there are no free lunches in maintenance; each activity must be justified. In zero-based budgeting there is no maintenance floor of funds that are carried forward from year to year just to keep the system operational. Each change must be justified. This concept will be explained in more detail in Chapter 7 on budgeting.

The calculation to justify the return on investment for maintenance should vary depending on whether the maintenance is small, medium, or large. These amounts will vary based on the size of the organization. For example, in a two-person data processing shop, 40-hour maintenance change is considered large, while in a multinational corporation it is considered small.

The suggested evaluative process for maintenance changes in the three categories are:

1. *Small Maintenance Changes.* The requester should be asked to conduct a personal investigation and then attest to the fact that the benefits of the maintenance will exceed the cost.
2. *Medium-Size Maintenance Changes.* For changes in this category, the cost of making the change should be calculated prior to identifying benefits. For these types of changes, a supervisor or the individual requesting the change should challenge whether or not the benefits from the change exceed the cost of effecting the change. The supervisor must agree with the requester that the benefits exceed the cost of the change.
3. *Large Maintenance Changes.* For larger maintenance projects, the cost should be calculated, and the benefits estimated and agreed to by two or more individuals in the requesting area. The same level of detail need not be prepared as was suggested in the six-step application justification process. The estimate can be based on judgment, but should be documented and its reasonableness attested to by a second party.

At some point, maintenance should be considered large enough to be covered by the six-step justification process. As long as the justification process applies to all maintenance and is proportionate to the size of the maintenance, there is little advantage in the requester breaking down a task into small parts to avoid a process of justification.

REVIEWING THE APPLICATION JUSTIFICATION PROCESS

Any process developed by management should be periodically reviewed to evaluate its effectiveness and usefulness. This review should be performed periodically and noted deficiencies corrected.

The responsibility for conducting process reviews resides with management. In larger organizations, this responsibility may be given to EDP quality assurance. It is less important who performs the review than the fact that the review is performed by a responsible party independent of the individual or group that developed the process.

The proposed review process is a review checklist. The checklist is designed so that yes responses are representative of good practices, while no responses should be investigated to determine whether or not the process requires improvement. Note that room is provided on the checklist to explain or comment on no responses.

The checklist for reviewing the application system justification process is provided in Figure 21. The items on the checklist have been discussed throughout this chapter. The user of the checklist is encouraged to read the

Item	Response			
	Yes	No	N/A	Comments
1. Is there a formal request system for new applications?				
2. If there a formal request system for all maintenance changes?				
3. Must new application systems be justified?				
4. Must maintenance changes be justified?				
5. Is the justification system consistent with the size of the application and maintenance change?				
6. Has data processing management identified the objectives of justifying application systems?				
7. Have the reasons for justification been explained to senior management?				
8. Have the reasons for justification been explained to the data processing staff?				
9. Have the reasons for justification been explained to the users?				
10. Has the process of justifying new applications been formalized?				
11. Does the justification process commence only after the requirements have been defined?				

Figure 21. Checklist for Reviewing the Application Justification Process.

Item	Response			
	Yes	No	N/A	Comments
12. Does the justification process quantify the benefits?				
13. Do the benefits include cost reduction, cost avoidance, and intangible benefits?				
14. Does the justification process provide a method for quantifying intangible items?				
15. Does the justification process require that more than one alternative be evaluated?				
16. Are project personnel instructed to consider the following alternatives in each application project: Modify, extend, or enhance the existing system. Purchase the application. Lease the application. Develop the application in-house. Contract the development of the application to a software house.				
17. Has the price to develop each alternative been calculated?				
18. Is project justification based upon a standard value of money?				
19. Does the justification process require that the life of the project be determined?				
20. Has a return-on-investment program been provided to project personnel to simplify the return-on-investment calculation?				
21. Is each proposed project required to develop a return on investment for each alternative considered?				
22. Are the decision factors for each application system formalized (e.g., decision factors such as staff availability, confidentiality of project, and return on investment)?				
23. Are special justification procedures established for maintenance?				
24. Do maintenance justification procedures vary with the size of the project?				
25. Are the justification calculations compared to the actual project results to measure performance?				
26. Is the application system justification process periodically reviewed to determine its effectiveness?				

Figure 21. Checklist for Reviewing the Application Justification Process (continued).

chapter in order to better understand the items on the checklist as well as the means to improve processes deemed deficient through the review process.

RECOMMENDED ACCOUNTING AND AUDITING PRINCIPLE FOR THE DATA PROCESSING MANAGER
The key to ensuring that any process is productive is to have it regularly reviewed by an independent party.

Chapter Five

Justifying Data Processing Support Activities

There are two main functions within the data processing area. These are the systems and programming functions, and the computer operations. All other activities are designed to support these two areas. In some organizations there are many small technical and administrative support functions, while in other organizations the support areas are consolidated into major departmental sections.

There is little uniformity in the data processing profession as to what technical and administrative support groups should exist, their specific function, and the value performed by those support areas. Some data processing managers feel specific support areas are essential, and some tolerate them. The question that all data processing managers face sooner or later is justifying the technical and administrative support staff.

The objective of this chapter is to identify the support areas and to propose a process for determining the need for the support staff. This need determination is a method of justification. The needs analysis process is designed to produce the justification for support staff. We will propose accounting as the tool for justifying technical and administrative support.

THE PHENOMENA OF SPECIALIZATION

Small data processing organizations have very few specialists. Large organizations have a large number of specialists. In a few organizations we are finding more technical and administrative support specialists than we are systems, programming, and operations personnel.

We can observe two distinct phenomena that occur with technical and administrative support.

Phenomenon 1. Technical and Support Staff Grow in Good Economic Times

Data processing managers recognize the need for individuals to champion certain causes. This need arises because certain activities seem to flounder without a catalyst to promote a concept. For example, in many data processing departments the standards program is in disarray and training is a haphazard function. Appointing someone to direct those activities brings order out of chaos. However, the managers wait until good economic times to establish the function. This is because justifying the function may be difficult. Therefore managers wait until more favorable periods when it is not as difficult to justify new positions or to rearrange staff activities.

Phenomenon 2. Technical and Administrative Support Positions Are Deleted in Poor Economic Times

Many of these technical administrative support positions are "yo-yo" positions. In good economic times they are established, and in poor economic times they are deleted. Whenever pressure is placed on data processing to delete staff or hold staff steady while increasing the workload, the data processing manager views these technical and administrative support systems with a critical eye. Many of the training and standards managers in an economic downturn find themselves back in systems and programming work.

The message in these two phenomena is that most managers are not really convinced that these administrative and technical support activities pay their own way. This book proposes that another administrative specialist be added to the data processing staff. This data processing comptroller position falls into this good time–bad time phenomenon. What is needed is to fully understand the economic return on investment provided by these administrative and technical support functions.

SPECIALISTS VERSUS GENERALISTS

The raging battle in all technical areas is whether to create generalist positions and have them perform all of the technical and support functions. The alternative is to take away from the generalists activities that can be more effectively performed by the specialists, and then create that specialist position. In general, in all technical fields the number of specialists is growing.

The argument for the specialist is that the technology is so complex that the generalist can no longer master it. The medical profession is moving rapidly into an area of specialists. As medicine becomes more complex, the generalist position is no longer able to keep up with all the new materials. Therefore, we are developing a body of medicine that is highly specialized. The generalist becomes a diagnostician who identifies a problem area, and then sends the patient to a specialist for examination and medical assistance.

The data processing field is experiencing the same growth in technology as is medicine. Twenty-five years ago the programmer couldn't do systems design work, code and test the program, place it into a production environment, and operate the computer. About 1965, technology mushroomed to the point where it was almost impossible for a single individual to perform the whole gamut of data processing activities.

All except the very small data processing shops have specialists. Some of these specialist functions were established in the mid-1960s and still survive. Other specialist functions are relatively new. Sometimes a specialist position is established, deleted, reestablished, redeleted, and so forth.

The general trend of business is to minimize the size of every function. In a world economic market, this trend is likely to continue for an extended period of time. This means that while technical and administrative staff has been viewed critically in the past it will continue to come under scrutiny in the future. On the other hand, many of these technical and administrative functions more than pay their own way.

Effective data processing managers will be able to cost-justify their technical and administrative support. It makes good business sense to know what is needed and to know that it can be supported economically.

AREAS OF SPECIALIZATION

Specialized support can be divided into the broad areas of administration and technical support. The size of these staffs will vary depending on the size of the data processing function. Let us divide and examine some of the functions performed in each of the two areas.

The tasks performed in the administrative function include:

- Personnel administration
- Accounting and budgeting
- Project administration
- Purchasing
- Office administration (e.g., telephones and copiers)
- Training
- Contracting
- Processing organizational administrative reports
- Administering secretarial pools
- Hiring, orienting, and terminating
- Mail and distribution of information
- Operation of libraries (e.g., magazines, books, self-study courses, and manuals)

The technical support areas vary with the hardware and software vendors selected, but tend to include:

Space managers
Information center
Help desk
Configuration management
Standards
System programmers (e.g., developing job control language, generating and operating systems)
EDP quality assurance
Data base administration
Communication specialists
Security specialists
Job schedulers
Documentation librarians
Computer media librarians
Input–output schedulers
Off-site storage
Disaster recovery specialists

These lists are not meant to be exhaustive but, rather, representative of the types of specialists that are being created within the data processing profession. Some are full-time jobs, some are part-time jobs, and some require large staffs to handle. For example, one large corporation with approximately 1,000 members to their data processing staff have over 150 of those 1,000 in data base administration.

MAKING THE SPECIALIST FUNCTION A PROFIT CENTER

The concept of a profit-making organization is to create organizational units that are designed to generate profit. Earlier in the book we stated that profit can be generated in two ways. One way is to increase revenue, which is generally out of the province of data processing specialists. The other avenue for generating profit is to reduce costs. It is in this aspect of generating profit that technical and administrative support groups can justify their existence.

The concept of a profit center within the data procesing area requires two premises to exist before the concept can work:

Premise 1. Data Processing Management Believes in the Profit Center Concept

Profit centers are a phenomenon of the accounting profession. The objective of a profit center is to demonstrate that it generates profits for the organizations by influencing one of the two profit variables. The counter-argument to a profit center within data processing is that it is too difficult to prove and not worth the time and effort. This argument states that many specialist functions, for example, a systems programmer or media librarian, are necessary and "intuitively obvious." To an accountant, nothing is intuitively obvious. Either the numbers support the function or they don't. Management must believe that putting the staff activities on a pay-as-you-go basis will be a key to improving the quality and productivity of the data processing function.

Premise 2. Staff Members Must Be Willing to Act as Entrepreneurs

The new concept in business is to establish individuals as small entrepreneurs. This concept states that if an organization can bring out the entrepreneurial instinct in individuals, their productivity and job satisfaction will increase. Many business schools have recently introduced courses on entrepreneurship. However, many individuals do not take readily to this concept. Some of the older technicians that are in specialist staff functions enjoy the technical aspect of what they are doing and do not want to be burdened with the financial paperwork aspect of entrepreneurship.

If the above two premises occur, the data processing function is ready to "unbundle" the technical and administrative support function. This unbundling is the same concept that the federal government forced on the IBM Corporation years ago. Until that point the IBM Corporation sold hardware and gave software away.

The charge against IBM was that customers had to pay for services that they did not want. For example, IBM built applications for special industries, yet charged the cost of developing those applications across its entire customer base. In addition, the charge stated that in a bundled environment the forces of the free market do not work, and therefore it was not necessary for IBM to develop highly efficient competitive software because in being given away the software did not have to compete against other similar software on the marketplace.

Let's look at how bundling data processing services leads to the same types of problems that proponents of unbundling charged had existed within the IBM Corporation. When staff functions are included in the overall data processing function, they do not need to justify their existence. The cost is absorbed in chargeout rates and customers pay for services whether or not they want them. For example, computer operations in many organizations establish a help desk. This costs money and is bundled into the overall operations charge. If as a user I do not need the assistance of the help desk, I still must pay for it.

One of the counterarguments states that if a service like the help desk is eliminated, then users will expend more resources getting the needed answers, and individuals within computer operations will again be pestered with inquiries for status information and help. On the other hand, if the service is really worthwhile, then people should be willing to pay for it.

Let's look at what has happened in the telephone industry. For years, the information service of the telephone company was a free service. If people wanted a number, they merely had to call information and they got that number. Since it was a free service for the customer, why should the customer be bothered looking up a number in the telephone book when they could get it free from information. Once the telephone company started charging for that service, the number of inquiries for information dropped significantly. When individuals found they had to pay for the service, they then evaluated the cost of the service against the time required to look the number up in the telephone book. However, those that still needed the service were more than willing to pay for it. In addition, and this is a very important addition, if the need for the service was caused by the telephone company, then there was no charge for the service. For example, if a number was not listed in the telephone book, then the phone number would be given to a customer without charge.

Let's look at the help desk from this perspective. Let's assume that the operations department is in a chargeout basis. Let us further assume that there is a charge for each inquiry to help them. However, if the application system processing is not delivered on time, or there are problems with the system directly attributable to the data processing function, then there should be no charge for the service. Note that the charge still exists, but it would be charged to computer operations, or the application project as opposed to the user.

Justification of the technical and administrative support function and putting those functions on a pay-as-you-go basis are two different concepts. However, they are closely related and should both be understood. Without a pay-as-you-go philosophy, justification is a one-time process. Once a technical function, such as the help desk, is justified, then it no longer needs to be justified. Pay-as-you-go is just another variation of zero-based budgeting. The objective of the profit center concept is to force a continual analysis of each function so that the viability of continuing that function can be demonstrated over time.

RECOMMENDED ACCOUNTING AND AUDITING PRINCIPLE FOR THE DATA PROCESSING MANAGER

The competition of the marketplace is a basic premise of free enterprise. Activities subject to marketplace pressures tend to offer higher quality products and are more productive in producing those products than activities not subject to marketplace pressures.

CASE STUDY EXAMPLE

Let us examine the attributes of a common data processing problem. This is a case from a large insurance company that had what it believed was a very effective data processing function.

The project leaders in this organization were responsible for the definition, allocation and management of disk space for their application. It was the project manager's responsibility to determine the expected volume of records, define the file structure, and then monitor activities and maintain or manage space in the same manner that the project maintains all other aspects of the system.

If space problems occur, for example, the application abnormally terminated because of space problems, project personnel were called in to remedy the situation. Over time, there were numerous space problems, abnormal terminations associated with space, and the problems were remedied as quickly as possible by project personnel. The costs for these services were borne by the project and charged to the users of the project.

After the data processing function established an EDP quality assurance group, that group analyzed abnormal terminations. The quality assurance function wanted to identify the type of problems the organization was having, and to do this took the job accounting logs for several months from an IBM software system called System Management Facility. The quality assurance group categorized abnormal terminations by type and frequency.

The result of this analysis was that space management was the number one cause of abnormal terminations, that is, approximately 40 percent of all abnormal terminations were caused by space management. The question then became: Was this problem being properly handled in the data processing department? In order to answer that question, an economic analysis was made to determine the cost of each space management abnormal termination.

The analysis showed the following two costs that were readily identifiable:

Cost 1. Eight hours of programming effort expended for each space management abnormal termination at $50 per hour equals $400 of programming time. (*Note*: Much of this time was associated with calling programmers during off hours and then not having them work the following day.)

Cost 2. Computer Rerun Time. The cost to rerun applications averaged $200 per abnormal termination. (*Note*: This cost involved rerunning the program from the most recent checkpoint.)

The economics for determining the total cost of the organization of space management problems was then an easy calculation. The total number of abnormal terminations due to space management was multiplied by the $600 ($400 programming cost plus $200 rerun cost) to produce the annual cost associated with space management problems. Needless to say, the number was huge and came as a shock to data processing management. A problem that was perceived to be minor, when quantified through accounting principles, became major.

The proposed solution to the problem was to establish space management specialists in computer operations. These individuals monitored space usage, and were able to modify space in most instances before abnormal termination occurred. The justification for space management specialists in computer operations was easy. Calculating the cost needed to add that service to computer operations was insignificant compared to the potential savings the organization was now realizing.

The next question that data processing management must face is: Is it still advantageous to keep that specialist function in compter operations? This requires an ongoing analysis, and a process to do that is provided later in this chapter. The key concept of the case is that economic analysis answered the specialist question.

WHAT COSTS ARE INVOLVED IN THE USE OF SPECIALISTS?

Accountants have terms for who contributes to the production of products and who supports those individuals. In accounting terminology, it is called direct labor and indirect labor. Direct labor represents those individuals and costs that are directly chargeable to the production of the products. In data processing, these would be the systems analysts, programmers, and computer operators. The indirect labor are those individuals who support the direct labor activities. In data processing, these are the technical and administrative staff, as well as departmental manager.

Accountants also have a term for the collection and allocation of the indirect costs. The term is overhead. The distribution of overhead to the direct cost is normally made or allocated based on the amount of direct cost. The accounting assumption assumes that all projects benefit equally from overhead. It is a reasonable concept because it would be very difficult, and probably impractical, to allocate such costs as electricity for lights, heat, insurance on the plant, and so on. On the other hand, there are many special services for which payment makes sense.

Most organizations provide copy machines throughout the data processing area for use by the staff. Other organizations charge those copy services back to the projects and individuals who use them. Most data processing managers are surprised at the dramatic reduction in copy services once those services go from a free to a chargeout basis. The concept of chargeout is to make one think of the value of the service being used. If the service is free, the perceived value need not be considered.

The premise of chargeout is that it is more economical to pay the costs of chargeout than not pay it because paying it will force people to consider the value of the service. If chargeout did not reduce the services rendered, the process probably would not be worthwhile.

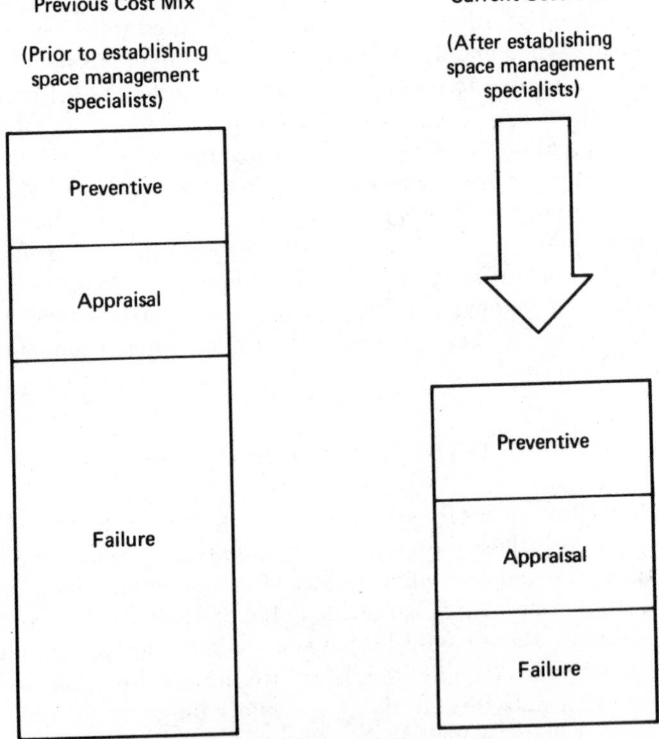

Figure 22. Reallocation Costs in the Case Study Example.

Much of the costs associated with staff services are the costs of quality. In our previous case study we saw that the major advantage to the organization was a reduction in abnormal termination. This is the failure cost component of the cost of quality.

There are three components of the cost of quality: preventive, appraisal, and failure costs. In the case study example, the benefit was primarily a tradeoff between failure costs and appraisal costs. The demonstratable benefit was a reduction in failure costs that was larger than the offsetting increases in appraisal costs. Figure 22 illustrates this phenomenon. It shows that the previous cost, comprising preventive, appraisal, and failure costs, is higher than the new costs after the change in procedures. However, the mix of cost has changed. In the current cost, preventive and appraisal costs are higher than they were in the previous cost. However, failure costs have dropped significantly.

As we begin the justification process for technical specialists, we will see the increased need for cost of quality accounting. Much of the problem associated with justifying technical and administrative specialists is that with the current chart of accounts we are unable to collect the needed information. For example, in our previous case study the quality assurance group had to undertake a special study to collect the information needed.

THE FIRST STEP: INSTALLING A PROJECT MANAGEMENT MONITORING FUNCTION

Error tracking or problem management is a prerequisite to cost-of-quality accounting. The objective of problem management is to identify the accounting buckets that should be used to collect cost-of-quality information. The principles of accounting state that you should only be collecting information on areas you want to measure. The areas that should be measured are those that are causing the problem. Error tracking is a means of identifying the problems so that the appropriate accounting mechanisms can be put into place to control those problems.

Most of the specialist divisions were established because of the problems associated with having generalists perform that function. For example, as operating systems became more complex the technical skills exceeded the capabilities and time availabilities of regular operations personnel. Operators generating operating systems were making problems or ran into difficulties that consumed too much of their time. Thus, the system programmer specialist was initiated to alleviate this problem situation. However, most of these evaluations were made intuitively as opposed to using accounting information. Error tracking is the science of identifying problem areas and then collecting statistical information about the frequency of those problems. Once the frequency is known, then accounting value can be attached to that frequency to produce the needed economic analysis for decision-making purposes.

The task being proposed is but one step in the problem management cycle. This cycle is illustrated in Figure 23.

The problem management cycle begins with error tracking. These errors can be tracked by error-tracking specialists, EDP quality assurance analysts, computer operations personnel, or general administrative personnel. One organization that found this concept to be very productive called their error-tracking team the "SWAT TEAM."

After the errors are tracked and recorded, they are quantified in economic terms. This is the same process that was illustrated in the previous case. Based on this economic analysis, decisions are made regarding solutions. Many of these solutions will be in establishing specialist functions or in rearranging job tasks and reassigning tasks to individuals more suited to dealing with those tasks.

The changing of the process or the reassigning of tasks is the second part of the problem management cycle. The accounting analysis made on the error tracking and recording information should be used to make recom-

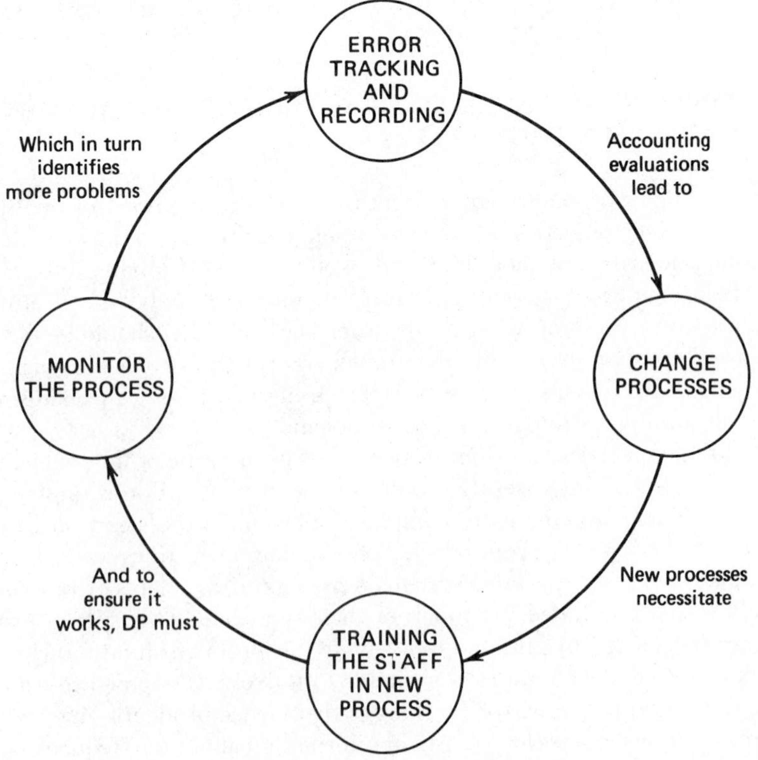

Figure 23. Problem Management Cycle.

mendations regarding changing job responsibilities and processes. The third step in the problem management cycle is to train data processing staff in new processes. If a new function is started, the function must be staffed and resources allocated. If a function is changed, this may involve changing job descriptions and work flows. Whenever change occurs, training must follow in order to ensure that the change is properly implemented.

The last step in the cycle is a monitoring or review of activities. This is essential to ensure that the activities remain economically viable. Out of the monitoring process, errors will be identified that will be tracked and recorded. The process then repeats itself and the cycle continues gradually to improve the organizational structure.

The key to this problem management cycle is the error tracking and recording function. It is through this function that the economics and viability of performing work in the existing way are determined. As the accounting analysis shows problems (Chapter 11 describes how to use accounting to identify data processing problems), solutions must be sought to those problems, staff trained, and their performance monitored.

Error tracking and problem analysis has been going on for years. The difficulty with the process has been the inability to quantify errors into a language understandable by all parties. Abnormal terminations mean nothing to senior management. Data processing supervision understands but has difficulty identifying the magnitude of bugs. The challenge of error tracking has been that when presenting the errors a "so what" attitude occurs. For example, in the previous case if we had stated that there were 137 abnormal terminations, management may have said, "So what." But once those 137 errors are converted into $600 problems that cost the data processing function $82,200 per year, it is now a problem requiring managerial attention.

RECOMMENDED ACCOUNTING AND AUDITING PRINCIPLE FOR THE DATA PROCESSING MANAGER
Statistics are only of interest to statisticians until they are converted into dollars. After the dollar conversion the statistics are of interest to management.

TECHNICAL AND ADMINISTRATIVE SUPPORT JUSTIFICATION PROCESS

Productivity refers to the rate of production. Quality refers to the standards or requirements to be met by those products. Both concepts are important in justifying technical and administrative support. We can justify economically a technical or administrative support system if:

It has a higher rate of production than occurs with direct labor.

The quality of the product is higher, thereby reducing the cost of quality for the data processing function.

The seven-step process proposed to justify technical and administrative support requires the economic assessment of both the productivity rate and the quality level of the technical and administrative support groups. These are the two bases by which these support functions can be justified.

RECOMMENDED ACCOUNTING AND AUDITING PRINCIPLE FOR THE DATA PROCESSING MANAGER
The key to justifying technical and administrative support is twofold. The group either is more productive and/or produces a higher quality product than the generalist function can accomplish.

The seven-step process is listed below and each step is then described in more detail.

Step 1. Identify all products.

Step 2. Identify the cost of products and then identify the current cost to produce the product.

Step 3. Identify the effect of the support group on productivity.

Step 4. Identify the effect of the support group on quality.

Step 5. Prepare a support T account.

Step 6. Transfer economically effective products to a support group.

Step 7. Maintain product records.

Step 1. Identify All Products

The key to quality and productivity is identifying and monitoring products. Productivity is the rate at which products are made. Quality consists of the predetermined standards and requirements that products must meet. Both concepts are product oriented.

Every activity produces products. The end result of any activity is a product. For example, the products of the data processing manager may be decisions, policy statements, and long-range plans. On the other hand, the products of the computer programmer are program listings, flowcharts, and unit test plans. Products of a standards manager are specific data processing standards, changes to standards, memorandums on new standards, reviews of new standards with appropriate parties, and disposition of requests to deviate from standards. There is no activity within a data processing function that does not produce products.

The objective of this exercise is to identify all of the products in the area under review. In our abnormal termination case, as it related to space management, the specific products were:

Notification of abnormal termination due to space

Computer rerun

Notification to project team (e.g., programmer) of the problem

Documentation of the space problem

Change to correct the space problem

Change to program or system documentation

Authorization to rerun the system

Notice to the user of late delivery of system outputs (optional in the event the rerun cannot occur in time)

Discrepancy explanation report (may be optional)

Payroll-related products (e.g., the individual correcting the problem may be paid overtime and/or provided compensatory time off)

A list of many of the products produced in the data processing function is listed in Figure 24. This listing can be used as a checklist to help individuals performing this analysis to identify products. However, it should be adapted to the specific area and organization.

Step 2. Identify the Cost of Products

The cost of producing each product to the group now producing it should be calculated. In general, it will only be necessary to identify the direct costs (those charged directly to the product) and not identify indirect costs. The indirect costs include costs that are prorated to the entire organization such as space and telephone. In most cases, the responsibility for creation of the product is transferred to another activity within the data processing function, so that the indirect costs are normally not a consideration.

The direct costs to produce data processing products are normally limited to those listed in the product cost worksheet (Figure 25). This worksheet can be used to calculate the cost of each data processing product. The total cost per product can then be multiplied by the quantity of products produced per year to develop the annual cost to produce this product.

Action item list
Administrative notice
Budget estimate
Business strategy meeting
Change order
Configuration change status report
Contract data requirement list
Contract status report
Contracts
Construction program reporting
Cost analysis
Cost estimate
Data change request form
Data item description form
Data management report
Delivery order
Determination and finding
Executive management review
Financial management board review
Fiscal reports
General briefing
Graphic aids
Incident reports
Inspection and acceptance document
Internal management review
Invitation for bid
Letters
Life-cycle cost study
Logistics support plan
Management reports
Memorandums
Messages
Personnel action request
Personnel reports
Phase-out plan
Position description
Printing request
Procurement plan
Program change request form
Program management plan
Program management review
Program management system checklist
Program review
Project status reports
Purchase order
Purchase request form
Quality assurance group review
Quarterly financial review
Quarterly resources reports
Request for proposal
Resources utilization committee action
Security classification guide
Security violation form
Staff meeting agenda (and report)
Statement of work
System specifications
Technical reports
Telephone calls
Terminal learning and prompting
Time card
Training plan
Travel request form
Weekly activities reports
Work order request

Figure 24. Typical List of Products.

Note that while Figure 25 is designed to calculate the cost of a single product, it may actually be more practical to group products and calculate the total cost. This can be done if the products are a family of products that are produced almost as a single unit. However, if the revised process adds or deletes items from the product list, there may be some confusion in comparing the two processess and in justifying transfer and/or establishment of a new technical and administrative support activity.

Step 3. Identify the Effect of the Support Group on Productivity

Improving productivity means that more products are produced per unit of cost. The cost of producing a product under a new process (e.g., moving space management from the application project team to computer opera-

PRODUCT: ______________________________

PRODUCED BY: ______________________________

QUANTITY PRODUCED PER YEAR: ______________________________

COST CALCULATION:

_________ @ $ __________ /hour	$ __________
Computer time	__________
Supplies	__________
Contract expenses	__________
Travel and meal costs	__________
Other (specify)	
______________________________	__________
______________________________	__________
______________________________	__________
TOTAL COST PER PRODUCT	$ __________
ANNUAL COST TO PRODUCE PRODUCT	$ __________

Figure 25. Cost to Produce a DP Product.

tion) must be calculated. Note that in doing this, some products are eliminated, other products may be added, and some are produced faster.

The effect on having a technical and administrative support group produce the products deals only with the cost to produce. This calculation does not take into account the quantity of products produced. Again, the justification for technical support is based on productivity and quality. Productivity deals with the rate of production, while quality is more concerned with the number of quality products produced.

This step requires the recalculation of the product cost using Figure 25. If a product is eliminated, the cost should be zero; if a new product is added, its cost should be calculated.

Step 4. Identify the Effect of the Support Group on Quality

This step evaluates the effect of reassigning and redesigning product development. The impact of quality is measurable through cost-of-quality calculations. In many instances, this can be readily determined by a reduction in the number of products that need to be produced. In our space management example, both benefits were achieved. The number of space management problems were reduced significantly (this is a reduction due to an increase in quality) and the effort required to correct the problem once it occurred was reduced (this is an improvement due to a productivity increase).

Quality as used to justify technical and administrative support functions can be defined as doing it right the first time. Quality preparation of job control language would involve developing the job control that meets system requirements. Quality in space management would be the elimination of space management problems, in other words, doing it right the first time. Quality in systems development and maintenance is producing defect-free products. Thus, the following questions need to be asked in determining the effect on quality of reassigning or redesigning the product production:

1. Will the defects be caught at the earliest possible point?
2. Will the defects be prevented from occurring?
3. Will the changes in the work process contribute to defect reduction?
4. Will the individuals performing the work be better qualified to produce defect-free products?

The end product of this step is a reevaluation of an increase in the number of favorable products produced, or a reduction in the number of unfavorable products produced. For example, in our space management case, the favorable products that were increased were the reallocation of space prior to abnormal termination; the unfavorable products decreased were programmer call-in, abnormal termination, and error analysis and explanation.

Step 5. Prepare a Support T Account

The justification analysis of the production of technical and administrative products can be done using the T account as used in accounting. On the debit side (left side of the T account) the costs associated with producing the product in the current way for the quantity of products produced can be arrived at. On the credit side place the cost of producing the quantity of products needed to do the same work. The difference between the amounts in the two sides of the T account represents the justification of having the task performed by a technical support group versus having it performed by direct labor.

An example of a T account analysis for the space management case is illustrated in Figure 26. This example shows the result of moving space management from the projects to a computer operations based on 200 abnormal space management terminations per year.

The result of this step shows that there is an accounting economic advantage of $104,500 for moving the function from a generalist to a specialist group.

Step 6. Transfer Economically Effective Products to a Support Group

The decision must now be made by management whether or not to transfer the function. As stated in the case example, the function was moved, and the benefits realized. Note that in this calculation there may be several alternatives, as was discussed in the application project justification chapter. If so, there would be several T account presentations for use in the decision-making process.

Notification of abnormal termination due to space	$ 25.00		$ 25.00
Notification to project team (e.g., programmer) of the problem	10.00		10.00
Documentation of the space problem	50.00		50.00
Change to correct the space problem	140.00		140.00
Change to program or system documentation	75.00		75.00
Authorization to rerun the system	25.00		25.00
Notice to the user of late delivery of system outputs	50.00		50.00
Discrepancy explanation report	25.00		25.00
Computer rerun	200.00		200.00
Total Cost Per Product	$ 600.00		$ 600.00
Times 200 abnormal terminations per year	×200	Times 10 abnormal terminations that cannot be handled by computer operations	×10
TOTAL PRODUCT COST	$120,000.00	TOTAL	$ 6,000.00
		Space management review report	25.00
		Change space allocation	15.00
		Notification to project of space reallocation	10.00
		Total Products Cost	$50.00
		Times 190 space reallocations per year	×190
		TOTAL	$ 9,500.00
		TOTAL PRODUCT COST	$15,500.00
		THIS ITEM CALCULATED AMOUNT USED TO JUSTIFY CHANGING SPACE MANAGEMENT MONITORING FROM THE APPLICATION PROJECT TO COMPUTER OPERATIONS	$104,500.00

Figure 26. Case Study Justification for Moving Space Management From the Project Area to Computer Operations: A T Account Analysis.

Step 7. Maintain Product Records

Technical and administrative support units should maintain records on their activities in sufficient detail to support those activities. The individual responsible for each technical and administrative support product, or group of related products, should maintain records on:

Number of products produced and the cost allocated to produce those products.

This basic cost information is essential in justifying, retaining, and explaining the purposes and objectives of staff functions. Senior management, users, auditors, or any other investigative group understands work products and the cost to produce the products.

When technical and administrative support staffs are described in this manner, their function is justified from a work perspective. If management, either data processing or senior management, requests the deletion of staff, or deletion or reduction of specific services, then the implementation of those edicts can progress in the following manner:

1. *Determine the Importance of Work Products.* Priorities among the work products produced by the technical administrative staff functions should be established. Important work products need to be produced, regardless of whether the technical and administrative staff functions remain. If the function is to be cut, then the least important work products should be eliminated.
2. *Determine Where the Needed Work Products Can Be Most Economically Performed.* In a period of economic cutbacks, it would be foolish to eliminate a staff function and then transfer the work of that function to other individuals who cannot perform it as effectively. The result of this inappropriate transfer will be a cascading of work while reducing the work force. The reduction process should eliminate the least important work products and not functions that are deemed expendable.

RECOMMENDED ACCOUNTING AND AUDITING PRINCIPLE FOR THE DATA PROCESSING MANAGER
One must be careful to avoid being penny wise and pound foolish in reassigning work. A knowledge of where work products can be most effectively produced is essential before work is reassigned.

EVALUATING THE PERFORMANCE OF CURRENT SUPPORT GROUPS

The previously described seven-step process is an evaluative process for determining where to best place the development of work products. It is an economic evaluation that will place those products at the point where they are most economically produced. However, most data processing functions already have many technical and staff support units in place. These units must also be evaluated to determine whether or not they are economically productive.

The same seven-step process can be used in evaluating and justifying the continued existence of existing staff units. The first step requires existing support units to identify their work product. The second step requires them to develop the cost of producing the current product. The totality of the cost times the number of products produced should equal the annual budget for that staff function.

The third and fourth steps require a rethinking of whether or not that product could be produced at less cost or at a higher quality level by another function. For example, the product could be returned to the project or operation personnel, products could be eliminated or the production could be transferred to another staff unit. In many instances, data processing management does not know all of the products produced and, if they did, they might want to stop producing many of them. Also, some work products fall to a staff group by default, but really do not belong there.

The fifth and sixth steps are an economic evaluation and a decision based on that economic evaluation. If it makes sense to delete products, they should be deleted. If the products can be produced more economically by another organizational function, the production of that product should be transferred to that function.

Finally, the staff unit should maintain records on the work performed and the cost of performing that work. Staff units on a pay-as-you-go basis should be subjected to zero-based budgeting. This means that annually the functions must rejustify their existence or be eliminated. Note that in the chapter on chargeouts, we will discuss charging for technical and administrative services. This is a self-policing marketplace concept that lets the marketplace justify the existence of technical and administrative support staff.

TECHNICAL AND ADMINISTRATIVE SUPPORT FUNCTION JUSTIFICATION PROCESS CHECKLIST

It is good practice to periodically evaluate the process of justifying staff functions. When initially installed, most processes follow the objectives and

Item	Response: Yes	No	N/A	Comments
1. Have each of the technical and administrative support functions been identified?				
2. Is a project management (i.e., error tracking) function established?				
3. Have the data processing defects been categorized and quantified by frequency?				
4. Is a single individual or group responsible for identifying and quantifying data processing defects?				
5. Have the products produced by each staff function been identified?				
6. Have the costs associated with producing each product been identified?				
7. Has the desired quality of each product been defined?				
8. Are records maintained on the type and frequency of products produced by each staff group?				
9. Does each staff group operate as a profit center?				
10. Does a process exist for evaluating the appropriate location for producing each work product?				
11. Is this evaluation process performed periodically?				
12. Does data processing management support the profit center concept for staff groups?				
13. Do the staff group supervisors or managers accept the entrepreneurial approach to operating a staff group?				
14. Have priorities for staff work products been established?				

Figure 27. ***Technical and Administrative Support Justification Process Evaluation Checklist.***

intent of using a process. However, as time progresses and people turn over, the purpose and intent are frequently forgotten. People perform steps because they have to be performed, not to meet the objective of performing the step.

A checklist for evaluating the technical and administrative support justification process is presented as Figure 27. The checklist contains a list of items for use by data processing management in evaluating this justification process. Yes responses on the checklist represent good justification practices, while no responses warrant investigation. If the investigation of no responses indicates that the process is defective, it should be changed.

RECOMMENDED ACCOUNTING AND AUDITING PRINCIPLE FOR THE DATA PROCESSING MANAGER
In addition to economic evaluation, management should use the "smell" test. If a particular staff function doesn't smell right, its existence should be challenged with its usefulness evaluated.

Chapter Six

Justifying Computer Operations

The operation of the computer center is an essential part of the business of the organization. Information and the processing of information is the lifeblood of many organizations. Industries such as banking are primarily information processing organizations. Without the computer, they are out of business.

The justification of computer operations is one of justifying workload forecasts and processing alternatives. Much of the need to justify additional processing facilities is based upon the credibility of the forecasting process. However, some services provided by computer operations will be subject to the same economic evaluation as other administrative and technical support services.

This chapter explains the unique accounting-related activities of computer operations. These include lease or buy decisions, performing tasks such as hardware maintenance in-house versus contracting for the services, and competitive bidding for vendor services. The chapter includes an evaluation checklist for assessing the effectiveness of the use of accounting in justifying computer operations and computer center services.

OPERATIONS COSTS ARE BASED ON USAGE FORECASTING

Computer operations is a service operation. Its primary mission is to provide capacity for those activities requiring computer processing. The amount of processing capacity provided by the computer operations group is based on forecasts of capacity usage. Capacity planning, therefore, is an important function within computer operations.

The task or usage forecasting begins with collecting and analyzing resource usage data. Collecting the data entails surveying the users, validating the users' responses, collecting the current usage accounting data, retrieving all pertinent historical usage accounting data, and readying the data for analysis. Wherever possible, the data should be collected in terms of the service, work, or resource units defined for purposes of charging services to users. After the current and projected usage data has been collected, the data should be analyzed using regression and trend analysis techniques or other mathematical modeling processes.

The results should provide a projection of the amount of usage for each service provided by computer operations. The science of forecasting data usage is not discussed in this book. That topic is adequately addressed in numerous other books and in specially designed software packages.

The economic accounting and justification of computer operations is based on usage forecasts. The same data will also serve as one of the primary inputs to a chargeout system (see Chapter 9, "Building Chargeout Systems" for the process of developing chargeout rates).

The remainder of this chapter describes the use of that forecast information in the justification of the resources within computer operations. Those economic considerations are based upon whether the current capacity is sufficient, too much, or too little capacity.

If the forecast analysis determines that there are discrepancies between the forecast in usage and available capacity, then the discrepancy must be resolved. There are three possible resolutions if the forecast in usage exceeds the capacity:

Resolution 1. More resources can be acquired to increase the capacity of the data processing facility.

Resolution 2. The extra work can be sent to another data processing facility.

Resolution 3. The projected usage can be cut back.

If projected usage is below available capacity, there are three possible solutions:

Solution 1. Reduce the capacity of the services and resources for which usage is unacceptably low. This should be done if the trend of declining usage has continued for a long period or if the data processing facility is incurring a substantial cost for the excess capacity.

Solution 2. Assuming that usage has temporarily declined and will pick up later, leave the capacity unchanged.

Solution 3. Share the excess capacity with other computer centers in the organization (if applicable).

Regardless of the actions taken, declining usage should be monitored very closely, because it could indicate an operating deficiency in the data processing facility. Operating deficiencies can range from not offering competitive rates to providing unacceptable levels of services. The decisions required to resolve discrepancies may require extensive interaction with, and compromises among, all of the data processing facility users.

Forecasts are used to establish a chargeout rate for operations in addition to equipment ordering. Much of the integrity of any economic accounting analysis is dependent upon the integrity of the forecast. Therefore, it is important that forecasts be closely monitored and adjusted as soon as any significant trend away from the projected forecast is noted.

COMPUTER OPERATIONS CONCERNS

The value of accounting to the computer operations manager is to assist in fulfilling the operations mission. Since accounting cannot directly assist in processing, its benefits will be in providing information to reduce operations defects and concerns. The problems that computer operations tries to solve lead to opportunities for using accounting in computer operations.

Let us examine some of the operations concerns and discuss how accounting can provide information to assist the computer operations manager in reducing them.

Scheduling Concern

The computer operations manager is charged with providing the needed capacity for computer processing. This normally means mixing regularly scheduled jobs with unscheduled jobs. In many instances, schedules will need to be changed from minute to minute to accommodate changing workloads.

Accounting is a period-oriented discipline. The cycles imposed by accounting drive most operations. The hourly, daily, weekly, monthly, quarterly, and annual accounting cycles provide the basis for scheduling most operations. In addition, many of the unscheduled activities cluster around the accounting cycles.

Smoothing Concern

Scheduling is allotting time sequences for operations. While computer operations have some leeway in scheduling, much of it is fixed by accounting cycles. Smoothing is a process of adjusting schedules so that the workload is steady.

Two accounting concepts can work together to facilitate smoothing. These are the chargeout concepts of charging users for services and a variable rate charged, such as that used by the telephone system. The accounting process collects statistical information about work cycles. Based on this, operations can develop variable rate charges to make it financially advantageous to users to process work during low-charge periods, which coincide with traditionally low-volume periods.

Capacity Planning Concerns

Ensuring adequate capacity is a major concern of computer operations. In larger installations, the wait period for hardware may exceed 12 months. Thus, organizations in need of hardware on short notice may have to pay marketplace premiums to acquire that hardware.

Accounting can help with capacity planning through the budgeting process. While it may be difficult to get the needed information from users through normal means, those same users normally ensure adequate funds for their operations through the budgetary process. Computer operations managers monitoring user budgets can obtain valuable data to help project expected capacity requirements.

Performance Management Concern

Managing a performance of the operations area is a responsibility of the operations manager. Performance can be rated against operations objectives, against industry standards, or against previous performance.

Accounting information provides the capability to measure performance. Organizations using job accounting systems collect detailed information on resources and facilities used. This computer-collected data can be analyzed through analysis programs. In addition, budgetary information provides information on economic performance.

Operations Processing Control Concern

The key concern in operations is the accuracy and completeness control over processing. It has been said that to really foul up, one needs a computer. Murphy also said that what can go wrong will go wrong and at exactly the worst moment. Controls are the means used by operations to ensure the ongoing integrity of processing.

Accounting systems and comptroller procedures incorporate a system of internal accounting controls into most application systems. These controls are designed to develop and verify totals of key financial fields. Many of the controls are self-checking, while others require the operations control clerk to verify the accuracy and completeness of the processing.

Data Handling Concern

Data handling is the movement of data from the media library to the computer during computer processing. Much of the media handling is automatic when the appropriate disks and data bases are mounted. The two concerns are that the correct files are mounted and that the integrity of data is retained during processing. This is particularly challenging in a large data base.

Accounting-type information is helpful in ensuring the integrity of data handling. Sequential control numbers, batch numbers, version numbers, file header and trailer labels are all controls helping to ensure the correctness of data handling. In some file-handling systems, trailer records contain totals or hash numbers of key fields.

Security Concern

Security is a growing issue in computer operations. It involves protection within the computer center, over communication lines, and the information in the possession of users. It also involves security over computer programs and operating systems.

The key accounting concept that is most beneficial in security is accountability. Under accountability, records of usage are maintained, and those users are held accountable for the resources addressed and processed. In addition, many of the normal financial controls are helpful in identifying security violations.

IDENTIFYING THE APPROPRIATE ACCOUNTING INFORMATION FOR OPERATIONS

The information that can be accumulated about systems development, maintenance, and technical support is relatively limited. It is a people-intensive function, so that most of the challenge is estimating and accumulating people time. In most organizations, this is done manually, and may or may not provide reliable information.

Computer operations is a highly automated part of data processing. Organizations that use mainframe computers incorporate numerous software packages with communication networks and multiple hardware devices.

The net result of this operations maze is the opportunity to collect millions of pieces of information per month. The problem in operations is not one of collecting information or of collecting reliable information, but rather which of the multitude of available information should be collected.

Computer operations management should establish the objectives for collecting accounting information. Accounting information is needed for the purposes of accumulating and charging costs; it is also needed to assist in managing computer operations. It is for this latter objective that requirements need to be established.

The computer operations concerns described earlier in this chapter provide a basis for establishing accounting objectives. Each of these concerns should be evaluated, and management should be asked what type of information would be helpful in managing those concerns. What is needed to manage is the type of accounting information that should be collected.

Listed below are examples of the types of information that would prove helpful in managing the concerns of computer operations:

Job accounting logs (e.g., IBM's SMF job accounting log)
Security software logs (e.g., IBM's RACF log)
Communication logs (e.g., IBM's TSO log)
Operators logs
Applications system control total reports
Data movement records in and out of media library
Long-range plans
Long-range budgets
Computer operation budget reports (i.e., budgeted amounts versus actual expenditures)
Error-tracking reports (used for performance monitoring)

SPECIAL COMPUTER OPERATIONS ACCOUNTING CONSIDERATIONS

In the early days of data processing, hardware costs far exceeded people costs. At that time, people would spend extensive system and programming effort in order to reduce hardware usage. During the mid-1960s people costs began to exceed hardware costs, and have ever since.

However, while the majority of the data processing annual resources may go into systems and programming, the majority of the discretionary spending normally falls to computer operations. Operations must acquire hardware, provide maintenance on that hardware, acquire extensive supplies, and contract for a variety of services to support computer operations.

Computer operations has the following three accounting decisions to consider in their day-to-day operations:

1. Lease versus buy decision
2. Competitive bidding
3. In-house versus contract decision

These accounting decisions are primarily economic decisions. The objective of the decision is to get the most product per dollar. Note that while systems and programming is also involved in this same economic analysis, most of the negotiations of this type involve computer operations.

Lease–Buy Decision

The lease–buy decision is one primarily involved in hardware. This decision involves deciding whether to purchase or lease hardware. The decision is almost pure economics and has very little to do with the actual ownership of the hardware.

The decision can even be complicated by third-party lessors. These are organizations such as banks or other financial organizations who have purchased the hardware from the vendor, and then leased it back to the organization that needs it.

Part of the decision is a tax decision. If the equipment is purchased, the U.S. Internal Revenue Service permits an investment tax credit of 10 percent. This means that 10 percent of the purchase price is paid for dollar by dollar from taxes. Thus, for tax purposes, the organization gets a 110 percent write-off.

In the lease from vendor, or third-party lease, the concerns involve avoiding paying a purchase price and the current interest rate. Another important decision is the length of the lease. Normally, the monthly rental will be dependent upon the number of months or years in the lease.

Let's look at an example and some of the considerations involved in the lease–purchase consideration. Note that the exact figures should be worked out by your organization's accountant and take into account federal, state, county, and local tax legislation.

Some of the major considerations in the purchase–lease consideration are listed in Figure 28. Let's look at the two options individually.

Purchase Option

Purchasing a piece of hardware involves the following considerations:

The organization must pay the purchase price at the time the equipment is delivered. In this example, we assume computer hardware at a purchase price of $50,000.

The federal income tax laws of the United States allow an organization to deduct 10 percent of the purchase of a certain type of assets from their tax dollars. In our example, this would be a $5,000 investment tax

Equipment Needed—$50,000 Computer

Purchase	
Purchase price	$50,000
Investment tax credit	5,000
Depreciation:	
Straight line—5 Years (assumes no cash value)	10,000/year
Lease	
Lease to run 5 years	
Assume 15% interest rate	
Assumes no value at end of 5 years	
Annual rental $14,000/year	

Figure 28. Lease Versus Purchase Consideration.

credit. This is a dollar-for-dollar deduction from taxes; therefore, the federal government is in effect paying $5,000 toward the purchase of the hardware. The net purchase price then becomes $45,000.

The acquired asset can now be depreciated. The organization must decide which depreciation method should be used for the computer. The more common depreciation methods are straight line, sum of the years digits, and one or two other accelerated rates. Accelerated depreciation, such as that obtained from the sum of the years digit method, enables the organization to write more of the computer off against taxes in the early years.

Let us assume that the organization has decided to use straight-line depreciation for five years. If we assume there is no cash value at the end of five years, then under the straight-line method one-fifth of the total cost, or $10,000, would be taken each year for depreciation. (Note that the investment tax credit has no effect on the value of the equipment.) In this example, the organization could deduct $10,000 per year from their taxes. However, while the investment tax credit was a dollar-for-dollar credit, the depreciation is a deduction.

The amount of tax savings that the corporation would obtain from this option is dependent upon their tax rate. If we assume that the corporation is in the 50 percent tax bracket, then 50 percent of their depreciation is applied to reducing taxes. In the five-year period, taxes would be reduced by $30,000 (i.e., five years of $10,000 per year depreciation, and a 50 percent bracket, results in a $5,000 tax reduction per year, plus the $5,000 investment tax credit).

Lease Option

The variables in a lease are the period of the lease, the interest charged, and the value of the equipment at the end of the lease period. In this example, we assume the lease will run five years, the assumed interest rate is 15 percent, and further assume that the equipment will have no cash value at the end of five years. Under these assumptions, the annual rental would be approximately $14,000 per year.

In the 50 percent tax bracket, this would equate to $7,000 in tax reduction per year, or $35,000 over the five-year period.

The advantages of leasing over purchasing are primarily the savings associated with not having to come up with the purchase price. In the purchase example, there was a $50,000 up-front cash payment, for which the tax benefits accrued over five years. In the lease example, there is no up-front cash payment, and the entire lease amount is deductible in the year in which it is paid.

There are advantages to both options. It is an accounting decision regarding which option the organization should make. However, most organizations opt for the lease option.

Competitive Bidding

Competitive bidding requires two or more vendors to bid on the same contract. Under this process, the organization establishes its needs and then invites vendors to bid to satisfy them. In this situation, it is assumed that the bidder who can satisfy all the requirements at the lowest price will be awarded the contract.

The following criteria usually occur in a competitive bidding situation:

- The requirements are defined in written form.
- The vendors who can satisfy the requirements are normally identified, although in some instances the bid may be advertised on the open market.
- A date is established by which the vendor must submit the bid.
- Normally criteria are established for determining who will be the winner.
- The winning vendor is normally the one who has met the bidding requirements at the lowest price.

The advantages of competitive bidding are threefold. First, and normally foremost, it is designed to acquire a product or accomplish a task at the lowest possible price. Second, it provides an opportunity to gain insight from the vendors in options and alternatives that may not have been included in the bidding. Third, it can enforce the rigid definition of requirements.

In most competitive bidding situations, the method for determining the winning bidder has been preestablished. Many organizations establish criteria and a weighting system to select a winner. The incoming bids are evaluated against this tie-breaking system, and the winner is the vendor who gets the most points.

Note that in most instances, the product will be examined or tested during the bidding process. The establishment of benchmarks, and measuring performance against the benchmark, can be an important part of the competitive bidding process. This may take longer but helps ensure that the winning vendor meets the contractual needs of the bid.

In-House Versus Contract

Computer operations is a function that requires numerous support services. Among the services that can be separately identified within computer operations are:

- Housekeeping (i.e., cleaning the computer room)
- Hardware maintenance

Software maintenance

Security

Communication services (e.g., moving telephone lines)

Operations services (e.g., organizations that will run the computer center and run specific applications)

A decision that must be made on these services is whether to perform them in-house or contract them to outside contractors. In some instances, for example, where hardware maintenance is included in the rental fee or the cost of the hardware, the source of the service is fixed. In other instances, such as security, a decision can be made whether or not to hire a security service or to perform those services with employees. Part of the decision will be based upon the economics of the decision.

The economic evaluation using accounting information is a T account type of evaluation. All of the costs associated with performing a service in-house are put on one side of the T account, and all of the costs for the contractual service are put on the other side of the T account. The accumulated amounts show which of the two alternatives is least expensive. This process can also involve competitive bidding to get the lowest possible contract bid.

The danger with this type of accounting comparison is that frequently oranges are compared to apples. The cost of the contract is normally known, but the cost of in-house services may be difficult to obtain. For example, we sometimes figure the cost of in-house services on a per-hour rate, which includes all of the departmental overhead as part of the hourly rate. However, if one more person is added, departmental overhead normally does not increase, therefore the question becomes: Should the comparison be made against the full billing rate, or made against out-of-pocket costs?

The specific considerations that need to be included within the calculations are:

Should unfunded costs, such as unfunded pension costs, be included in the calculation?

If the service is stopped, what are the costs of terminating the in-house service, versus terminating the contractual service?

What type of support services will the organization have to provide the contractor, and should they be included in the comparison of costs (e.g., physical quarters, telephone, staff time used to provide direction and answer questions, etc.)?

What are the problems of the service that needs to be expanded quickly in-house versus contractor?

There are no easy answers to these questions. Many of them are arbitrary, as is accounting. The general rule is to ensure that like costs are being compared. It is easy to exclude some in-house costs that may make an alternative appear more attractive, when in reality it is not.

The method to make this decision is as follows:

Step 1. Identify all of the costs associated with the desired service.

Step 2. Obtain from the contractor a detailed list of all of the services that will be performed by the contractor.

Step 3. Calculate the in-house costs based on the actual services to be performed by the contractor, not the services needed to fulfill the requirement.

Step 4. Verify with the organization's accounting department that the in-house-developed costs are reasonable (e.g., all employee benefits are included).

RECOMMENDED ACCOUNTING AND AUDITING PRINCIPLE FOR THE DATA PROCESSING MANAGER
When using accounting to compare two or more alternatives, extreme caution must be exercised to ensure that the costs being compared are the same costs.

USING ACCOUNTING TO MAKE COMPUTER OPERATIONS DECISIONS

This chapter will emphasize the unique accounting considerations associated with computer operations. Many of the decisions and uses of accounting within computer operations are similar to those made by systems and programming, and technical support areas. In fact, many of the technical support areas may be physically part of the computer operations area.

The two major functions of computer operations are providing computer processing capacity and services that support that processing capacity. For many users, there are alternative sources for processing capacity, and many of the services are provided at the discretion of the computer center. For example, processing capacity can be in-house or contracted through a service center; and services such as downloading data on diskettes for personal computers may be an optional service which the computer center can offer if resources are available.

We will look at these two considerations separately. In considering the processing capacity we will focus on selecting among alternatives or using mixes of alternatives. We will address the services supporting processing capacity from some of the unique accounting perspectives of those services.

Evaluating Processing Capacity Alternatives

The traditional challenge of computer operations is to provide sufficient capacity when needed, but at the same time minimize excessive capacity. The process of accomplishing this feat is called capacity management. It operates in the same way that organizations attempt to control any other inventory.

Inventory is managed in organizations using accounting as a management tool. Computer capacity is in effect an inventory of capacity stored and awaiting usage. When viewed from this perspective, it can be subjected to the same type of accounting controls as any other inventory. The objective of using accounting controls is to provide the type of information needed to effectively manage the inventory of computer capacity. Like other inventories, if it is not effectively managed the resource can be lost or degradated.

There are five accounting controls used to manage inventory:

Turnover. The number of times the average inventory is sold per year.

Stockout. The number of times an item in inventory is requested but is not available.

Economic Order Quantity. The most economical quantity of inventory to order based on usage and carrying cost.

Carrying Cost. The amount of funds required to keep a certain quantity of inventory on hand.

Aging. The average time period that inventory has been on hand. (Note that this can be for a specific item of inventory or inventory in general.)

Let's look at how each of these five accounting controls can be applied to the management of processing capacity.

Turnover

Capacity usage is frequently measured in terms of chargeable hours. In the multiprogram environment, this can be a difficult number to fully understand. Also, many of the computers are operating 24 hours a day, seven days a week, and thus we add additional confusion to the traditional usage analysis. Turnover requires the following three pieces of information:

A definition of available capacity (this could be expressed in instructions per second or other work units)

Workload processed measured in the same work units as capacity

Length of average workday

This information enables the calculation to be made of maximum processing capacity per workday. The total work for an accounting period can then be divided by this maximum capacity per workday. The result is the number of times that capacity is used during an accounting period or, in other words, the turnover of capacity. This becomes a measure that senior management understands and provides another measure to evaluate the effectiveness of the use of capacity.

Stockout

This measure would show the frequency by which users requiring service are unable to obtain that service. In computer operations, the definition of stockout, particularly for on-line systems, would have to be defined in terms of wait time for service. Industrial psychologists tell us that two minutes is a maximum desirable wait time; therefore, a stockout definition may be a service that cannot be provided within two minutes after being requested.

An inventory control stockout is an important measure. While it may be thought desirable to have a zero stockout level, in practice it is not. If an organization is never out of inventory, they most likely are overstocked and spending too much money to carry the inventory. Therefore, this is a measure that is predetermined by management as a means of controlling the amount of inventory on hand, or in the case of the computer center, the amount of available capacity.

Economic Order Quantity

Buying computer capacity is similar to buying inventory. Capacity is usually purchased in magnitudes of capacity, as opposed to buying exactly what is needed. For example, adding additional computer memory, new optimizing software, or more disk space may increase available capacity by 25 percent in a single day. On the other hand, usage rarely jumps that quickly. Therefore, when capacity is increased there is a period of overcapacity until the workload increases sufficiently to consume that capacity.

The economic order quantity calculation for inventory is a complex calculation. It takes into account the value of money, carrying cost of inventory in space and people time, expected usage gross, and price breaks in ordering larger amounts.

These same variables should be considered when computing capacity is increased. The accounting questions to consider are:

Is it better to have many small increases in capacity, or one large?

Which of the multiple alternatives to increase capacity are the most economical?

Are there alternatives to increasing in-house computer capacity? (Note that this will be discussed later in this chapter.)

Carrying Cost

This accounting measure defines the cost of providing capacity, both used and unused. The objective is to identify the income that the corporation could make if those same funds were invested. For example, if the organization has $100,000 worth of equipment that provides computer capacity, and money is worth 15 percent, then the carrying cost of the computer is $15,000 per year. This can be broken into carrying cost for capacity used, and carrying cost for unused capacity. The number serves two purposes. First, it shows the minimum return on investment that the organization should be receiving versus the return obtained by using outside suppliers and, second, the figure can be used in evaluating various capacity alternatives.

Aging

Inventory generally loses value the longer it sits on the shelf. Turnover is one measure of evaluating this potential loss, and another is the average specific age of inventory items. Using this concept for computer capacity, we could calculate the average age of the computer equipment. For example, we could know that half of our available capacity is 2.5 years old, and the other half is 1.2 years old. This enables management to assess expected lives and replacement times for computer capacity.

Using the Accounting Measures

These measures applied to capacity are designed to help manage capacity as an inventory of the organization. The measures are rarely used individually, but are used in conjunction with one another. Some of the measures are designed to indicate the usage of capacity (e.g., turnover and stockout) while others are designed to help determine and plan capacity changes (e.g., economic order quantity, carrying costs, and aging).

The primary advantage of restating computer capacity in accounting terms is to open a dialog with nondata processing management. These five accounting measures are well known to senior management and, if capacity is expressed in those terms, communication will be facilitated. However, data processing management must identify reasonable standards against which to measure these accounting statistics. For example, when discussing inventory turnover, management knows what is a desirable turnover rate for different categories of inventory. This would not be known for computer capacity unless data processing management established specific goals. Therefore, it is suggested that these numbers be used internally for some period of time before using them with management as a basis of controlling and managing computer capacity.

Using Measures to Select Capacity Alternatives

Providing computer capacity for an organization is becoming more complex. The complexity is due to the alternatives available for meeting capacity needs. For example, among the alternatives that can be considered for satisfying processing capacity requirements of an organization are:

Central computer centers
Commercial data processing service centers
Decentralized computer centers
Timesharing services
Personal computers
Contracted computer operations
Distributed processing networks

One type of capacity no longer satisfies the computer processing needs of an organization. What now must be evaluated is the mix of processing capabilities offered. Some computer center managers have lost control over computer capacity. For example, users can now order at their discretion personal computers to do computer processing. This loss may have been attributable to the failure to consider the mix of capacity requirements, and how to best manage the acquisition of that capacity resource.

The accounting measures presented provide a tool for that purpose. Data center managers should inventory their entire organization's computing capacity, and then present methods for managing that resource as an inventory. If the accounting principle of "you cannot control what you cannot measure" is applied to organizational-wide computing capacity, then it will become obvious that some sort of measures must be applied to this growing capacity inventory. The five measures previously discussed become that tool.

Accounting is a science that has matured over hundreds of years for the purpose of providing information to management to control their resources. These same concepts need to be applied to technology for both control and communication with other managers. Measures that were effective when all computing was done in a single center are no longer effective because of the dispersion of that capacity in the organizations. New measures and controls are needed, and accounting can fill that gap. The challenge to data operations management is to select and put into place the measures it needs to manage operations capacity before senior management develops its measures and takes control away from computer operations.

RECOMMENDED ACCOUNTING AND AUDITING PRINCIPLE FOR THE DATA PROCESSING MANAGER

He who measures first, wins. It is far better for data processing management to put in place accounting measures that are effective for its control needs, rather than to lose that opportunity to senior management, which will develop its own accounting controls.

EVALUATING OPERATIONAL SERVICES ON A PAY-AS-YOU-GO BASIS

The computer center as a monopoly on computer processing in the organization is over. The large, central mainframe computers of 15 years ago can now be acquired by any user for a few thousand dollars and, in addition, can become operational in a few days or weeks.

The key to the survival of the data center as it is now known will be service and technical expertise. For example, the computer center will be able to provide backup and recovery services, round-the-clock processing capacity, secure processing and numerous generalized software packages just to name a few capabilities that users may have difficulty matching.

The more services that the data center performs, the higher their cost of operation. The higher the cost of operation, the less likely it will be that users will select those services, and the more likely they will install their own because processing will be cheaper. Thus, a data center dilemma arises of they lose if they do and they lose if they don't.

The solution is to provide services for which the users are willing to pay and not to provide services for which users will not pay. In order to accomplish this objective, accounting principles must be employed to price data center services.

The decision for the data center manager is which services are essential, and which services should be considered optional and charged for. Gasoline service stations faced this issue several years ago when they unbundled attendant gas pumping, cleaning windshields, and checking oil from sale of gasoline. The services are still available, but if customers want them they pay for them.

Let's just look at a few of the services offered by the data center and ask a question about the need for that service:

Item	Response Yes	No	N/A	Comments
1. Is a forecasting system used to project capacity requirements in the future?				
2. Is the forecasting system automated?				
3. Have the estimates produced by the forecasting system proved reliable?				
4. Does computer operations management periodically identify concerns that need to be addressed in the data center?				
5. Is the data center's accounting system used as a tool for identifying those concerns?				
6. Is the data center's accounting system used as a tool for determining the magnitude of the concerns?				
7. Does the data center use accounting to evaluate lease–purchase decisions?				
8. Does the data center use accounting to evaluate competitive bidding?				
9. Does the data center use accounting to evaluate in-house versus contractual services?				
10. Is an evaluation made in accounting comparisons to ensure that the items being compared are calculated on the same services and using the same cost makeup for those services?				
11. Are tax considerations included in economic evaluation?				
12. Is computer capacity managed as if it was an inventory?				
13. Is the turnover rate for capacity calculated?				
14. Is the stockout rate for computer capacity calculated?				
15. Are economic order quantity principles used in increasing computer capacity?				
16. Is the carrying cost of computer capacity calculated?				
17. Is the computer equipment's age recorded and monitored?				

Figure 29. Justifying Computer Operations Checklist.

Item	Response			
	Yes	No	N/A	Comments
18. Are the above five accounting measures (questions 13–17) used in discussions with senior management in justifying additional capacity?				
19. Is computer capacity managed from an organizational perspective, as opposed to the central data center?				
20. Have all the data center services been identified?				
21. Has a decision been made as to which services are essential to the success of computer operations?				
22. Are the nonessential services charged to customers on a usage basis?				
23. Is the use of accounting in computer operations periodically evaluated to ensure that it is used effectively?				

Figure 29. Justifying Computer Operations Checklist (continued).

Off-Site Storage. Does every user of a data center need off-site storage?

Disaster Planning. If the computer center was destroyed, would it have an impact on every user's business?

Customer Service (e.g., Help Desk). Should customers who do not want this service have to pay for it?

Physical and Software Security. If a user's information does not require protection, should they have to pay to have that data protected?

Input–Output Control and Preparation. Should users be charged for the amount of preparatory work required for their jobs?

Computer Media Storage. Would a rental charge for each media item retained in the data library be a reasonable way to allocate those costs?

These are just a few of the areas for which the data center may want to consider unbundling and charging. Generally, users do not mind paying for services they need, but do object to paying for services they don't need. If the data center manager can differentiate the essential from the unessential, then accounting provides the tool for identifying an appropriate method for identifying costs, and then distributing those costs.

This same concept is applicable, whether or not computer operations charges users for services. Data center management should still know what services cost and if users consume these services. Until this information is known, data center management will not be in a position to manage and control the use of their resources.

JUSTIFYING COMPUTER OPERATIONS COSTS CHECKLIST

The checklist to evaluate the process of justifying computer operations costs is provided as Figure 29. The checklist is designed to be used by computer operations management to evaluate periodically the use of accounting in computer operations. Yes reponses to the checklist are representative of good accounting practices, while no responses represent areas where the increased use of accounting and accounting principles might prove beneficial.

RECOMMENDED ACCOUNTING AND AUDITING PRINCIPLE FOR THE DATA PROCESSING MANAGER
Accounting is a tool that can be used to help organizations survive. Studies by the Better Business Bureau indicate that a major cause of business failure is the inability of businesses to identify and control their costs.

Part Three

GENERATING FUNDS TO OPERATE THE DATA PROCESSING FUNCTION

Organizations allocate a portion of their revenue to the data processing function. The amount of the revenue allocated may be dependent upon the ability of data processing management to build the appropriate case. In most organizations, revenue is allocated through the budgeting process, which is described in this part. The reallocation of funds to the activities using data processing services is an important aspect of acquiring revenue for the data processing functions. These chapters explain strategies for pricing data processing services and building and using chargeout systems.

Chapter Seven

Budgeting the Data Processing Function

Budgeting is a process by which management allocates available funding among departments and projects. Some view budgeting as an annual rite or exercise undertaken to punish the poor performers and reward the good. Many view it as a game that pits subordinates against managers. In reality, budgeting is a control exercised by management over the activities of subordinates.

The process of budgeting and then operating within the budgeted funds is the data processing manager's most important accounting activity. The ability to accomplish the data processing mission within the allocated budget is a major measure of the performance of the data processing manager. It is a process by which performance of senior data processing management is judged and, at the same time, a tool that senior data processing management can use to control data processing project leaders and activities.

This chapter describes the importance of budgeting and its relationship to planning. Many of the common data processing budgeting strategies are explained and one is recommended for use. A step-by-step process is described for preparing an effective budget, together with the concerns that the data processing manager should have about budgeting. Finally, a self-assessment checklist is provided to help the data processing manager evaluate the effectiveness of his department's budgetary process.

PLANNING VERSUS BUDGETING

Planning is the process of determining "what" should be performed by the data processing function. Planning determines how the data processing mission is accomplished. Like budgeting, it is an annual rite, but its purpose deals with tasks and objectives as opposed to funding.

Planning normally precedes budgeting. Planning includes both the internal data processing activities, such as operation of the data library, as well as external activities, such as developing and maintaining user applications. Planning, like budgeting, involves the collection of information from those activities involved in fulfilling the data processing mission.

Data processing planning should be tied to the plans of the organization. The data processing plan should be a subset of, and supportive of, the organization's plan. Unless the two are tied together, the data processing plan may not fulfill the information processing needs of the organization.

Many organizations like to separate the planning and budgeting function. If the two are tied together, it is possible that budgeting would take precedence over planning. People might become too influenced with the dollars involved and want to change the plans to meet what they believe would be acceptable dollars. If planning is done separately, then the needed plans will be developed regardless of the budgeted costs for those plans.

The budget should be tied directly to the annual data processing plan. If three- or five-year plans are developed, then normally three- and five-year budgets are prepared. It is generally preferable to have budgeting lag planning. However, this does not preclude the plan from being changed during the budgeting process.

DATA PROCESSING BUDGETING STRATEGIES

The actual budgeting process comes from senior management. In many organizations, budgeting is a comptroller responsibility. Thus, the comptroller procedures spell out when and how budgets are to be prepared. In many organizations, this includes the instructions and forms to be completed during the budgetary process.

These organizational budgetary processes define what the data processing department must do, but rarely explain how to do it. There are some unique budgetary aspects to data processing that few budgetary processes address. These unique budgetary characteristics of data processing include:

Multiyear projects, which are not capital projects in the sense of other major organization multiyear projects.

Projects that involve the use of new and frequently unproven technology.

Projects that are subject to continually changing technology. (This requires projects to be continually modified to take advantage or utilize currently installed computer technology.)

Projects that are interrelated, meaning that a change to one project may change multiple projects.

Projects and services that involve all major activities within the organization.

Projects that are subject to the demands of all major activities within the organization.

The bottom line of these unique budgetary aspects is that data processing is highly susceptible to any change in current organizational activities and future plans. This means that the budget must be closely tied to current proposed business activities of the organization. Failure to take into account or estimate what might happen to the business activities of the organization subjects the data processing budget to gross error.

The strategies that data processing departments take in dealing with these unique characteristics vary significantly from organization to organization. Many data processing managers are not privy to organizational plans and activities. Therefore, they frequently must "guess" what might happen to the organization and budget accordingly.

Among the strategies used by data processing management to prepare a budget that will handle most contingencies are: crystal ball, bare bones, double-cut, dartboard, breadboard, consensus, and ground-up budgeting.

Crystal Ball Budgeting

This budgeting strategy requires the data processing manager to anticipate what might happen to the organization's business. While the process is called crystal balling, many managers use a more scientific process to develop estimates. Among the techniques that can be used are:

Trend Analysis. Showing rates of growth based on past performance.

Interviewing. Discussions with users regarding their opinion on the growth of their activities.

Economic Forecasts. Projected growths, both of the national economy and the industry in which the organization resides.

Corporate Guidelines. Many organizations provide general guidelines on budgets outlining acceptable levels of growth. (Note that data processing need not comply with these guidelines, but they are indicators of acceptable levels of growth.)

Bare Bones Budgeting

This budgetary approach attempts to define the minimum level of funding needed to accomplish the organization's mission. The objective of this type of budgeting is that people work better when they are under budgetary pressure. If projects or activities are given more funding than they need, management believes Parkinson's law will come into effect. This law states that the work expands to consume the totality of the allocated resources. If organizations have just what they need or slightly less, then individuals will work harder to accomplish their goals and objectives than if they had more than enough funding.

Double-Cut Budgeting

This strategy assumes that senior management will cut the budget, regardless of what it is. Therefore, the stategy is to ask for significantly more funds than are needed, so that management can make its traditional budget cuts, leaving the data processing function with still adequate funds to accomplish its mission. The double-cut connotation means that you ask for twice what you want so that management can cut it in half and you still end up with the needed funds. In practice, the actual amount of overbudgeting should equal the projected cut by management. For example, if data processing management believed that their budget would be cut 10 percent, then it would pad the budget items by a sufficient amount so that when the budget was cut by 10 percent, the final budget would equal the amount of funding that data processing believed it needed to operate throughout the year. This strategy is a cat and mouse game played with senior management. If the padding becomes too obvious, then management will cut more than the anticipated percent, leaving the function with inadequate funds to accomplish its mission.

Dartboard Budgeting

This is a variation of crystal balling without the investigation. The strategy is usually undertaken by data processing managers whose philosophy is that budgeting is a futile exercise, and they will be allocated whatever funds management wants to allocate regardless of the exercise. Given this philosophy, the expenditure of large amounts of data processing resources on budgeting appears to be a waste of time and effort. Thus, only minimal effort is expended on preparation of the budget. This precludes any analysis and encourages pulling figures out of the air (i.e., the equivalent of throwing darts at a budgetary dartboard) to create a straw man from which senior management can do with what it has already intended to do. For example, many data processing managers believe that next year's budget will bear some predefined relationship to this year's budget, so regardless of what data processing submits, the amount of funding they will get has already been predetermined.

Breadboard Budgeting

Breadboarding is a process of comparing the resources required to do a known project with another similar yet to be performed project. For example, if project A and B are similar, and project A has been completed while project B is planned, the budget for project B can be based on the actual expenditures for project A. Let us assume that project A took 1,000 hours to complete, and project B is about the same size in complexity as project A. Therefore, using breadboarding, the budget for project B would be the 1,000 hours that it took to do project A. If project B was slightly more complex some additional hours would be allocated, for example, 1,100 hours might be allocated, while if it was slightly less complex then perhaps only 900 hours would be included in the budget for that project. Breadboarding can be applied to maintenance, new projects, the acquisition of new technology, the budgetary estimate for outside contracts, or any other activity for which similar activities have previously been performed.

Consensus Budgeting

Consensus budgeting is normally a by-product of consensus management. Consensus management is managing by majority rule. Whenever the majority of involved parties believe that an appropriate action is correct, then that action is taken. This is sometimes referrred to as the "Nasser Rule," Nasser, as president of Egypt, once said that the responsibility of the rule was to find out which way the mob was going and then get out in front and lead it.

Consensus budgeting involves extensive interaction with all the parties involved in budgeting. This includes subordinates within data processing, user management, as well as senior management. This process attempts to gain approval and support for the budget before it is formally submitted for approval. It is generally immaterial what the actual costs might be; the rationale behind this approach is to get agreement that the amount of money budgeted is realistic. Projects will then be molded to fit those budgetary estimates.

Ground-Up Budgeting

This process closely parallels that recommended by most organizations' budgetary procedures. It identifies the budgeted items or categories and then collects data for those categories. For example, it lists budget categories such as personnel, benefits, hardware contracts, maintenance contracts, and employee benefits. The objective of budgeting is then to identify the costs associated with those budget categories and then accumulate them to develop a grand budgetary total. The ground-up concept implies that budgeting is performed at the lowest levels and then that all budgets are consolidated as the grand budget is arrived at.

Recommended Data Processing Budget Strategy

The recommended data processing budget strategy is to budget at the data processing project level. The projects are the activities within the data processing function that are defined in the mission and plan of the data processing organization. This equates budgeting to specific mission items for which the data processing manager is responsible.

Normally, the organization's budgetary procedures neither require nor imply that budgeting should be done at the project level. This is because budgeting is a senior management control, and it is designed to control the activities with which senior management is concerned. An organization's budgetary procedure is not designed to assist data processing managers in performing their functions.

RECOMMENDED ACCOUNTING AND AUDITING PRINCIPLE FOR THE DATA PROCESSING MANAGER
Systems are built to serve their user. The primary user of an organization's budget is senior management. Therefore, to be effective in data processing the budgetary process must be restructured to complement the characteristics of the data processing function.

This approach requires data processing to develop a budget under one structure, and then resequence the accounts into the organization's budgetary structure. The purpose of doing this is to develop a budget that is of maximum benefit to data processing. The benefit of a project-oriented budget is that the budget is more closely matched to the work performed in data processing; moreover, the work performed becomes the focal point of justifying and adjusting budgets based upon managerial decisions.

In a budget that is line item-oriented, budget changes are usually at the line item level. For example, most budgets call for people to be budgeted at a line item. Thus, if management wants to cut the budget, they can cut the people line item. However, this cut is not directly translatable into projects. Therefore, data processing management may be held to complete the same number of projects even though the line item people is cut. When the budget is at the project level, then data processing management can quickly translate that line item budget cut to projects, which transfers the responsibility for mission changes to the individual that cuts the budget.

Project-oriented budgeting takes more time than line item-oriented budgeting. However, the benefit of planning at the project level is usually returned in fewer problems because of greater managerial direction in project planning. It also makes budgeting a more effective control tool for the data processing manager.

BUDGETING IS AN ORGANIZATION'S NUMBER ONE CONTROL TOOL

Senior management is responsible for all of the operations within the organization. This includes general administration, marketing, production, administration, data processing, legal, public relations, and any other organizational activity in which the company is involved. No one individual can fully understand the intricacies of all of the activities within the organization. This is particularly true of technical functions such as research, production, and data processing. However, even without understanding those functions in detail, management must control them.

When asked what is the primary tool for controlling their organization, most senior management respond that it is the budget. This tool translates all problems, needs, and solutions into a common term—money! Thus, by controlling a single variable, management can exercise maximum control over the activities within their organization. For example, it is difficult for senior management to intelligently discuss the advantages and disadvantages of moving to newer technology, but management can intelligently discuss alternative tradeoffs in the use of funding.

If budgeting is that important to senior management, it should be as important to data processing management. The mechanism by which its activities are controlled should be understood and effectively utilized. For the data processing manager to fail to devote adequate attention to the senior management's primary tool of control is not only negligent, but foolhardy.

Once the importance of the budget is recognized, then it is not only the tool by which management controls data processing, but the tool that data processing management can use to achieve its objectives. Some of the previously described data processing strategies illustrated how budgeting can be abused. Data processing management can also effectively use the same process to accomplish its mission.

DATA PROCESSING MANAGEMENT'S TRUE BUDGETARY CONCERNS

The budget is a means for communicating requests to management and receiving resource allocation from them. If budgeting is unsuccessful, at least part of the reason can be attributed to data processing's inadequate communication of its needs to senior management. Procedures that clarify and clearly explain the tasks to be accomplished with the budgetary resources provide a vehicle for facilitating communication of budgetary needs.

There are three major concerns that the data processing manager should have regarding budgeting.

Concern 1. Budgetary Requests Are Denied or Cut

Requests for funding within the budget may be rejected by senior management, or the funding for those projects cut. The denial may relate to specific projects, or consist of across-the-board cuts. For example, management may not want a specific project undertaken and delete that project from the budget, the funding for a project may be cut, or there may be an across-the-board cut. The across-the-board cut leaves the discretion of where to cut the funds to data procesing management. This latter situation may prompt data processing management to attempt to undertake all the existing proj-ects, but to scale them down within the new budgetary amounts. Note that these across-the-board cuts lead many data processing managers to consider using the double-cut budgetary strategy.

Concern 2. Management Assigns a New Portfolio of Work

Senior management may rearrange or substitute new projects for budgeted projects. In the heat of the budgetary battle, a give and take must go on between the participants. Projects that senior management may want, or think necessary, may not be included within the proposed data processing budget. During the budgetary cycle, which includes not only the preparation and approval, but also the usage of funds, management may add new work that alters the ability of data processing management to perform the tasks perceived as necessary.

Concern 3. Budgeting Estimates Are Incorrect

This is a data processing problem, not a senior management-related problem. In preparing the budgetary estimates, data processing management has stated that it believes it can accomplish certain tasks with certain resources. If the budgetary estimates are incorrect, the credibility of data processing management is affected. It can be equally inappropriate to complete projects that are significantly under budget as over budget. This is because in budgeting, management makes tradeoffs among projects. In allocating funds for a data processing project, management may have deleted a project in another area. If the funds are not used, management may not have the opportunity to reinstate a project that could have helped the organization, but was deleted due to budgetary constraints.

RECOMMENDED ACCOUNTING AND AUDITING PRINCIPLE FOR THE DATA PROCESSING MANAGER
Good budgeting is indicative of good management.

STEPS IN BUILDING A DATA PROCESSING BUDGET

Senior management defines the timetable and procedures to be followed in developing the organization's budget. These procedures describe the information that senior management wants, and the time schedule in which this information is wanted. However, it does not address the information that data processing may need to control its function. The objective of the budgetary process described below is to provide data processing management with the budgetary information it needs. At the end of this budgetary process, the information may have to be transcribed into the format and cost items described by senior management.

The six-step process for customizing the data processing budget are listed in Figure 30 and described below.

Step 1. Identify the Work Tasks to Be Accomplished During the Budgetary Period

Data processing is a task-oriented function. The use of resources can normally be associated with the satisfaction of some need or requirement. Even functions designed to help a wide variety of individuals and users, such as help desk or information center, can be tied to the accomplishment of specific tasks or requirements.

Accounting budgets tend to be line item budgets, as opposed to task or objective-oriented budgets. Accounting systems, including budgets, are constructed around a chart of accounts. A chart of accounts is a predefined list to which the request for, or use of resources, can be charged. The budgetary chart of accounts is normally closely related to the general ledger chart of accounts established by accountants. These generalized accounts, such as payroll, employee benefits, and utility charges, become a

Step	Step Name	Description
1.	Identify the work tasks to be accomplished during the budgetary period.	The objectives, activities, or projects to be performed by data processing must be identified.
2.	Develop a budgetary bridge.	A method needs to be established for ensuring that both the organization and data processing budgetary information will be collected.
3.	Train the data processing staff in budgeting methods.	The data processing personnel involved in budgeting must be trained in how to perform those budgetary processes.
4.	Develop budgets at the project or task level.	The information needed for budgeting must be collected.
5.	Consolidate and approve the data processing budget.	The information collected must be consolidated in the formats needed and then approved by data processing management.
6.	Present and defend the budget to senior management.	The budget must be presented and defended to senior management.

Figure 30. Data Processing Budgetary Customizing Process.

convenient way of consolidating costs from multiple activities into common categories.

The "buckets" or accounts into which data processing can request funds and charge activities are not designed to facilitate managerial control within data processing. In this process, activities like data libraries, systems programming, and disaster recovery programs are buried along with user-related production activities.

To adequately address data processing needs, numerous new accounts would need to be established. This is generally impractical in most organizations. Therefore, the most desirable alternative is to develop a structure for accumulating the available chart of accounts into subcategories that can be managed and controlled by data processing management.

The recommended categories are data processing projects, activities, or tasks. These include such items as:

- Data processing applications (user projects)
- Maintenance activities
- Internal projects such as data libraries, off-site storage, and disaster planning
- Operation activities
- Technical support activities, such as generating and maintaining operating systems
- Administrative and managerial functions

Step 2. Develop a Budgetary Bridge

Data processing management should collect and use budgetary information at the project or task level. For example, a budgetary line item will be salaries, while a project or task accumulates salaries in terms of developing projects, as opposed to bodies.

The method for collecting information at the project level and converting it to line item level must be established. The most common method of doing that is to collect information at the line item level within projects. For example, personnel hours or days to do a project are collected and then at the departmental level converted into people for line item budgeting purposes.

The transition from approved budget back to project–task levels must also be developed. This permits data processing management to allocate funding at the task level and control it at that level. It must also be done in the event there are across-the-board line item cuts, so that those line item cuts can be translated directly to individual projects and tasks.

Step 3. Train the Data Processing Staff in Budgeting Methods

Few data processing organizations train their staff in how to collect, present, and use budgetary information. It should be little surprise then that there is a lot of bad budgeting. It is unrealistic to expect people to do a job in which they have not been trained.

The most common training tool for budgets are forms and organization-developed guidelines and procedures. These usually accompany budgetary information, but are not explained and taught. When taught, they are rarely instructed by a competent instructor. The bottom-line implication that is given to the data processing staff is that budgeting is neither important, nor need it be done by any formalized process. Thus, many staff members resort to one or more of the data processing strategies discussed earlier in this chapter.

Good training encompasses the following activities:

1. *Establishing Training Objectives.* In educational terms, this involves determining what skills the trainee should learn. In budgeting, this might include use of forms, budget estimating techniques, interviewing practices if data needs to be collected from users, and instruction on the makeup of the accounts used in the budgetary process.
2. *Developing Instructional Material.* Material should be developed to teach the stated course objectives and skills.
3. *Developing Case Studies.* The student should be given materials on which skills can be practiced.
4. *Evaluation of Mastery of Skills.* A process should be developed (usually testing) to ensure that the students have mastered the appropriate skills.

Step 4. Develop Budgets at the Project or Task Level

As a general rule, budgets should be developed by the individual to be held accountable for the operation of the project or task involved. For example, a project leader for an application system should develop the budget to build or maintain that project. Likewise, the data librarian should develop the data library budget, and the system programmers the project support budget. If the responsible individual has yet to be named, then data processing management will have to assume that responsibility.

The objective of having the responsible individual collect the information is that this individual will have to perform the defined tasks within the allocated budget. The individual involved becomes part of the budgetary process and thus both understands the budgeting process and is involved in determining the amount of funds allocated for the project.

The collection of data should always be task oriented. For example, software maintenance should not be done by block allocating funds. Block allocation means that if $100,000 was used last year, then a block of funds (i.e., $100,000) is allocated the following year for unknown purposes. It is difficult to justify a block allocation budget; it is not difficult to justify a budget that is designed to accomplish specific tasks.

The task-oriented budget is more difficult to develop. It is easy to do a block allocation budget, or a gross estimate of what a project might cost.

Wherever possible, the projects and tasks should be broken into business components and not data processing components. For example, it is far better to divide an application project into tasks to process transactions, produce reports, provide planning information, and so on, than it is to divide the project into design, programming, and testing. While the project leader may actually perform design, programming, and testing, it is more difficult to justify testing than the inclusion of certain activities.

RECOMMENDED ACCOUNTING AND AUDITING PRINCIPLE FOR THE DATA PROCESSING MANAGER
The budget is a tool for management. Thus, it should not be built around the technical issues but, rather, around management issues and business objectives.

The budget preparers should be instructed that the budget is a vehicle for justifying funds and implementing managerial objectives. Therefore, while project personnel perform technical tasks, they accomplish business objectives. It is just common sense when one thinks about it that management is much more likely to approve budgets that provide for the accomplishment of business objectives, than budgets that appear to address technology. Businesses are not in the business of building computer systems but, rather, accomplishing business objectives.

Step 5. Consolidate and Approve the Data Processing Budget

Individual project or activity budgets must be consolidated into data processing departmental budgets. This involves two activities. The first is the approval of the individual budgets by data processing management. Management should approve budgets at the individual project level and not at the departmental level. However, after the budget is consolidated, some additional adjustments may be necessary.

The second activity is the consolidation activity. It is during this activity that the budget is converted from the task-oriented perspective to the organizational budgetary line item perspective. This is normally not a difficult transition and in many instances can be computerized.

Data processing management must again review and approve the consolidated budget. At this point in time, it should view the budget with a critical eye of senior management. The process should be a postdevelopmental challenge.

The challenge should include the type of questions with which senior management will challenge the budget. For example, this challenging would include:

Is the budgetary amount consistent with last year?

Is the data processing budget consistent with the organization plans?

Is the budget consistent with managerial budgetary guidelines?

Do the items within the budget appear to be reasonable?

Are the items included within the budget reasonable?

If the challenging questions cannot be adequately answered, then either additional information should be collected or the budget changed. Data processing management must feel comfortable with the budget they present to senior management. Unless data processing managers are committed to the budget, it is difficult for them to be convincing in the support and defense for the budget. It also requires data processing management to be conversant in the budgetary details.

Step 6. Present and Defend the Budget to Senior Management

The last step should not be difficult if the previous steps have been properly performed. A well-constructed and challenged budget should be highly defensible to senior management. The more specific the budget, the easier it is to defend; the more general the budget, the more difficult to defend.

This step involves the following three activities:

1. Consolidation of the budget into the format and style desired by the organization. This is normally well specified by the budgetary procedures.
2. Embellish the formal budget with the data processing story. What needs to be said that is not provided for in the formal presentation process should be included as an appendix or addendum to the presented budget.
3. Prepare and present the budget formally to senior management. Note that sometimes this is required, sometimes it is optional, and in some instances senior management will not permit such a presentation. If permissible, it should be made. This gives data processing management an opportunity to appeal to the eye through a visual presentation and to the ear through an oral presentation. The process should be looked at as a marketing process and the best marketing tools used to convince management to adopt the proposed budget.

The six-step budgeting process has been designed to provide the evidence needed to "sell" the budget to senior management. It is difficult to sell line items; it is not as difficult to sell projects, particularly if the projects are business oriented as opposed to technology oriented. In the project-oriented budgets, cuts result in reduced projects, not reduced line items.

RECOMMENDED ACCOUNTING AND AUDITING PRINCIPLE FOR THE DATA PROCESSING MANAGER
Senior management is less likely to cut business-oriented objectives than they are technological-oriented objectives.

DATA PROCESSING BUDGET SELF-ASSESSMENT CHECKLIST

The creation and use of the budget is a major accounting function for the data processing manager. The success that the manager has in budgeting may directly affect his or her personal performance. Time and effort expended in budgeting is usually rewarded in improved data processing performance.

A checklist for evaluating the effectiveness of the data processing budgeting process is given in Figure 31. This checklist is designed so that yes responses are indicative of good budgetary processes, and no responses are indicative of items that data processing management should investigate. Improvements in the budgetary process should prove helpful in improving the performance of the data processing function.

	Responses			
Item	Yes	No	N/A	Comments
1. Has data processing management accepted budgeting as one of its primary responsibilities?				
2. Has data processing management established the data processing objectives to be achieved through budgeting?				
3. Is the data processing budget task or activity oriented as opposed to line item oriented?				
4. Do the individuals responsible for each task or activity determine the initial budget for that activity?				

Figure 31. Data Processing Budgetary Process Checklist.

Item	Responses Yes	No	N/A	Comments
5. Are sufficient time and resources allocated for budgeting?				
6. Has data processing management established a budgetary process for the data processing (DP) department)				
7. Is the DP budgetary process directed toward data processing objectives as opposed to organizational objectives?				
8. Has the data processing staff been trained in how to budget?				
9. Have the educational objectives of the budget training course been established?				
10. Is the data processing staff involved in budgeting evaluated to ensure that it fully understands the process?				
11. Has a bridge been developed to cross-reference the data processing budgetary requirements to the organization's budgetary requirements?				
12. Is each data processing project or activity fully justified (i.e., no block estimating permitted)?				
13. Does data processing management fully understand each item in the data processing budget?				
14. Does the data processing management supplement the organization's budgetary requirements with sufficient evidence to support the uniqueness of the data processing budget?				
15. Does data processing management prepare presentations (if possible) to senior management, explaining the information included in their budget?				
16. Is the budget used by data processing management to control the day-to-day operations of the data processing department?				
17. Does data processing management challenge the budget from a senior management perspective prior to issuing that budget to senior management?				

Figure 31. Data Processing Budgetary Process Checklist (continued).

Chapter Eight

Data Processing Pricing Strategies

In the beginning, data processing departments did not charge for their services. Data processing was considered part of the organization's overhead, and put in the same category as the mailroom. However, the cost for data processing escalated quickly, and senior management felt the need to control those costs. One of the most popular methods selected for controlling data processing costs was to charge those costs to the user's budget. This made the user accountable for the costs, as well as the data processing function.

Chargeout provided senior management with two controls over the expenditure of the same dollar. First, data processing had to justify the resources needed to provide the user services. Second, the users had to justify the services received.

It was relatively unimportant to senior management how the services were charged. Management's concern was that costs were distributed to the users of the service. In many instances, the methods picked were detrimental to the long-range success of the data processing function. Many DP managers still suffer from the chargeout decisions made 25 years ago.

This chapter explains the two primary methods of charging services: cost and price. The chapter describes the advantages and disadvantages of each method. Pricing is the recommended alternative, and a step-by-step process is provided to help data processing managers establish a price for their services. The chapter concludes with a self-assessment checklist of chargeout practices.

WHAT DOES CHARGING FOR SERVICES MEAN?

Many data processing departments hold their users accountable for the data processing resources they consume. However, many data processing departments do not. Those that do have an obvious need to value their services so that those costs can be transferred to user budgets. On the other hand, the data processing organizations that do not transfer costs to users should still place a value on the services consumed by their users.

The arguments against charging users for value received include:

Time is involved to calculate and prorate costs.

Services need to be provided whether or not costs are allocated.

Charging discourages the use of automated activities and encourages the use of less efficient manual procedures.

Cost can be controlled through the data processing department budget; therefore, charging users is not necessary.

In putting a value on services provided to users, there are two considerations. The first is whether a value should be placed on those services, and the second is whether users' budgets should be charged for those services. We will examine the advantages of these two issues separately.

Among the advantages for calculating the value of services provided users are that these calculations:

Demonstrate whether or not the service is cost-beneficial.

Assist users in selecting among alternatives.

Provide a basis to cost-justify projects to senior management.

Provide a basis for rejecting noncost-effective user requests.

The following two advantages accrue when those services are charged to users' budgets, as follows:

Users are made accountable for the services they consume.

Senior management is given two opportunities to evaluate whether or not to provide data processing services within the organization.

The question as to whether services are charged to users' budgets is an organizational decision. It assumes a budgetary process is established so that costs can be transferred. However, the practice of calculating the value of services provided a user appears so beneficial and such a good management practice that it is recommended that all data processing groups follow this practice.

RECOMMENDED ACCOUNTING AND AUDITING PRINCIPLE FOR THE DATA PROCESSING MANAGER
If you do not know what a service costs, you do not know whether it is worth providing that service.

WHAT PRECISION IS NEEDED IN VALUING SERVICES?

An easy assumption to make is that services must be charged to the last penny. The implied 100 percent precision implies a time-consuming and cumbersome process.

Proponents of valuing user services argue that:

1. Costs are "funny money" meaning that it is not real money but, rather, internal allocations of money.
2. They are not very accurate and thus should not be used.

The latter argument deals with precision. Whenever costing of any type is used, the implied precision is down to the last penny. However, this type of precision is unnecessary in valuing services provided to users.

The level of precision needed is the level required to make decisions. Normally, to the nearest $100 is sufficient and, in larger organizations, to the nearest $1,000 may be sufficient. All one needs to know is that:

1. The maximum cost is less than the minimum benefit.
2. The maximum benefit is less than the minimum cost.

If either of these above two criteria are met, the desired precision is present. For example, let us assume that the benefit of making a maintenance change to a system was estimated to be $50,000. In this instance, it would be immaterial whether the cost was estimated to be $5,000 or $35,000. Either would lead to the same decision that the change was worthwhile. On the other hand, if the costs were estimated at $100,000 or $1 million, the decision would be not to install the change. Too frequently, chargeout systems are not designed based upon management's needs.

RECOMMENDED ACCOUNTING AND AUDITING PRINCIPLE FOR THE DATA PROCESSING MANAGER
The expected precision from any internal accounting system need only be as precise as needed to make effective management decisions.

PRICE VERSUS COST

The value according to which data processing charges users of services can be based on either cost or price. The differences between the two concepts are significant. While price is highly recommended, most data processing departments use cost as a basis for valuing user services.

The concept of cost is one in which the total costs of the date processing department are allocated to users based on services they are provided. Some means of defining services must be made. (How to do this is described in Chapter 9). The total units of services are then divided into the total cost to calculate the cost per unit of service. This calculated unit cost is the value assigned to that service. The user then is charged that cost for each time the service is utilized. In practice, it is more complex, but this simplistic explanation should suffice to explain the cost concept.

Under the cost concept, the user is in control. The data processing department provides the service, and the user decides whether or not to accept that service. Under this concept, any activity relating to the user's application and services becomes a user decision. If data processing believes some modification or action is desirable and the user does not, that action is not taken.

The concept of price is one in which data processing establishes a fair value for services. Under this concept, the data processing function becomes an entrepreneurial activity. The objective is still to allocate all of the data processing costs to users of that service, but the method of doing it is significantly different than in the cost illustration.

Under the pricing concept, the data processing department must still identify the basis of service. However, the price established for that service is one set by the data processing department and need not be based upon an equal distribution of costs.

Under the concept of pricing, the data processing department can:

Charge different prices for service at different times of the day, or days of the week, or weeks of the month.

Make technological improvements to users' applications without their approval, because the technological updates are not charged to the user but, rather, absorbed into the pricing algorithm.

Charge users different rates for similar services based upon unique attributes of the application system; for example, the per-hour cost to make changes to systems written in assembler-type languages may be higher than the per-hour charge for working on statement-level language systems.

Establish price leaders for using newer services, such as data base technology.

Provide services deemed highly beneficial by the data processing manager at no cost, and charge for services deemed not beneficial by the data processing manager.

Based on a system of valuing user services at cost, many applications have become technologically obsolete. Under the cost concept, the data processing manager cannot improve the technological currentness of systems without the user's approval. The technological deterioration of those systems has added to the maintenance costs, and has been at least partially attributable to users wanting to replace those systems with purchased applications and/or microcomputer systems.

Under a pricing concept, data processing management would remain in charge of the technological aspects of systems. Just as computer operations have not given up the ability to move to new hardware and software at the discretion of operations management, neither should systems management give up their prerogative to improve the technological currentness of systems.

USES OF PRICING

Establishing a value for services provided to a user may satisfy many needs of the organization. Price in this context means two different prices. The first price is the estimate of what it will cost to complete a task, and the second price is the actual amount charged the user for that service. These may or may not be the same amount.

The two prices are calculated by different methods. For example, the estimate may be based on a generalized estimating algorithm, while the actual cost may result from totaling actual expenditures. Later in the chapter we discuss the various methods for determining price.

The uses of price by a user of a data processing service include:

Establishing Priority. With limited funding and much work, priorities need to be established. One factor in establishing priorities is the price of doing a task. The price may help establish priority through cost–benefit analysis, or determinations may be made that there are insufficient resources to do a project of a certain cost level.

Planning Work. Price includes two variables: resources and time. Price will vary based on the time schedule for completion. Generally, very short time spans increase price, while longer time spans tends to reduce it. An understanding of these variables helps build plans involving information systems.

Selecting Among Alternatives. Price is an important factor in determining which alternative to select. For example, if two alternatives appear approximately equal, but one costs significantly less than the other, the lower cost alternative is normally selected.

Make or Buy Decision. The price of developing a project in-house can be used to determine whether it would be more economical to buy the product or make it. It also becomes a basis of comparing to determine whether a vendor is giving appropriate value for the services offered.

Shifting Responsibility. Pricing product establishes the base for shifting the responsibility of using the resources from the data processing function to the user. Until a price is established, it is hard to transfer the responsibility for the use of resources. This shifting makes users accountable for both the use and also partially for the justification of a centralized data processing function.

Centralized Versus Decentralized Decision. Many users are now going through a process to evaluate whether or not they should acquire and use computers in their own area. The microcomputers have extensive capabilities, and those capabilities are increasing. Thus, the possibility now exists of users doing projects themselves versus having them performed centrally. Knowing the price of the function centrally helps to determine whether it is more economical to do it centrally or to acquire and install computers in the user area.

Control of Data Processing Resources. The establishment of a price provides a vehicle for management to use to control the use of data processing resources. Until management knows where data processing resources are being consumed, they cannot initiate control procedures to control those expenditures. Without accurate information, the controls may be exercised over the wrong data processing variable.

DATA PROCESSING PRICING STRATEGIES

Most organizations have two distinct pricing strategies. One is for estimating, and one is for accumulating actual costs. The data processing decision is which type and how much effort should be expended on each of the two types of systems.

Both systems are equally important. If an improper estimate is developed, it may result in an erroneous management decision. Many thousands of dollars may be lost or wasted if the wrong decision is made. Thus, some argue that the estimating system is the more important of the two systems. The cost collection system is merely an after-the-fact basis of telling what happened and may not be instrumental in the decision-making process.

The actual collection of cost data is normally factual. It is more a process of establishing the appropriate buckets, and then collecting the data as required. Chapter 9 will describe this cost collection process.

The pricing strategies relate to the amounts provided users of data processing services. In a costing system, the collected costs are what the user gets. In a pricing system, there are a variety of options available to data processing management in how they want to allocate costs among the services provided.

The more common pricing strategies used in data processing are:

Strategy 1. Division of Costs

The division of cost is the simplest of all pricing strategies. The objective is to transfer all of the data processing costs to users of data processing services. The allocation of costs may be in total or by general activities such as computer operations, software maintenance, and project development.

This pricing method first determines what will be included in data processing overhead. Overhead means activities that are indirectly charged to users. These normally include data processing management and services that aid all users, such as training, standards development, and quality control. The price is then composed of two variables: The fixed amount or overhead that users are charged per unit of service, plus the variable cost, which is the cost of the resource itself that is utilized.

Strategy 2. Cost Plus

The cost plus strategy is a variation of the division of cost. In division of cost the distribution is based exclusively on units of work performed for users. In the cost plus concept, a percent of cost is added for internal activities. Both methods will allocate all costs to users. Under the division of cost concept, the user has control of where all of the costs go, while under the cost plus strategy the data processing department reserves a predetermined percent of resources for their own internal activities. (Note that the amount allocated for internal usage is the plus percentage added to cost.)

The objective of cost plus is to permit the data processing department to perform those activities believed needed to keep their "shop" up to date technically. These extra funds can be allocated to bring applications up to existing technological standards, to improve applications performance, to improve the skill level of the data processing staff, to establish new functions such as configuration management or change management, and to do research into better ways to perform data processing. These costs could have been included in the overhead part of the division of cost strategy. However, when done so, it partially undermines the entrepreneurial aspect of data processing.

Strategy 3. Negotiated Price

Under this method, price is not directly related to cost. The price that a service will be performed at is whatever price data processing management and user management agree upon. This is equivalent to bidding for jobs as is common in many industries that build products.

The negotiated price provides the data processing manager with a series of options not available in the division of cost or cost plus strategies. For example, negotiated price can be used to smooth work. If data processing experiences cycles of work, the price can be raised during the busy points of the cycle, and reduced during the low ebbs of the cycle in order to smooth and equalize work throughout the entire business cycle.

Negotiated price does not guarantee that the data processing function will recoup all of its cost from users. Under negotiated pricing, the data processing function may make an internal profit or loss. This provides the manager with more leeway in bidding against contractors. The performance of the data processing manager can then be partially based upon the ending budgetary position of the function.

Strategy 4. Risk-Related Pricing

Risk is the probability that an unfavorable event may occur. Understanding the risk enables one to determine the probability that an unfavorable event will or will not occur. For example, if an organization is relying upon delivery of new equipment to run a system, and can determine that the risk of the equipment not being delivered is very high, then they could state that the probability of the system being installed on time is very low.

The three risk dimensions in developing and maintaining a computerized application are:

1. *Structure.* Degree of predetermined structure inherent in a system.
2. *Technology.* Degree of technological expertise required and its availability within the organization.
3. *Size.* Expressed in terms of man-hours of development effort.

If these three risk dimensions can be measured, then the impact of those risk dimensions on pricing can be measured. For example, if it is estimated that one project has twice the risk of another project, then the price to perform the second system may need to be twice that of doing the first system. In other fields, the ability of a contractor to adequately measure risk may determine whether or not that contractor stays in business.

The concept of estimating the cost of data processing service using risk has been incorporated into commercially available estimating packages. One such package is ESTIMACS.[1]

The ESTIMACS package asks 25 questions about data processing projects developed for mainframe systems. These 25 questions are listed in Figure 32. The answers to the questions are then fed into the ESTIMACS software package, which produces the following:

Estimate of the number of hours of effort by the project manager, systems analyst, and programmer

The mix of staffing that should be applied for the optimum development cost

A scheduling window indicating when specific tasks should be started and stopped

Strategy 5. Fixed Price (Guaranteed Price)

The last strategy is one in which data processing guarantees its estimate. What is stated as the estimate will in fact be the cost of doing the work. In construction this is called a fixed price contract.

Some data processing organizations use the fixed price as the upper limit guaranteeing that the cost of the project will never exceed that amount. If the actual costs collected are less than the fixed price, then the user is charged for the actual cost. If the actual cost is higher than the fixed cost, then the user is charged the fixed cost. The data processing department must account for these overruns in a category entitled "poor performance."

The fixed price contract is a sign of maturity of the data processing profession. Organizations that feel confident enough in their pricing procedures and work procedures to guarantee prices are either extremely skilled and well organized or foolhardy. Fortunately, the foolhardy will not last long.

ESTABLISHING A DATA PROCESSING PRICING POLICY

The establishment of a data processing pricing policy is the DP manager's responsibility. The policy must address the following three areas:

1. Will the value of services charged to users be calculated?
2. If so, what method will be used to calculate the value of services consumed by users?
3. Will users be charged for the services they consume?

[1]This is a software package available from Management and Computer Services, Inc., Valley Forge, PA.

Questions	Answers
1. How many user organizations must sign off on requirements definition?	________
2. Identify the number of company locations that require travel for information gathering.	________
3. Identify the number of hundreds of people in each organization identified in Question #1.	________
4. How familiar is the development group with this business application?	________
5. What is the level of user management agreement on system objectives?	________
6. How significant will commuting be to the project site?	________
7. Will staffing be by developer, or developer and user?	________
8. How many people might conceivably be relocated for this effort?	________
9. How many major business functions are being implemented?	________
10. How many unique logical business inputs will the system process?	________
11. How many unique logical business outputs will the system generate?	________
12. How many logical files (views) will the system access?	________
13. How many major types of on-line inquiry are envisioned?	________
14. Will the user's knowlege of data processing aid the application effort?	________
15. What % of proposed business functions does the user already perform?	________
16. What percent of these are already automated?	________
17. Is a system of this type in operation anywhere?	________
18. Will the operational environment be distributed, on-line, or batch?	________
19. Is this a critical business system?	________
20. Is a back-up system being developed?	________
21. Will the system require any special disaster-recovery mechanisms?	________
22. Will performance or load levels be specified as explicit design criteria?	________
23. Is the proposed system primarily batch, on-line, or real-time?	________
24. Does the procesing logic seem to be simple, average, or complex?	________
25. Will automated error detection and correction be required?	________

Figure 32. Twenty-Five Questions.
(Reprinted with permission from Management and Computer Services, Inc., Valley Forge, PA.)

The answers to these questions form the basis of building a pricing policy. While not necessary, it is good practice to document these policies. A documented policy forms the basis of developing procedures to accomplish the stated intent of the policy.

This policy needs to be reevaluated periodically. For example, organizations currently may not charge for their services, but may see value in developing costs even though these are not transferred to user budgets.

A proposed five-step policy for developing and implementing a pricing strategy is listed in Figure 33 and described below:

Step	Step Name	Description
1.	Set pricing objectives.	Data processing management must identify their expectations from a pricing policy.
2.	Identify estimation strategy.	The recommended pricing strategy for estimating data processing tasks should be determined.
3.	Identify the chargeout price.	The recommended pricing strategy for allocating costs to users should be identified.
4.	Market the pricing strategies to users.	The proposal should be discussed with all involved parties and adjustments made based upon the comments received in those discussions.
5.	Implement and monitor the pricing systems.	The process should be initiated and modified as more pricing experience is obtained.

Figure 33. Steps to Establish a Pricing Policy.

Step 1. Set Pricing Objectives

An entrepreneur establishes price as a basis of continuing in business and making a profit. The entrepreneur must establish a price which will permit that individual not only to service customers and make a profit, but to provide plant, equipment, and skills needed to meet those user needs. Entrepreneurs that do not look toward the future do not stay in business very long. The entrepreneur that sold at cost would not survive long in the marketplace.

Pricing provides numerous options for the data processing manager. The manager must decide which of those options are desirable for the data processing function. It would appear that the same options available to the entrepreneur (i.e., to keep the plant technologically current and to upgrade skills) should be the pricing objectives of the data processing manager. Unless the data processing function can add resources and services not readily available to the user from other sources, there will be no need in the future for the centralized data processing function. If, as many data processing departments have permitted, the applications and skills of the data processing staff become obsolete, users will leapfrog to newer solutions, such as microcomputers and purchased applications.

Step 2. Identify Estimation Strategy

Data processing departments that do not bill for their services still must price their services. Sooner or later users or management are going to ask what it cost to do X or Y. The answer to that question is a price. The decision on whether to undertake X or Y is dependent upon that price. Therefore, data processing management needs an estimation pricing strategy.

A good estimate is one that is reproducible by a second person given the same input. Estimates that are people dependent are not reliable estimates. The estimating process should permit two or more individuals to produce approximately the same estimate given the same requirements.

The variance in most estimates is risk. People intuitively or through a process estimate the amount of risk associated with a project. If one individual determines that a project will be difficult, the estimate may be higher than that of another individual who does not perceive the project as difficult.

The recommended estimating pricing strategy includes risk. The process should be well defined and laid out so that it is easy to follow and will produce a reproducible estimate. It is normally more important to have a process that produces consistent estimates than one that produces totally accurate estimates. If estimates are consistent, they can be relied upon but, if they are inconsistent, it is difficult for users to rely upon them. Note that project leaders can make inconsistent estimates come true more easily than they can make consistent estimates come true. This is because the project variables can be altered so that the actual hours will equal the estimated hours.

Step 3. Identify the Chargeout Price

The decision to charge for services is frequently a senior management decision. Data processing management is charged with implementing the process that will allocate data processing costs among the users of the service. In determining how to do this, several decisions need to be made as follows:

1. *Will Senior Management Underwrite Part of the Data Processing Cost?* If so, then future-oriented projects such as research and modernization of data processing plant and upgrading of skills may be borne by the organization for the benefit of the organization. This decision helps to make the centralized data processing function competitive with outside organizations.

2. *Must Estimates and Actual Costs Be Comparable?* If so, then the chargeout system must be comparable with the estimating system. While the algorithms to produce the estimate, and the algorithms to produce the chargeout costs do not have to be the same, the result may be.
3. *Must All Users Be Charged at the Same Rate?* If so, data processing management is limited in its ability to lead users to more desirable services.
4. *What Level of Precision Must Be Used As a Billing Parameter?* The less precision used, the more economical the chargeout system. However, the cost of the system should never exceed its value so that the precision should be related back to the objectives established in Step 1.

The pricing strategy selected for charging users for services consumed is dependent upon the answers to the above questions. Once the questions have been answered, the chargeout method should be easy to select. The manager should select from among the previously described pricing strategies the one that best suits the constraints placed by senior management on the pricing system.

Step 4. Market the Pricing Strategies to Users

This chapter has described the pricing strategies, and not the detailed implementation of those strategies. There are many methods that could be utilized to accomplish each of the described strategies. It is these methods that need to be discussed and worked out with users.

Failure to gain user support for pricing strategies provides three negative results as follows:

1. *Users Reduce Services Requested.* If the pricing seems unrealistic or unsatisfactory, the users will find alternative means to have their needs satisfied.
2. *Develop Systems to Minimize Pricing.* Systems analysts will study the pricing algorithm and alter their systems accordingly. For example, if the pricing algorithm uses lines printed as the basis, systems will minimize the number of lines printed.
3. *Build Alternative Processing Capabilities.* Users unsupportive of a pricing structure will tend to create alternative data processing sources. This may involve acquiring their own computers, using timesharing services, or contracting work with outside contractors.

The objective of marketing pricing strategies is twofold: first, to identify problems in the system from user perspectives and then adjust the pricing system to minimize those problems; and second to explain the objectives of the pricing system and to attempt to gain user support for those objectives. Obviously, users would prefer free services to charge services, but most are business people and can understand the purposes and objectives of a well-laid-out and implemented pricing strategy.

Step 5. Implement and Monitor the Pricing Systems

Conditions change and so should pricing strategies. Concepts that are applicable with today's technology and business environment may not be applicable tomorrow. Therefore, the strategies should be installed, but their use and effect closely monitored. If the pricing strategies are not achieving the desired pricing objectives, they should be changed.

The purpose of putting in a pricing system is not to recoup costs but, rather, to change behavior on the part of users. For example, making users accountable by charging their budget should make them more cognizant of the effective use of data processing resources. If this is a stated objective of pricing, and the pricing strategy is not accomplishing that objective, then the strategy should be changed. It is the objective that is desired, not the creation of the price.

RECOMMENDED ACCOUNTING AND AUDITING PRINCIPLE FOR THE DATA PROCESSING MANAGER
Pricing is established to accomplish specific objectives. If those objectives are not achieved, then the pricing strategy should either be modified or eliminated.

PRICING STRATEGY SELF-ASSESSMENT CHECKLIST

Much of the success of the data processing function is upon its ability to adequately price its services. If this accounting function is shortcutted, business may be lost due to overpricing, or acquired due to underpricing when it should not have been. Good contractors provide good prices.

A self-assessment checklist on pricing is presented as Figure 34. This checklist is designed so that yes responses are indicative of good pricing practices, and no responses warrant investigation to determine if pricing strategies should be adjusted. Even organizations that do not charge customers should evaluate those items applicable to the estimating part of pricing.

Item	Response: Yes	No	N/A	Comments
1. Has data processing management established the objectives of pricing for their function?				
2. Is data processing management familiar with the alternative strategies for pricing?				
3. Have pricing strategies been selected based upon management's pricing objectives?				
4. Has the precision for pricing been defined?				
5. Has the consistency between estimating and pricing been defined?				
6. Will the estimate pricing strategies produce consistent and reliable estimates?				
7. Does the pricing strategy permit data processing management to smooth production?				
8. Do the pricing strategies permit data processing management to maintain the technological currentness of application systems?				
9. Does the pricing strategy permit data processing management to keep their physical plant technologically current?				
10. Does the pricing strategy provide funding for maintaining the skills of the data procesing staff?				
11. Are users in agreement with the pricing strategies?				
12. Are pricing strategies maintained to ensure they are consistent with current business needs?				
13. Are the pricing strategies meeting the pricing objectives?				
14. Are the pricing strategies consistent with the desires and intent of senior management?				

Figure 34. Pricing Strategy Self-Assessment Checklist.

Chapter Nine

Building Chargeout Systems

The common practice within the data processing profession is to charge users for services. The objective is to make users accountable for the resources they consume in fulfilling their mission. The concept requires data processing to charge users for all services provided by the data processing function.

The charging system should be viewed from two perspectives, operational and developmental. The operational perspective examines the tasks required to operate a charging system that has been developed and implemented. The developmental perspective addresses the tasks required to develop and implement a charging system. The key to a successful charging system is to develop an equitable and easy-to-use system. The danger in a charging system is that it will change users' behavior (e.g., cause them to develop systems to minimize billing to them, or to use alternate methods that are not cost-effective), so great care must be taken in developing the system to ensure that any behavior change that occurs is a desired change.

This chapter explains how to develop and operate a billing system. A fourteen-step process is proposed and briefly described. An in-depth description of the fourteen-step process is provided as Appendix A. The chapter also explains how to evaluate the billing system to ensure it is performing correctly.

WHO SHOULD USE A CHARGEOUT SYSTEM?

Many organizations use a chargeout system. On the other hand, a large number of data processing organizations do not charge for their services. Therefore, guidance is needed as to when a data processing function should commence charging users for their services.

The following three guidelines are suggested as the point at which a data processing function should commence charging users for their services. If any of the three following criteria are met, users should be charged for the services:

Criterion 1. The data processing facility provides service to more than one user.

Criterion 2. The cost of operating the data processing facility exceeds $100,000 per year for the full cost of operation.

Criterion 3. It is believed that some users are requesting services that are not cost-effective.

The decision regarding charging for services can be made by either data processing management or senior management. It is recommended that the two groups of management be in agreement before a charging system is implemented. Data processing management should agree because they have the responsibility for designing and implementing the chargeout system; and senior management should agree because they have the obligation to enforce the use of the chargeout system.

CREATING A TEAM TO IMPLEMENT THE CHARGEOUT CONCEPT

Chargeout systems are complex accounting systems due to the intricacies of data processing. Anyone can develop a chargeout system. However, to develop an easy and equitable system requires a multidisciplined approach to the problem.

Data processing management should establish a group of people with the responsibility to develop and implement the charging system. This group is commonly referred to as the "charging team." The team not only has responsibility for developing and implementing the system, but should also be responsible for monitoring the operational process.

The charging team may not do the actual detailed implementation. It is more of a planning and designing team as opposed to detailed implementation team. It operates in the same manner as a systems analyst in designing and overseeing the implementation of the systems, though a programmer may actually do the coding under the direction of the systems analyst. Likewise, data processing may have an implementation team of programmers and operators who work under the direction of the charging team.

The charging team should be composed of individuals from senior management, data processing, accounting, budgeting, and user department. The team should be composed of all of those organizations that have a vested interest in the charging system. It is particularly important to have users involved in the charging team as they will be the groups who are charged. If a system is unequitable, the users may perform undesired acts because of the charging system. Involving them in the charging team should minimize the undesired behavior changes.

One of the main functions of a charging system is to help senior management better manage the data processing facility. It is, therefore, important for senior management to take an active role in the development and implementation of the charging system. Such a role will help ensure that the charging system provides senior management with the data needed to manage the data processing facility and influence user behavior in appropriate ways. Also, there are many major decisions that need to be made in developing a charging system, and it is important that management be involved in those decisions.

RECOMMENDED ACCOUNTING AND AUDITING PRINCIPLE FOR THE DATA PROCESSING MANAGER
People believe that you get what you pay for. If data processing services are free, it could be argued they are not worth much. Those making that argument are the ones that will tend to abuse the offer of "free" data processing services.

PROCESS OF CHARGING FOR DP SERVICES

A charging system consists of the work activities used to calculate billing rates, to monitor the use of DP services, and to report to or bill users according to their utilization. Related work activities have been grouped into procedures, and the procedures have been separated into two subsystems—rate-setting and billing. Figure 35 illustrates the procedures contained in each of the subsystems. The billing rates that are charged for DP services are established during the rate-setting subsystem and are then fed into the billing subsystem. The billing subsystem monitors service utilization and applies the billing rates to compute the amount that should be reported or charged to a user. When viewed operationally, the rate-setting and billing subsystems are cyclical; that is, the work activities of each subsystem are repeated on a regular basis. The rate-setting subsystem is used whenever billing rates need to be changed. In most DP facilities, this will occur on an annual basis. The billing subsystem operates almost continually when the DP facility is offering services, because service usage must be monitored whenever a service is utilized.

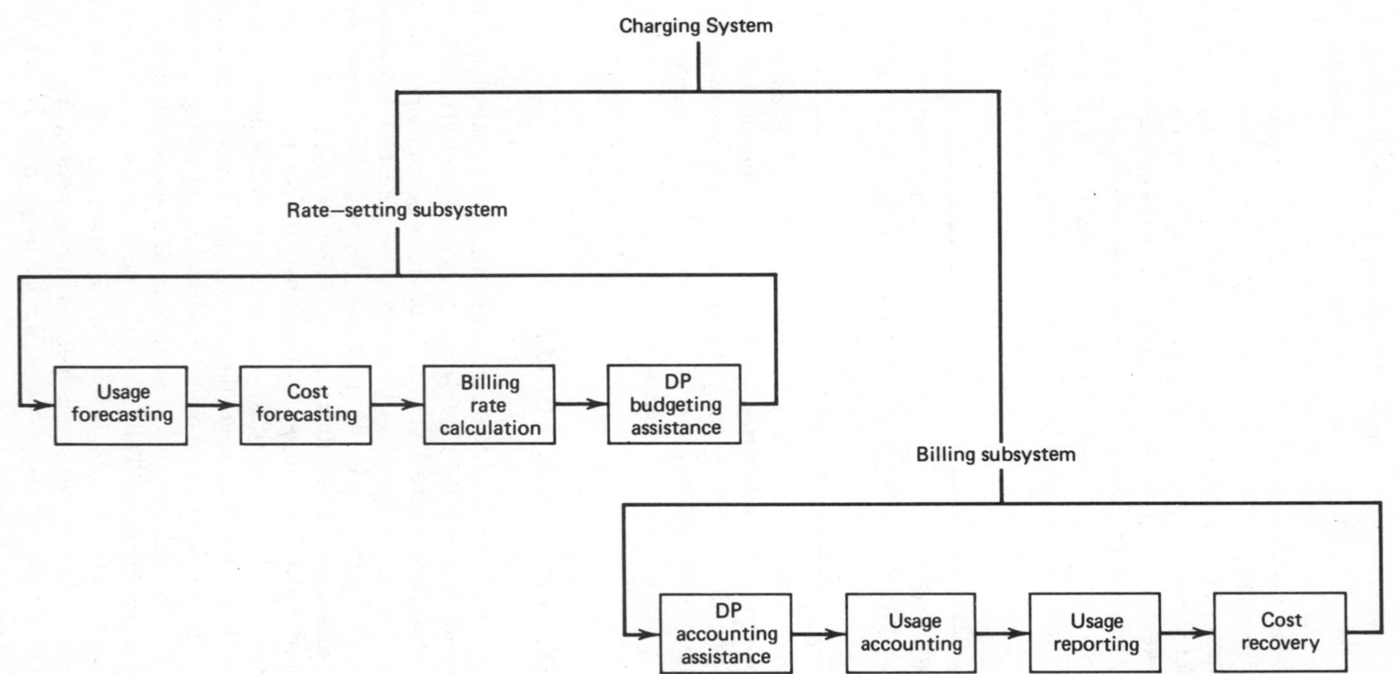

Figure 35. Components of a Charging System.

Each of the work activities of the rate-setting and billing subsystems is designed to satisfy one or more of the four primary objectives for promoting efficient and effective management of DP facilities. The four primary objectives are:

1. To increase the accountability of the DP facility and the users to senior management.
2. To keep an accurate accounting of the costs of operating the DP facility.
3. To allocate and report the costs of service utilization to the users.
4. To facilitate better DP planning and controls.

Rate-Setting Subsystem

The ultimate objectives of the rate-setting subsystem are to identify and group the resources and their associated costs that are used to support particular work areas of the DP facility; to identify and group the work areas and their associated costs that are associated with each DP service; and to develop a billing rate for each service that reflects the cost to the DP facility of providing that service.

Figure 36 illustrates the relationships among the important concepts involved in the rate-setting subsystem. The rate-setting subsystem is the most difficult and time-consuming part of a charging system to develop. It involves (1) identifying the resources to be included in the charging system, (2) forecasting the cost of these resources, and (3) distributing the costs of the resources to the subfunctions and, subsequently, to the service centers.

1. *Work Activities.* The first step in the rate-setting subsystem is to forecast the volume of usage of each DP service. These usage forecasts will normally be in terms of the number of service units (CPU seconds, checks printed, analyst hours, etc.) of each DP service that will be used for a given rate period. Next, the costs of all the various resources (hardware, software, personnel, etc.) used to provide the services are forecasted. These individual resource costs are then distributed into DP facility work areas, called subfunctions, according to a predetermined formula. A subfunction is the bottom level of a DP facility's work area hierarchy, which consists of areas of management responsibility (AMR) at the top, work functions in the middle, and subfunctions on the lower level. This work area hierarchy is used for the purpose of categorizing costs in terms more relevant to the DP facility. An example of a work area hierarchy is an area of management responsibility (computer processing operations) with three work functions (computer operations, reporting, and technical support) each containing two subfunctions (CPU and

storage devices for computer operations, microfiche and printing for reporting, and data base management and equipment maintenance for technical support). Another way of viewing the work area hierarchy of a DP facility is to think in terms of cost centers. Each AMR, work function, or subfunction can be viewed as a cost center for some part of the DP facility specifically and for the whole DP facility generally. The total cost of each subfunction is calculated and then distributed into individual service centers (groupings of related services) according to a predetermined formula. The total cost of each service center is calculated and then, based upon individual service forecasts and certain other factors, the billing rate for each service is calculated. The billing rates are then distributed to the users and fed into the billing subsystem where they replace the current rates.

2. *Objectives of Work Activities.* Each of the work activities in the rate-setting subsystem is performed to achieve one or more of the four primary charging objectives. Forecasting resource costs helps allocate and report the costs of service utilization to the users, keep an accurate accounting of the costs of operating the DP facility, and improve DP planning and control. Distributing the resource costs

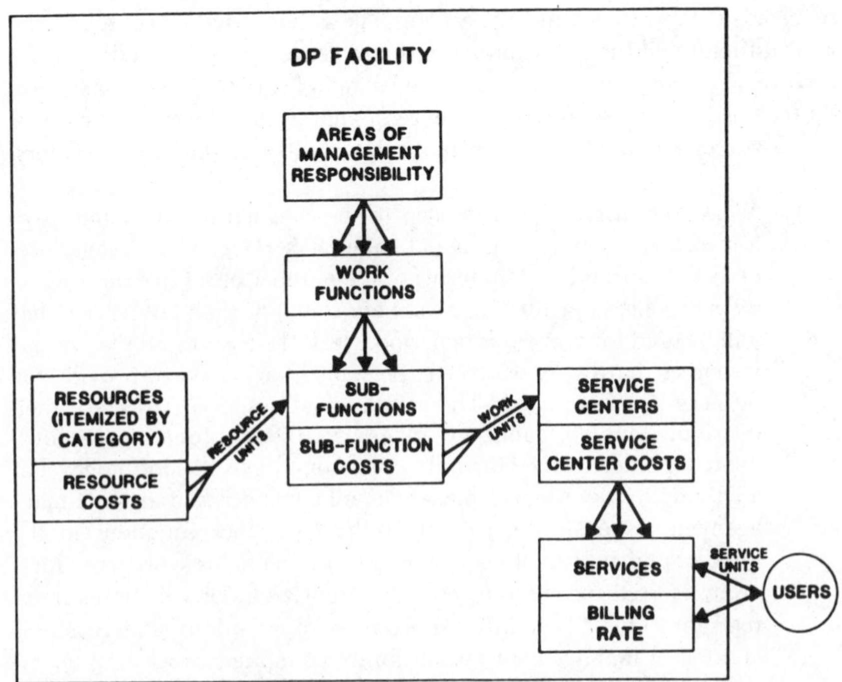

Figure 36. Relationships of Important Concepts of the Rate-Setting Subsystem.

into subfunctions, before distributing the costs to service centers, provides senior management with information on the cost that the DP facility incurs in performing particular areas of work, that is, the subfunctions, work functions, and areas of management responsibility. Consequently, providing senior management with cost information facilitates better DP planning and control and increases the accountability of the DP facility to senior management.

Billing Subsystem

The objective of the billing subsystem is to inform users of, and/or bill users for, the services that they have utilized during a particular billing period. When a charging system is being developed, the billing subsystem's development is relatively straightforward, as opposed to the rate-setting subsystem. It is assumed that the development of the billing subsystem will be less difficult to users of this book.

1. *Work Activities.* The first work activity that is performed in this subsystem is to monitor the usage of services. This monitoring is performed with manual and automated techniques, according to the type of services being monitored. The data collected on service usage are stored in service logs. Next, these service logs are analyzed and reduced to obtain service usage figures by user. The service usage figures are then multiplied by the billing rates for the services used in order to calculate the charges for each user. Service usage and charges are then reported to the users. If the DP facility is recovering its costs, users are billed for the amount reported.
2. *Objectives of Work Activities.* Each of the work activities of the billing subsystem, like the work activities of the rate-setting subsystems, is performed to achieve one or more of the four primary charging objectives. The work activities of the "Assist with DP Accounting" procedures facilitate the interface between the DP facility and the accounting department in the organization. The remaining work activities of the billing subsystem help to allocate and report the costs of service usage to the users.

IMPORTANT DEVELOPMENTAL CONCEPTS FOR A CHARGEOUT SYSTEM

The following six concepts are important to the development of an effective charging system:

1. Senior management involvement
2. Incremental development and implementation

3. Resource charging algorithms
4. User's DP budgets
5. Documentation of charging system development
6. Developmental cost/benefit tradeoffs

The charging team should review and consider the following discussions on each of the concepts when developing its charging system.

Senior Management Involvement

Senior management involvement refers to the degree of participation by senior management in the planning, design, development, and implementation of the charging system. The degree of senior management involvement is important to the charging system project for three reasons.

First, the involvement of senior management provides the charging team with the authority to implement all aspects of the charging system. This authority is extremely important, since a charging system may require changes in company policies or practices and may result in additional work for the involved groups.

Second, through its involvement, senior management will be able to inform the charging team of the type of information that it needs from the charging system. This is important since the main purpose of a charging system is to enable senior management to better manage the DP facility.

Third, senior management's involvement ensures that any changes in the work environment caused by the charging system will be under its control. When implemented for the first time, charging systems can cause extensive changes in work environments and budgeting processes; thus, senior management should be able to control any disruption of the working environment.

Incremental Development and Implementation

DP facilities, especially those that have been providing services free to their users, should consider an incremental development and implementation of the charging system. It is not always possible, or desirable, to develop and implement all parts of a charging system at once. Rather, it may be better to implement parts of the system as they develop, instead of waiting for the entire system to be developed. Incremental development and implementation will also enable the users and the DP facility to better plan and budget for the new charging environment.

Although there are many different ways to separate the development and implementation of a charging system, some of the more common methods are listed below.

Develop and implement the manual procedures first and then the automated procedures.

Develop and implement a system that charges for the most frequently used services first and that later charges for the remaining services provided by the DP facility.

Develop the entire charging system and stage implementation of the various procedures.

Develop and implement a charging system that only monitors and reports the use of services; later develop the procedures for budgeting and transferring funds.

Each company must determine the best approach to be used in its particular environment.

Resource Charging Algorithms

Resource charging algorithms refer to the equations often employed to aggregate the use of computer-related resources into a single artificial service with a single service unit. An example of this type of service is a DP facility that charges its users only according to the number of Computer Accounting Units (CAUs) utilized. In the past, this method has been one of the most common methods of billing users of DP facilities. Recently, a number of deficiencies in this charging method have become generally recognized, some of which are:

The artificial billing units (e.g., CAUs) have little real or intuitive meaning for most users. Thus, users have little incentive and virtually no information with which to plan for future DP usage or to improve the efficiency of DP usage.

The algorithms are often so complex that even sophisticated users have difficulty understanding the actual amount of resources utilized.

The algorithms can become extremely expensive to develop and maintain both in terms of dollars and the amount of time expended.

The current trend in state-of-the-art charging systems has been away from the artificial resource charging algorithms and toward techniques that are more understandable by the users, such as transaction or output charging. It is recommended that the charging team not select a resource charging algorithm as the basis for its charging system. Of course, it is recognized that there are a limited number of situations that encourage the use of this charging method. And, if the charging team determines that it must use a resource charging algorithm, then it should make certain that all formulas, loading factors, and billing rates for the formula variables be made public. Making this information available to the users will enable them to determine for what and how they are being charged.

User DP Budgets

User DP budgets refer to the amount of services authorized to each user during a rate period. After an organization has implemented a charging system, it is important that it enforce the DP budgets allocated to users. Adherence to DP budgets can be enforced in one of several ways, depending on whether or not funds are being transferred. One frequently used technique is to authorize users a set dollar or "pseudo" dollar amount for a rate period and allow users to exceed that amount only by obtaining approval from senior management. An organization should require users to justify all major expenditures over or under their limit, regardless of the technique selected.

Documentation of Charging System Development

Although the development of a charging system is essentially a one-time activity, a number of development tasks are repeated during the operation of the charging system. Therefore, it is important for the charging team to produce good documentation for the procedures developed. Whenever feasible, this documentation should meet the organization's standards. Good practice suggests that the charging team produce thorough documentation for at least the following tasks and procedures:

- The development of the distribution matrices
- The charging system general design
- Usage forecasting procedure
- Cost forecasting procedure
- Billing rate calculation procedure
- Usage accounting procedure
- Reporting procedure

Developmental Cost/Benefit Tradeoffs

Determining the appropriate size and complexity of the charging system is an important and ongoing task of the charging team during its developmental efforts. It is important that the charging team keep the cost of developing the charging system in line with the overall budget and size of the DP facility. Unfortunately, there are no good metrics that the charging team can use to determine the proper ratio of the charging system cost to the size and budget of the DP facility. Therefore, the charging team will have to analyze the costs and benefits of each decision that concerns the structure of the charging system. The charging team should adjust its level of effort for analyzing each decision to the potential additional cost of the decision. Some of the major decisions that the charging team will have to analyze have been identified and listed below.

Size of the charging team
Quantity and level of detail of the costing data
Level of detail of the distribution matrices
Quantity and level of detail of the usage data
Proper mixture of the charging system characteristics
Sophistication and expense of the billing package
Level of detail for reporting charges

OUTLINE OF A STEP-BY-STEP METHODOLOGY FOR DEVELOPING A CHARGING SYSTEM

The charging system contains two subsystems: rate setting and billing. The step-by-step methodology presented below has been organized around the procedures of each subsystem. The methodology consists of 14 steps separated into four phases. Figure 37 illustrates the separation of the steps into the four phases. A brief discussion of each phase and a summary of the tasks involved in each step follows. (A detailed description of each step is presented in Appendix A.)

Planning Phase

The planning phase consists of preparing the developmental plans for the charging system and is the most important of the four phases.

Step 1. Establish the Project Structure

Establish the management structure for the charging system project.

Establish a charging team.

Step 2. Determine Charging System Characteristics

Clarify the characteristics of the DP facility in order to determine the type of DP facility that exists within the organization.

Clarify the organization's reasons for charging for its DP services.

Decide on the desired mixture of the major characteristics of the charging system.

Reconcile the charging system characteristics with the characteristics of the DP facility and the organization's reasons for charging for its DP services.

Planning Phase

1. Establish the Project Structure.
2. Determine Charging System Characteristics.
3. Prepare the Project Plan.

Design Phase

4. Initiate a Cost Accounting Project.
5. Establish the Distribution Matrices.
6. Design the Charging System.

Rate-Setting Phase

7. Forecast Usage.
8. Forecast Costs.
9. Calculate Billing Rates.
10. Assist With DP Budgeting.

Billing Phase

11. Assist with DP Accounting.
12. Account for Usage.
13. Report Usage.
14. Recover Charges.

Figure 37. Charging System Development Phases and Steps.

Step 3. Prepare Project Plan

Prepare a formal project plan for the design, development, and implementation of the charging system.

Design Phase

During the design phase, the characteristics and reasons for charging set forth in the planning phase are used to direct the conceptual development and general design of the charging system. During this phase, the requirements for the charging system must be identified and the alternative techniques used to satisfy the requirements explored. The cost accounting system, distribution matrices, and general design of the charging system provides a starting point for the detailed design, development, implementation, and operation of the rate-setting and billing subsystems. The general design of the charging system also serves to coordinate the individual steps and tasks of subsequent phases.

Step 4. Initiate a Cost Accounting Project

Design and develop a DP cost accounting system to complement the chargeback system.

Step 5. Establish the Distribution Matrices

Determine the services, service units, and service centers.

Determine the areas of management responsibility, work functions, subfunctions, and work units.

Itemize the resources and define the resource units.

Test and adjust the distribution matrices.

Step 6. Design the Charging System

Define the functional requirements of the charging system.

Use the functional requirements to define and document the data requirements of the charging system.

Explore the alternative techniques that can be used to satisfy the functional and data requirements of the charging system.

Compile, review, and approve or disapprove a general design document based on the decisions made in the first three tasks.

Rate-Setting Phase

During the rate-setting phase, the four procedures of the rate-setting subsystem are developed and implemented. Your organization's standard DP systems development techniques should be used in conjunction with the steps in this phase to structure the detailed design, development, implementation, and operation of the rate-setting subsystem.

Step 7. Forecast Usage

Collect and analyze the data forecasting usage for services, subfunctions, and resources.

Determine and resolve any discrepancies that may exist between the forecasted service usage and the current resource capacity.

Reevaluate the distribution matrices and, if necessary, restructure them to incorporate the resolutions between the users' forecasts and available capacity.

Step 8. Forecast Costs

Obtain or establish the trial budget that will be proposed for the DP facility for the rate period.

Collect and analyze cost forecasting data.

Reevaluate and update the distribution matrices.

Step 9. Calculate Billing Rates

Determine the proportion of each resource that supports each subfunction and the cost of that proportion.

Determine the proportion of each subfunction that supports each service center and the cost of that proportion.

Calculate the base rates.

Calculate the billing rates.

Step 10. Assist with DP Budgeting

Develop techniques that will instruct users in how to use the data from the charging system to develop their DP budgets.

Develop techniques that will provide to the DP facility the data from the charging system that will facilitate the preparation of its budget.

Develop techniques that will provide to the organization the data from the charging system that will facilitate the preparation of its budget.

Billing Phase

During the billing phase, the four procedures of the billing subsystem are developed and implemented. These procedures directly affect the users, the DP facility, and the organization's accounting activities. The organization's standard DP systems development techniques should be used in conjunction with the steps in this phase to structure the detailed design, development, implementation, and operation of the billing subsystem.

Step 11. Assist with DP Accounting

Develop techniques for establishing and maintaining user DP accounts.

Develop the techniques for providing billing data to the accounting department.

Develop techniques for assisting in the maintenance of accounting information.

Establish billing techniques for handling aborted work.

Step 12. Account for Usage

Design the DP usage accounting procedure.

Develop and implement the usage accounting procedure.

Step 13. Report Usage

Design the billing reporting procedure for users.

Develop and implement the reporting procedure.

Step 14. Recover Charges

Design, develop, and implement the cost recovery procedure.

IMPEDIMENTS TO A CHARGEOUT SYSTEM

Generally, the world is not waiting for a data processing chargeout system. Although it offers many advantages to an organization, it does not facilitate the use of data processing services, which occurs when those services are not charged to users. The very act of charging for services can evoke strategies to undermine the effectiveness of the chargeout system.

Here are some impediments to an effective chargeout system and suggested counterstrategies.

Impediment 1. The "I Can Get It Cheaper Elsewhere" Attitude

Many users are natural-born shoppers. If you give them a price, they will find somewhere that it can be done cheaper. Business tends to reward individuals who can cut costs; therefore, this attitude may result in work being transferred from the data processing function to other sources.

There is nothing wrong with this attitude if the prices being compared are equitable. Unfortunately, in many instances the price for performing a service in-house is not comparable to the price quoted by another organization for a similar service. For example, the in-house price may include extensive documentation, compliance to in-house standards, and user training. Users may find if they accept an outside organization to perform the same task that they will pay extra for items included in the in-house price and, thus, in the end pay more for the same service.

COUNTERSTRATEGY

Involving users in the charging team is a method of educating users on the basis for charging. This helps ensure that users fully understand the in-house charging system. In addition, management may want to establish a policy that all work be done in-house; or if not, at least it may provide adequate guidance to users so that they can accept bids for the equivalent service that will be provided in-house. Under this latter method, the services would be reasonably comparable. In some organizations, the data processing function will set up bidding requirements and/or review bids to ensure equality in services.

Impediment 2. Build a Departmental Computer Processing Capability

The low cost of computers makes it easy for users to establish a departmental computer processing capability. The capacity of microcomputers today was considered adequate to perform most corporate computer needs 10 years ago. In fact, the small computers available to users today are powerful enough to perform most processing needs.

Pricing for services helps to justify the establishment of departmental computer processing facilities. In terms of budget, organizations may be able to demonstrate that the net cost of services to them is less if they build a departmental facility. The concern, of course, is that all of the costs are appropriately accounted for. For example, in an in-house facility, people's time may be diverted to that facility and yet not charged as is true in a central site.

COUNTERSTRATEGY

Computing as a capability in an organization needs to be controlled. This does not mean that departments should not have their own computer facility but, rather, that the use of computers in an organization should be centrally directed. This would help ensure that what is done within a department is best done there and what is done centrally is best done centrally. This excludes the chargeout rate from the decision of where to perform computing services.

Impediment 3. Building Requests to Minimize Chargeout Costs

Both data processing systems personnel and user personnel may design requests for the sole purpose of minimizing chargeout costs. For example, if a charging algorithm includes lines of printing, users may develop extra routines or subsystems to minimize printing. Unless this is a business objective of the organization, it is an undesirable side effect of a chargeout system.

Funds expended for the purpose of minimizing billing rates may lead to wasted effort on the part of organizational personnel. If the billing algorithm has arbitrarily picked a billing method, it may not want systems optimized around that method. For example, it may appear that lines of printing are a reasonable method for billing, but not a desirable system design consideration. Since the purpose of billing is one of accountability, the organization will not increase its profits by optimizing systems to take advantage of "quirks" in the billing algorithm. In fact, it will reduce the income because funds are expended on an unnecessary chore.

COUNTERSTRATEGY

The billing algorithm should be constructed in such a manner that the machine-dependent characteristics of applications are unidentifiable. At a minimum, billing characteristics should be sufficiently clear so that an attempt to take advantage of one would be offset by increases in charges of another. This type of algorithm can best be constructed by a team of individuals representing all parties with a vested interest in data processing chargeout costs.

RECOMMENDED ACCOUNTING AND AUDITING PRINCIPLE FOR THE DATA PROCESSING MANAGER
The negative effects associated with chargeout systems must be considered in developing and implementing a data processing chargeout system.

CHARGEOUT SYSTEM SELF-ASSESSMENT CHECKLIST

A responsibility of the charging team is to periodically assess the effectiveness of the chargeout system. If weaknesses are detected, then changes should be made to the system. Two methods can be used to evaluate the charging system. One is to interview the involved parties, such as users and data processing project leaders. The other is to perform a self-assessment.

A self-assessment checklist for a charging system is provided in Figure 38. This checklist is designed to be used by the charging team. Note that the team will have to do some investigation to find answers to the questions. The questions are constructed so that yes responses are representative of good charging practices, while no responses represent a potential weakness in the charging system. No responses should be investigated to determine whether or not changes need to be made in the charging system.

Item	Response			
	Yes	No	N/A	Comments
1. Have objectives been established for developing a chargeout system?				
2. Has a chargeout team been establilshed for developing and implementing a chargeout system?				
3. Has the chargeout team been provided with the objectives for establishing a chargeout system?				
4. Does the chargeout team include a member of senior management?				
5. Does the chargeout team include a member of data processing management?				
6. Does the chargeout team include all major users?				
7. Does the chargeout team include someone with accounting knowledge?				
8. Has a charging system rate-setting subsystem been established?				
9. Has a charging system billing subsystem been established?				
10. Has senior management involvement in the charging system been established?				

Figure 38. Chargeout System Self-Assessment Checklist.

Item	Response			
	Yes	No	N/A	Comments
11. Has the incremental development and implementation plan been considered by the chargeout team?				
12. Is the chargeout system simple to understand?				
13. Is the chargeout system equitable to all users?				
14. Are users limited to the amount of resources included within their data processing budget (unless specifically authorized by senior management to override their budget)?				
15. Has the charging system been documented?				
16. Has the cost of developing the chargeout system been considered in relationship to the benefits achieved from the system?				
17. Does the methodology for developing a chargeout system include a planning phase?				
18. Does the methodology for developing a chargeout system include a design phase?				
19. Does the methodology for developing a chargeout system include a rate-setting phase?				
20. Does the methodology for developing a chargeout system include a billing phase?				
21. Is the chargeout system automated?				
22. Have the potential impediments to the chargeout system been identified?				
23. Have counterstrategies been put in place to overcome any potential negative effects of the identified impediments?				
24. Is the chargeout system monitored to ensure that it is meeting the stated objectives?				
25. If the chargeout system is not meeting the stated objectives, will it be changed?				
26. Is an independent group established to assess the effectiveness of the chargeout system (e.g., charging team)?				

Figure 38. Chargeout System Self-Assessment Checklist (continued).

RECOMMENDED ACCOUNTING AND AUDITING PRINCIPLE FOR THE DATA PROCESSING MANAGER
A chargeout system is designed to accomplish specific objectives. If those objectives are not being met, the chargeout system should be changed.

Part Four

ACCOUNTING AS A MANAGERIAL TOOL

Accounting provides the information management needs to manage and, at the same time, becomes a common language for communication with nondata processing personnel. This part explains how to use accounting to identify problems in the data processing area. The material addresses using accounting as a managerial tool for managing unrecorded data processing assets, as well as a tool for communicating with management in the accounting language.

Chapter Ten

Accounting for Unrecorded Data Processing Assets

In the early 1960s, a group of major corporations banded together to lobby against capitalizing data processing costs. The group argued that funds expended for data processing systems were no different than funds expended for manual systems. The work produced procedures and rules but nothing of tangible value. Therefore, they argued, the costs should be expended rather than capitalized.

The real intent was to minimize corporate taxes. Expenses reduce current profits. Capitalized items take several years before the expenditure has the same tax effect as an immediate expense. Corporations won, and the systems and programming costs have been expenses ever since.

The loser in this situation has been the data processing profession. Rather than develop a capital asset that could be managed in the same context as any other capital asset, it produced an expense. People do not manage expenses.

This chapter describes the impact that expensing the creation of programs and data has had on the data processing profession. Recommendations are made on how to place a value on this major unrecorded asset of organizations. Once systems and data are recognized as assets, the recommendations in the chapter regarding managing these assets can be put into place. The chapter concludes with a self-assessment checklist regarding the care given to programs and data by the organization.

ARE PROGRAMS AND DATA REALLY WORTH ANYTHING?

Data that is recorded, stored, and maintained on computer media and computer programs is not recorded as assets on the books of organizations.

The costs involved to create and maintain those items were charged to expense. The question that needs to be asked is "Are these items worth anything? If so, should they not be recorded on the books as an asset?"

As described in an earlier chapter, accounting is a science which assumes that organizations will continue in existence. The accounting system does not try to record a resale value of the corporation but, rather, prepares a financial picture using generally accepted accounting procedures applied on a consistent basis. Thus, the books of the corporation are not truly representative of the value of the corporation. For example, some extremely valuable buildings may be fully depreciated and shown at near zero value on the books, while in fact they are worth many times the cost to acquire them years ago.

Data and programs are not the only major corporate asset not recorded on the books. People are not given a value, yet it is generally recognized that they are normally the single most valuable asset of the organization. However, people are managed. There is normally a personnel director, a salary administration program, employee benefit programs, and so on. Thus, even though some assets are not recorded on the books, they are still treated as assets.

Data and programs are frequently left to deteriorate. Programs written are not subject to capital management programs, nor do many organizations have a director to oversee the assets, as they have personnel directors to oversee the management of people.

It is difficult to calculate the value of programs and data using conventional accounting practices because they do not address data processing activities. Therefore, we must look for another accounting concept to serve as our basis for valuing. The one that has the greatest acceptance is replacement cost. This accounting concept states that we can value an asset by the amount of funds it would take to replace that asset if the asset should be lost.

Replacement Cost of Programs

We can calculate the replacement cost for programs by identifying the lines of code in use and then multiplying by the cost to develop a line of code currently. The range of cost to develop a single line of code ranges from $12 to $50. Obviously, there are many variables affecting the cost to develop a line of code including:

- Use of preprogrammed routines on libraries
- Whether the code was developed using structured or unstructured methods
- Complexity of logic

Style of programmers
Data processing standards
Skill of systems and programming personnel

Listed below is a process for calculating the replacement cost of the organization's programs. We will use $20 per line of source code as the replacement cost, as it represents a conservative value for lines of code. The lines of code in use can be taken from your source master, deleting duplicate programs and programs that would not be replaced should they be lost. The calculation is as follows:

Number of lines of code on the source master	______
Multiply by $20 per line	×20
Replacement cost of programs	______

In many organizations, this becomes the second or third largest asset in the organization. It is a surprisingly large figure, but represents the value of an asset sitting within the data processing function. Once the value has been established, the need to manage that asset should become obvious.

Another interesting calculation is to determine the number of man-years of effort required to replace that code. We can calculate this by dividing 1,600 into the total number of lines of source code in the replacement calculation. Individuals can produce about one line of source code per hour, and a programmer can deliver about 1,600 productive hours per year.

Once the number of man-years of effort required to replace the code has been calculated, this figure can be divided by the number of professional analysts and programmers within the data processing function. The result then shows how many years it would take if the full data processing staff were devoted to replacing the source code. Again, this is normally a staggering figure, which demonstrates the need to manage the source code because it is basically irreplaceable.

Once it is understood that the source code is a valuable asset and that it is irreplaceable, attitudes change. If one had a building that could not be replaced, the management of that building would be of paramount importance. So it should be with an organization's programs.

Replacement Cost of Data

Data comes in many types and formats. Some of the data obviously has minimal or no value, while other data is of extreme value. For example, a file of orders after those orders have been filled is of no value. On the other hand, a listing of customer name, address, and characteristics may be one of the more valuable assets of the organization.

Several years ago a very large organization lost its accounts receivable file. The loss was due to incorrect handling of recovery procedures by the operator. The net result was that the current file, the immediate backup, and all other backups were destroyed in the recovery process. The consequence was that many of the receivables were never collected. This meant that while the organization should have shown a profit for the year, it in fact showed a loss. In that instance, the value of the data was apparent to senior management of the organization—painfully apparent!

We calculated the replacement cost of programs using a method that showed what it would cost to replace those programs. Even though it was demonstrated that it would be impractical, if not impossible, to replace the programs, a value was not added for the processing loss. However, in terms of data, the data itself may have a value above and beyond the actual replacement cost of that data. As with our corporation that lost its accounts receivable, the data represented the value that was lost. Thus, losing the data lost the value represented by the data.

Data that has value tends to be managed as an asset. For example, the accounts receivable file in most organizations is very well-managed. It generally is not permitted to deteriorate. There are sufficient people assigned the responsibility to ensure the currentness and legitimacy of transactions on that file, which makes it difficult for the information to deteriorate.

We will not attempt to put a value on the data, although like the program it must be recognized that organizations may not be able to continue business without their data and programs. The value assigned to data will be the replacement cost to collect and reenter the data onto automated media. Normally, this cost is large enough to warrant considering formal management of data.

The replacement cost of data should be calculated as follows:

1. Identify the computer files or data bases needed on an ongoing basis. This would include such files as product masters, customer masters, and personnel files.
2. Calculate the number of characters of data on each file, and then accumulate.

This should be multiplied by the average cost to enter one keystroke of data into a computer file. If no figure is readily available in your organization, one-fourth of a cent per keystroke is a good figure for rough calculation purposes.

This rough estimation will develop an asset value for data. The actual figure is probably much greater because of the cost to collect and the management and storage costs of data. However, the one-fourth of a cent per character cost is a conservative method of valuing data maintained by the data processing organization.

HOW ARE ASSETS MANAGED BY CORPORATIONS?

Senior management of an organization only reads two documents. These are the balance sheet and statement of income and expense. Management's interest in the statement of income and expense is to increase income and decrease expenses. Management's interest in the balance sheet is to preserve the value of the organization's assets.

Senior management is charged with the responsibility of safeguarding the assets of the organization. This is one of management's primary responsibilities. Management is also charged with proving from time to time the existence of assets. These responsibilities require management's continual attention.

The asset management program normally includes the following steps:

1. *Management Approval to Acquire an Asset.* The acquisition of assets is usually covered in a separate budget. Management prepares the normal expense budget, and then prepares a capital acquisition budget. Thus, special procedures are required to acquire an asset.
2. *Record Assets in a Special Ledger.* Management provides special bookkeeping for assets. Each asset is usually individually recorded and then records are maintained on that asset until its useful life has concluded.
3. *Assets Are Tagged.* Management physically identifies the assets with a tag. These might be an etched-on number, a paste-on number, or some plaque or unique identifier physically attached to the asset. This is done so that management can ensure that its assets are properly identified.
4. *Assets Are Inventoried.* Periodically, a team of individuals physically examines all assets to ensure that they do, in fact, exist. In a physical inventory the recorded assets are compared against the actual assets located throughout the organization.
5. *Asset Maintenance Budgets Are Prepared.* Annually, management prepares a budget for the improvement and maintenance of capital assets. Through examination it is usually determined whether repairs to the asset need to be made, if so, they are provided for through a capital maintenance budget.
6. *Assets Can Only Be Disposed of Through Management Approval.* Individuals are not free to throw away assets. There is normally a special form that needs to be completed and approved by management before a capital asset can be physically disposed of. This is to prevent individuals from removing valuable assets from the organization for personal gain.
7. *Assets When Disposed of Are Usually Sold.* Most assets have value at the end of their useful work life, and can command some value

when disposed of. Some organizations make assets available to employees if they would be of interest to employees, such as with typewriters and office furniture. Others may be accumulated and sold as scrap to individuals who acquire such products.

8. *Physical Assets Are Usually Managed by a Single Individual.* Someone is appointed accountable for overseeing physical assets. This individual has responsibility for the asset maintenance budget, and in many instances is also responsible for the asset acquisition program.

HOW ARE UNRECORDED DATA PROCESSING ASSETS MANAGED?

The answers to this question are as varied as are organizations. Some organizations manage data and programs well, while others provide no central direction and leave it up to individual project leaders to make asset management decisions. In other words, in addition to defining and implementing project specifications, these same individuals are also financial asset managers.

We can best understand how data processing unrecorded assets are managed if we compare some of the differences between the physical assets of a corporation and the data processing program and data assets:

Difference 1. Physical assets of an organization are normally managed by a member of senior management who is usually at a comptroller or vice president level. Data processing programs and data are normally managed at the project leader or systems analyst level. While the vice president is of a senior pay grade and respect, the data processing project leader may be a new member of the organization at a relatively low pay grade in comparison to the senior vice president.

Difference 2. There is a formal program for managing the physical assets of an organization, and no program for managing data or programs.

Difference 3. Physical assets are individually recorded and controlled. Data processing assets are rarely recorded in an asset ledger, and rarely controlled as an individual entity. In most organizations there is not even an inventory of systems and data.

Difference 4. Physical assets have planned maintenance and planned replacement based upon anticipated physical deterioration. Data processing programs and data have no planned termination date, or no formal means to determine when they should be replaced. In many instances, the individual who can make the decision to replace a computer system has not been identified.

These four differences are neither the only differences, nor are they applicable to every organization. They are merely representative of the types of problems that are occurring in data processing because of the inability to manage these major unrecorded assets.

PLAN OF ACTION FOR MANAGING UNRECORDED DATA PROCESSING ASSETS

The data processing assets of program and data need to be managed in the same context as any other organizational asset. This management, like management of physical assets, requires a plan of action. Putting this plan into place should be the responsibility of the data processing manager.

The plan of action must elevate programs and data from the status of an expense to an asset. The success of the plan will be dependent upon the ability of the data processing manager to change attitudes about the importance of these data processing assets. A plan to do this is listed in Figure 39 and is individually described below:

Step	Step Name	Description
1.	Identify the items to be managed as assets.	Determine which items in the data processing area of responsibility are to be managed as assets.
2.	Record data processing assets.	The items selected for management should be recorded as assets. (Note that they will have no value on the books of the corporation.)
3.	Determine the value of the new assets.	A value must be assigned to the asset. (Note that normally this will be replacement cost.)
4.	Advertise the value of these new data processing assets.	Senior management must be advised and agree that the items and values assigned are reasonable. This is necessary to obtain management support for the remainder of the program.
5.	Appoint someone accountable to manage the assets.	An individual should be appointed accountable for each of the identified and valued assets. It is this individual who will be responsible for managing the asset.
6.	Develop a data processing asset plan.	A capital management plan must then be developed to manage these new assets.

Figure 39. Plan of Action to Manage Unrecorded Data Processing Assets.

Step 1. Identify the Items to Be Managed as Assets

You cannot manage what you cannot identify. Data processing organizations have program libraries and data libraries. Each program is uniquely numbered in this library as is each computer file. However, these inventories are of items, not assets.

An inventory of assets would contain information such as:

1. Number of asset
2. Name of asset
3. Physical location of asset
4. Owner of asset
5. Date of acquisition
6. Brief description of purpose of asset
7. Originator of asset
8. Application system of which the asset is a part
9. Who can access asset
10. Value of asset

Many organizations have some of the above data. Other data would be easy to acquire if the need was established. However, some of the data, such as value, may be difficult to acquire and at best would only be an estimate.

A key decision in inventorying the asset is the primary identifier of an asset. The three recommended identifiers are:

1. *Application System.* A group of programs or modules designed to accomplish a specific business objective.
2. *Data File.* A collection of records held together by a common bond.
3. *Data Bases.* A group of information managed by a single piece of software called a data base management system.

Step 2. Record Data Processing Assets

Records should be maintained indicating the assets within the data processing department. In a simple fixed-asset system, the information is contained on cards or in a ledger. In a data processing function, a simple generalized file management system should be used to maintain the records of data processing assets.

Many data processing organizations already have an asset system. This is used for the fixed assets required by the data processing department, such as computer hardware, storage area, furniture, and fixtures. It is possible that this same system would suffice to record the current unrecorded assets.

It must be remembered that while these are recorded and treated as assets, programs and data are not accounting-related assets of the organization. The fact that they will or will not be recorded on the balance sheet is a quirk of accounting theory. The programs and data can be recorded as assets, valued as assets, and treated as assets regardless of whether or not they appear on the organization's balance sheet.

Step 3. Determine the Value of the New Assets

It has been recommended that replacement cost be used as the value of assets. This is because replacement cost is relatively easy to calculate and is representative of the current value of assets. Note that other assets in the organization are not valued at replacement cost, but this is primarily because they are recorded on the balance sheet and replacement cost is an unacceptable method for balance sheet recording. On the other hand, programs and data are not recorded on the balance sheet and, thus, can be handled with whatever method is chosen, as they will not affect the official accounting records of the organization.

Organizations may choose to record the cost of data and assets at the actual cost of development. This presumes that the organization has maintained those types of records and that the records are available. The disadvantage of doing this has been discussed in accounting literature on inflation accounting. The argument for reporting assets at their current value is to show on the financial statements of the organization the real worth of assets and not the book value of assets. This is done because organizations may have assets many times more valuable than those shown on the books of the organization. Valuing computer systems at actual cost is not a truly representative cost valuation because of the increases in inflation over the past 20 years.

High precision is not essential in assigning a value to these assets. But it is important that the same method be used consistently from asset to asset. This value is designed at best to be an approximation to show an estimate of the value of assets if they are not currently recorded on the books. An estimate off by plus or minus 10 percent is relatively unimportant related to the objective of valuing the assets.

Step 4. Advertise the Value of These New Data Processing Assets

The primary objective of this exercise is to draw attention to large corporate assets that may not be properly managed. It is unrealistic to expect users, senior management, or other interested parties to contemplate the value of these assets. It is a relatively new concept to value programs and data. However, the concept is of growing interest because the value of the data processing assets is growing. Also, as discussed earlier, it needs to be recognized that an organization does not have the talent or resources to replace this asset should it fall into disrepute.

The methods of drawing attention to the value of these assets should be consistent with the style of management in the organization. The methods that should be considered include:

1. *Writing a Special Report.* The objective of a special report would be to explain the value of these assets and how that value was arrived at. The reports should explain the purpose of doing this and any change in the handling of these assets anticipated by the data processing department.
2. *Request for Action.* Data processing can prepare a proposal to senior management for more funding; different approaches, better protection for these assets, and so forth. The concept of valuing would be to build a case for the proposal.
3. *Formal Presentation.* Data processing management could convene the involved parties and make an oral presentation of the unrecorded asset story. It is frequently appropriate to draw the analogy between management or other fixed assets in the organization and the data processing assets. The story should show the entire process for managing fixed assets, versus the process for managing unrecorded assets. The value of the two can then be shown, and invariably the value of the data processing resources will exceed the other fixed assets of the organization.
4. *Footnote Financial Statements.* It has been suggested that if the value of the asset is large, it should be footnoted on the financial statements. This is the proposal for inflation accounting to show the actual value of assets as the footnote. Organizations can add any footnote they want to financial statements that they feel will be of value to individuals reading and interpreting those financial statements. If the value of data processing resources are included on the financial statement, it will draw continual attention to the need to manage those assets.

This advertising of the value of programs and data should be an ongoing process. The value will keep changing; it usually will be an upward increase in value. It is important to continually draw attention to the value of these assets, so that the funding expended to manage them is easier to justify.

Step 5. Appoint Someone Accountable to Manage the Assets

A key ingredient to asset management is to make one single individual accountable for each asset. In this manner, someone can be held accountable for the existence and condition of the asset. It is very difficult to hold a committee responsible for a deteriorated system.

The type of management that is needed is well known. Some organizations have already put into place the organizational structure that will manage these assets, even though they are not formally recorded on the books of the organization.

Managing the Data Assets

Many computerized countries are called information societies. Information or data is the primary product of these societies. As such, its value is recognized and the need to manage it understood.

The hierarchical structure for data begins with the data administrator or chief information officer. This is a senior manager of an organization who is responsible for information in the organization. The individual in the realm of information is the equivalent of the comptroller in the realm of financial assets. The responsibility of the chief information officer includes establishing information policy, defining and accounting for information, and resolving differences of opinion regarding the precision, content, and use of information.

The data base administrator is the custodian of data. This individual has the same responsibility over information as the treasurer has over financial assets. While the comptroller establishes policy and procedure, the treasurer actually maintains the financial resources of the organization. In data processing, this treasurer role falls to the data base administrator.

The data base administrator determines where the data will be stored, in what sequence, and how that data will be protected. Of course, the data base administrator must operate within the policies and procedures established by the chief information officer. This again is the same relationship as that of comptroller and treasurer. Note that in some organizations, there is a chief financial officer in addition to the comptroller. If there is a chief information officer, this position encompasses the functions of both the chief financial officer and the comptroller.

Managing Programming

Programs are actually managed. Individuals are responsible for either the development and/or maintenance of programs. However, the accountability concept applies to the management of the processes by which programs are developed in addition to the management of specific programs. It is the management of the processes in which organizations tend to be the weakest.

Some data processing organizations are establishing a quality assurance group to oversee and evaluate the process. Other organizations are establishing a manager of maintenance, and may already have a manager for new development. All of these individuals are involved in ensuring that the processes by which systems are developed and maintained provide them with the highest probability of success.

The groups are also attempting to identify the various risks inherent in building and maintaining systems. These risks can then be identified, measured, and managed. By identifying and managing risks, we can improve the probability of success.

The individual(s) accountable for the new data processing assets must initiate plans to manage those assets. In many organizations, the term software maintenance is being changed to systems management. This means that the portfolio of programs requires management. A major responsibility of any manager is planning.

Step 6. Develop a Data Processing Asset Plan

A plan of action is a series of steps designed to preserve the value of the new data processing assets. Organizations already have plans to preserve and maintain their capital assets. The data processing plan of action should parallel the corporate plan of action for capital assets.

These capital asset management plans have the following characteristics:

1. *Set Objectives.* The plan is designed to preserve the value of the assets and, in doing so, lay out some very specific objectives to be accomplished.
2. *Funding.* The plan includes the funds necessary to accomplish the plan.
3. *Assigned Responsibilities.* The individual or group responsible for implementing the plan is defined in the plan.
4. *Schedule.* The time table by which the individual tasks within the plan are to be accomplished is defined in the plan.

These plans for capital assets are then approved by senior management in the organization. They become an important part of the annual work plan of the organization. When applied to data processing, the plan formalizes the importance of preserving one of the major assets of the organization.

The plan of action for these new data processing assets should be prepared annually. It should be an integral part of the data processing budget. However, the capital preservation plan should be separate from the normal ongoing activities of the organization. This enables the capital preservation plan to receive appropriate attention and funding and, at the same time, be a plan that can be monitored by senior management.

RECOMMENDED ACCOUNTING AND AUDITING PRINCIPLE FOR THE DATA PROCESSING MANAGER
Without a plan to preserve the programs and data, other workloads will invariably take priority over ensuring the technological and business currentness of programs and data.

Item	Response			
	Yes	No	N/A	Comments
1. Has an inventory been made of the program and data assets managed by the data processing function?				
2. Does that inventory specify who is responsible for the asset?				
3. Does the inventory provide a description of the asset?				
4. Are there adequate attributes in the description so that a value of the asset can be calculated?				
5. Has a basis been established for identifying program assets, such as application systems?				
6. Has a basis been established for identifying each data item, such as data file and/or data bases?				
7. Has the value of each of these unrecorded data processing assets been assigned?				
8. Is senior management aware of the value of this unrecorded asset?				
9. Is someone accountable for maintaining these assets?				
10. Has an annual plan of action for preserving these assets been developed?				
11. Has funding been included in the annual plan of action?				
12. Is the data processing capital budget separate from its operating budget?				
13. Have objectives been established for preserving the data and program assets of the organization?				
14. Is the capital asset plan for data processing programs and data the same caliber of plan as for other fixed assets within the organization?				
15. Will the value of the assets be changed over time to reflect a changing value of the assets?				

Figure 40. Unrecorded Data Processing Asset Self-Assessment Checklist.

DATA PROCESSING ASSET SELF-ASSESSMENT CHECKLIST

Organizations continually evaluate the status of their assets. Many organizations conduct annual inventories to verify the existence and status of these major assets. Some organizations have departments whose sole responsibility is to maintain assets. All of these efforts are continually evaluated to ensure that the proper job is performed.

A self-assessment checklist for the new data processing assets is included as Figure 40. The checklist is designed so that yes responses are indicative of good asset management practices, and no responses may indicate areas where additional effort would prove beneficial. This self-assessment should be conducted at least annually by data processing management.

RECOMMENDED ACCOUNTING AND AUDITING PRINCIPLE FOR THE DATA PROCESSING MANAGER
You cannot manage what you cannot measure. Until data processing managers know the type and value of assets under their control, a plan of action for managing those assets cannot be developed.

Chapter Eleven

Using Accounting to Identify Data Processing Problems

Accounting is a universal managerial tool for measuring performance. It is used by senior management to measure the performance of data processing. It is equally applicable by data processing management to measure performance within the data processing function.

Accounting as a measurement tool works best when two criteria are met. First, the area or activity to be measured must be identified. For example, management must determine that it wants to measure the number of reruns in computer operations. Second, the appropriate accounts must be established in order to collect information to meet the desired measurement objectives. Measurement objectives cannot be met unless the correct information is collected, and collecting information for which there is no objective is a waste of time and effort.

This chapter describes how accounting can be used as a measurement tool within data processing. Areas of measurement are suggested, together with the types of information that could be collected to measure those areas. This information is summarized as types of accounting reports that can be used, and the analysis that can be made on those reports. Finally, the chapter provides a self-assessment tool for evaluating whether or not accounting is being used effectively to measure data processing performance.

ACCOUNTING IS A MEASUREMENT TOOL!

Accounting is a science developed over hundreds of years to measure performance of organizations. Practiced in the traditional sense, it is subject to generally accepted accounting procedures. These are the procedures developed by the accounting profession itself in order to regulate the consistency of results produced by accounting.

Self-regulation attempts to ensure that information is presented on a consistent basis from period to period. If information was not presented in a consistent manner, then it would not be comparable. Thus, it becomes more important in accounting that measurement be consistent rather than representative of marketplace values.

Accounting used as an internal measurement tool need not be subject to the same generally accepted accounting procedures. Using accounting for internal measurement merely means using the science of monetary units for measurement. However, even in internal measurement, consistency of measurement is one of the most important practices. Without consistency, the measurements cannot be relied upon.

Many data processing managers view accounting as the tool of senior management. They fail to recognize the value that data processing management can derive from measuring internal performance through the use of accounting. Unfortunately, the information collected by senior management for financial accounting may not suffice for the internal measurement needed. Data processing management may have to establish a new chart of accounts for its own internal measures.

The primary value of using accounting as an internal data processing measurement tool is that it measures in the same units used by senior management—dollars. Thus, while different criteria may be measured, the results can be equated to one another because they are both in dollars. Accounting is the only universal measurement tool because it can equate measures in any area of an organization to the same unit of measurement.

RECOMMENDED ACCOUNTING AND AUDITING PRINCIPLE FOR THE DATA PROCESSING MANAGER
The advantage of using accounting as an internal DP measurement tool is that the units of measurement are the same as that used by all other functions within the organization.

WHAT DATA PROCESSING ACTIVITIES CAN BE MEASURED BY ACCOUNTING?

Anything that generates or consumes resources can be measured through accounting. Accounting has the ability to measure the generation of revenue or the consumption of resources used to produce those revenues.

What is required is the conversion of units of revenue or units of consumption of resources into monetary units.

Within the data processing function there are two general categories that management measures. The first category is business functions, such as people, supplies, equipment, contracts, and facilities. The second are technical activities such as programs, testing activities, systems development processes, software maintenance, computer operations, communications, transmissions, and documentation. Business functions are readily translatable into monetary units, but technical functions require more thought and analysis in order to convert lines of code to monetary units.

The key to determining what can be measured using accounting is really: What does management want to control? If management is not concerned with monetary units, then accounting will not be the best measurement tool.

Nonmonetary measures are best when management wants to control the ways in which things are accomplished, the "how." Monetary units are the best measure when management wants to control "what" happens. For example, if management wants a specific set of forms completed during the development of an application, then it would measure that the appropriate variables on the forms had been completed. On the other hand, if it wanted to measure the development process did what was needed, it might want to measure the cost expended to correct not doing it right the first time.

WHAT YOU MEASURE IS WHAT YOU GET!

Measurement is a two-edged sword. On the one side it provides management with the information it needs to manage its activity. On the other side (i.e., the second edge) what is measured is what employees will strive to achieve.

Let's look at an example of how this two-edged sword of measurement works. Let us assume that management wants to improve the testing process. In doing it, it decides to measure the number of tests that a programmer takes to debug a program. From management's perspective, the objective of the measurement is to determine the efficiency of individuals in testing. From a programmer's perspective, management views this measurement as meaning that a few tests are good and a lot of tests are bad. Therefore, the programmers may expend an exorbitant amount of time in performing steps manually so that they do not have to have many program tests. Because of the measurement process the net result is that the number of tests undertaken will decrease. In other words, by introducing the measurement itself management has changed behavior. This phenomenon can be demonstrated over and over again in all aspects of performance. Whatever is measured is what people will strive to do better.

The lesson in this phenomenon is that the objective of the measure must be clearly determined before the measurement is made. It is important that management answer the following three questions before adopting any measure.

Question 1. Does This Area or Activity Need Measurement?

The answer to this question is determined by whether the activity is an end or a means to achieve that end. For example, testing is usually not an end by itself but, rather, a means to accomplish the desired objectives. Management generally should measure the end result and not the means to achieve the end.

Question 2. Will This Measure Accomplish the Measurement Objective?

Many times the information collected does not measure the desired objective. For example, many data processing managers measure whether or not a project achieves the stated budget for that project. The question becomes whether that measures the performance of the project team or whether it measures the ability of the estimator to develop a good estimate. Unless the estimate itself is highly reliable, all that measuring against a budget determines is whether the estimator can or cannot produce a reliable estimate.

Question 3. Will the Measurement Cause Any Undesirable Behavior Changes to Occur?

Because what you measure is what you get, management must carefully evaluate the impact of the measure on performance. Whenever people are measured, they are first suspicious about why they are being measured, and then attempt to change their behavior in order to produce a desirable measure. For example, if project people perceive that meeting a budget or schedule is a primary measure which most do in data processing, then they will strive to achieve that measure regardless of the quality of the work produced. Thus, measurement against budget may negatively impact the quality of the work people do, because they perceive the importance of meeting the budget as being much greater than the importance of producing a high-quality project.

One of the keys to successful measurement is establishing the proper measurement criteria. In many instances, the existing accounting system will not provide the appropriate measure. For example, accounting may record the number of hours that a programmer worked, but may not record the amount of time spent on testing, or the amount of testing time expended to correct defects caused by poor requirements or design.

The accounting measurement system may require the establishment of a new chart of accounts. Data processing managers should not be limited by the current chart of accounts. The accounting system can be easily changed to produce more information. What the accountants need from data processing management is an understanding of what is needed, and then the appropriate accounting "buckets" can be established to collect the needed information,

RECOMMENDED ACCOUNTING AND AUDITING PRINCIPLE FOR THE DATA PROCESSING MANAGER
Accounting as an internal measurement tool is only limited by the imagination of those using the system. If the current chart of accounts restricts measurement, then data processing management should request that that chart of accounts be expanded.

THE PROCESS OF USING ACCOUNTING TO IDENTIFY PROBLEMS

Accounting information can provide the basis for problem identification. It does not diagnose the cause of the problem but, rather, indicates that a problem has occurred. For example, a thermometer indicates an abnormal body temperature and a possible illness, but does not by itself diagnose the illness.

Problem identification through accounting does not occur through happenstance. It must be planned like any other data processing activity. The planning involves establishing objectives and then putting into place those mechanisms that will identify potential problems.

The process for using accounting to identify problems is illustrated in Figure 41, which gives the following four-step process:

Step 1. Identify the activity or event to be controlled.

Step 2. Develop a problem measurement plan.

Step 3. Implement the measurement process.

Step 4. Monitor the activity or event and make adjustments as required.

The measurement process is a tool of data processing management. The needs should be specified by data processing management, even though the process is implemented by subordinates. Only management knows the information it needs to properly monitor the function.

Step 1. Identify the Activity or Event To Be Controlled

Problem identification should be viewed as a project. As such, it has the same characteristics associated with any other project. The requirements

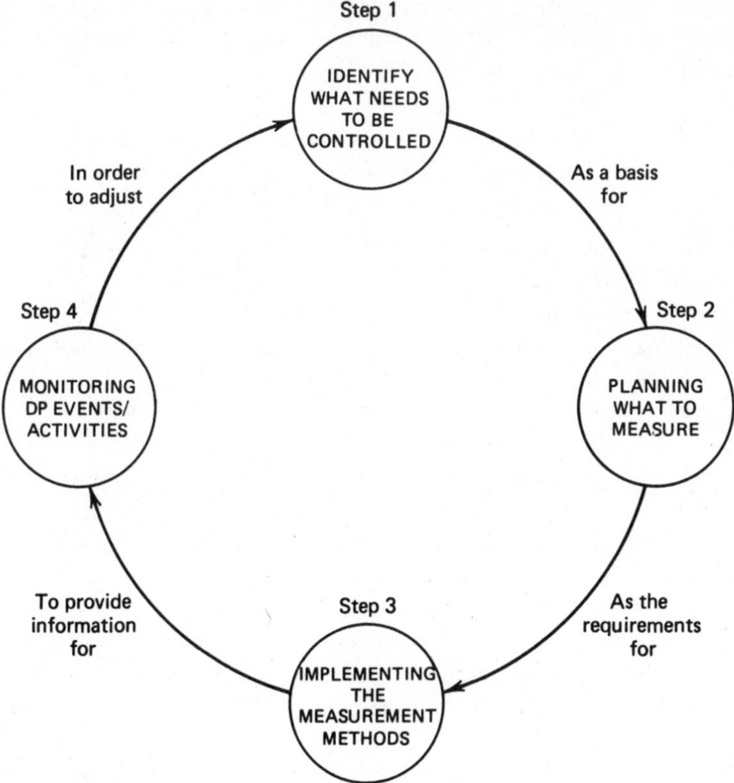

Figure 41. Problem Management Cycle.

must be stated, a design or plan developed to implement those requirements, and the requirements implemented and then utilized.

Problem identification in data processing is frequently referred to as "problem management" and "error tracking." It utilizes the scientific approach to problem solving. However, in all cases it begins by identifying what needs to be controlled, and then utilizes investigation measurement to determine if any adjustments are necessary.

The activities or events that data processing management needs to control are generally the major activities within the function, which include:

Systems development
Software maintenance
Software testing
Project management

Change management
Configuration management
Change control
Data base technology
Systems programming
Computer operations
Telecommunications
User interfaces
Data libraries
Backup and recovery procedures
Standards

The above list represents those areas that generally require managerial control. Note that most of them are items identified in the data processing literature and frequently are items that can be organizationally separated from the other activities in the list.

The accounting process is directed at the activities or events that senior management wants to control. Normally, there is an account in the chart of accounts for each activity that management wants to control. For example, if it wants to control petty cash, it will set up a petty cash account in a chart of accounts; if it wants to control training, then it sets up a special account for training; and, if it wants to control the use of microcomputers in the organization, it will set up a special account against which the organization will charge the cost to acquire microcomputers.

If the data processing manager were to compare the above list of controllable items to the organization's chart of accounts, very few items would match. On the other hand, if the data processing manager were to compare the chart of accounts to what senior management wants to control, there would be a very high relationship between those two lists. The fact that the chart of accounts does not address what the data processing manager needs to control merely shows that the chart of accounts may require changing.

The data processing department can expand the chart of accounts, without affecting the organization's chart of accounts. This is possible as long as what data processing wants is a subset of the organization's chart of accounts. For example, if the organization only controlled employees' salaries, the data processing department could subdivide salaries into as many categories, for example, job number, as is necessary in order for data processing management to control where its analysts and programmers are expending their time.

Step 2. Develop a Problem Measurement Plan

Accounting is a method for collecting information. Even in financial accounting, the information itself rarely has meaning. It is only when that information is used in a format that can be analyzed by people that the accounting system provides the basis for problem identification.

Let's look at an example. The accounting system collects payroll information. Knowing the dollars paid in payroll provides very little information for analysis and problem identification. However, when payroll dollars are compared to sales, compared to a previous period, or broken down by job, or accumulated in financial statements or compared to what other organizations spend for the same work, the data quickly pinpoints problems. For example, if the industry your company was in normally expended 30 percent of cost of sales for payroll, and your organization was expending 45 percent, it would be indicative of a problem within your process. Thus, it is the analysis of information that identifies the problem, as opposed to the collection of information.

Using accounting for problem analysis means the type of analysis must first be determined, and the data needed for the analysis determined second. For example, if it was important to know salaries as a percent of cost of sales, first a ratio would have to be established to show this figure and, second, the information needed to develop the ratio would be determined. Once the information has been determined, methods can be designed to collect that information.

The most common accounting analyses use financial statements, comparison against other similar accounting entities, ranking of costs, stratification, measures of central tendency, return on investment, trend analysis, comparison against a standard or goal, comparison against other organizations, and development of ratios, all of which we will discuss below.

Financial Statements

A financial statement is a consolidation of accounting information into a financial report. The two most common financial statements for a profit-making organization are the balance sheet and statement of income and expense. Within the data processing function, the type of financial statements that might be prepared include:

Cost to develop a project
Cost to conduct a study
Cost associated with a contract
Cost chargeable to a user
Budget statements

Any financial statement that the data processing manager needs can be prepared if the data is available. These statements are normally prepared no more frequently than once a month. However, this is convention and not a requirement.

Comparison Against Other Similar Accounting Entities

The costs associated with performing one activity can be compared to the cost to perform another similar activity or event. For example, two projects of similar size may be compared to show variances in the cost to develop. The comparison would show differences between the two activities or events, but not the cause for the difference.

Ranking of Costs

A very powerful analytical method is to rank the costs associated with some activity by all of the projects' individuals, or areas involved. For example, all development projects could be ranked by the number of overtime hours expended on the project.

The ranking can be in absolute or normalized terms. For example, overtime could be ranked according to the total hours of overtime, or it could be ranked as overtime as a percent of the project budget.

Ranking in some organizations is considered MBE, which stands for management by embarrassment. The object is to rank performance either in terms of most desirable to least desirable, or least desirable to most desirable. The report is then circulated without comment or interpretation. However, the individuals or projects that are at the top of the least desirable end of the ranking quickly get the message. It is a very effective use of accounting to change behavior. Much of the impetus for change is the result of peer pressure at seeing your name, or your project's name, at the top of an undesirable list.

Stratification

Stratifying places information into groupings or strata. It is helpful to analyze where activities cluster. For example, on a listing of overtime, we could stratify by categories such as:

Overtime up to 5 percent of the project cost
Overtime between 6 and 10 percent of the project cost
Overtime between 11 and 15 percent of the project cost
Overtime more than 16 percent of the project cost

This analysis places all of the projects into one of four strata. The number of strata is up to the individual performing the analysis. Stratification is generally used as a basis of determining problem areas, and then using those problem strata as a basis for determining what specific activities or events should be investigated further.

Measures of Central Tendency

The accounting information collected can be analyzed statistically. Among the first measures to be used would be the measures of central tendency: the mean, median, mode, and standard deviation. These measures of central tendency provide insight into analyzing the population for potential problems. Other measures that can also be used for analytical purposes are skewness and kurtosis.

Return on Investment

A return on investment shows the value received for performing a data processing service. In order to calculate return on investment, both the benefit of performing an act, as well as the cost, must be known. The calculation is usually expressed as a percent, which is the equivalent of profit in the traditional accounting sense.

It is not necessary to actually generate revenue in order to show a return on investment. For example, if a computer application replaces X people, and the application is significantly less expensive, then the cost of the individuals that replaced that application would show a positive return on investment through cost reduction.

The return on investment has to take into account the current value of money. For example, a dollar spent today to reduce costs by a dollar two years from now is not the same dollar. The dollar two years in the future must be discounted back to today's dollar. This is accomplished by subtracting the value of money, frequently the value is considered to be the prime interest rate, in order to show what today's dollar is worth.

Trend Analysis

Trend analysis shows the direction in which costs or benefits are moving. For example, a trend would be the increase in starting salaries for recent college graduates.

Trend analysis normally shows a single event over a period of time. The trends can be monthly, quarterly, annually, or over a several year period. Frequently, the trend is more important than the absolute value. For example, knowing the trend in hardware costs per millions of instructions processed per second can be helpful in determining in what year certain applications may become economical. It can also show that programmers are becoming less productive or that the costs of testing are decreasing. Knowing these trends can help management ward off potentially serious problems before they become serious.

Comparison Against a Standard or Goal

If accounting goals are established, then measurement can be made against those standards. The most common measurement using this method is budgeting. The amount of actual expenditures is compared against the budget to produce a variance from the budget. Both the dollar amount and percent of variance are measures that management can use to identify potential problems. For example, if the project is only half done, but salaries are three-fourths consumed, then management is alerted to problems regarding the inability of the project to be completed within cost expectations.

COMPARISON AGAINST OTHER ORGANIZATIONS

Many organizations share information, either individually or through associations. This enables the cost of doing certain work in one organization to be compared to what another organization spends for the same services, for example, the cost of hardware maintenance.

In conducting these types of comparisons, it is important to ensure that the items being compared are comparable. For example, hardware maintenance is normally a comparable cost, but the cost to test a program would not be comparable unless all of the testing tasks performed were the same.

DEVELOPMENT OF RATIOS

One of the most powerful measurement tools is the development of ratios. In normal accounting, the most common ratios are gross profit, net profit, return on investment, and inventory turnover.

A ratio is a relationship between two values. For example, net profit is a relationship between sales and cost of sales. Selecting the right ratio can show tremendous insight into performance. Some of the ratios that are being used in data processing include:

Maintenance dollars to development dollars

Rerun dollars to total operation dollars

Maintenance dollars to operation dollars for the system being maintained

The ratios selected should show a relationship in which there is a high correlation. For example, there should be a relationship between the amount of dollars expended to develop a system and the amount of dollars needed to maintain that system. On the other hand, there may not be a relationship between hours of programmer overtime per year and the cost to develop a disaster plan. Unless there is a definite correlation between the two variables, the ratio is meaningless. The more perfect the correlation (meaning a change in one variable will produce a corresponding change in the other variable) the more valuable the ratio will be to management in identifying problems.

Step 3. Implement the Measurement Process

The information needed to produce the accounting analysis must be obtained and put into a usable format. The analysis itself normally defines the information needed. For example, the ratio of development cost to maintenance cost identifies the two pieces of accounting information needed to produce the ratio.

In addition to the information, the time period for the information involved must also be determined. For example, trend analysis might require information over a several year period, while some ratios may need to be performed daily and others monthly.

The information needed for analytical purposes will normally be obtained from one of the following data processing sources:

- Budgets
- Time and attendance reporting
- Project status reports
- Invoices
- Responses to requests for proposals
- Operating logs such as:
  - Operator's log
  - Job accounting log
  - Data base management system log
  - Communications log
- Chargeout systems

It is preferable to use the standard data collection processes in the data processing function to collect the needed accounting information. If new information is needed, it is better to add it to one of the existing systems than to establish a new data collection system. For example, asking the data processing staff to expand their time and attendance reporting system is preferable to instituting another reporting system for allocating time among projects. In most instances, the information used for analysis can be taken from these reports without developing elaborate reporting systems.

Finally, automated methods for collecting data are far superior to manual methods. Not only are they more accurate, but they are normally preferable from a people perspective. The automated systems provide the needed data as a by-product of performing a normal job task, and are not systems that require extra work to report information.

Step 4. Monitor the Activity or Event and Make Adjustments As Required

Reporting, analyzing, and presenting accounting information to identify problems is a worthless exercise unless action is taken to correct those problems. Too frequently in data processing, information is available but no action is taken. For example, many of the warning messages produced by computer systems are left unused, when taking action could avoid serious problems.

The best method to ensure that action is taken is to make someone accountable and responsible for taking action. The measurement itself should indicate when and what action to take. For example, if the rerun costs in computer operations get too high, then action should be taken to eliminate or significantly reduce the cost of reruns. Making the computer operations managers responsible for taking action means that they would get the analytical information and be expected to act upon it.

Ensuring that action is taken can be facilitated by one of the following two processes:

> *Process 1.* Issue regular reports on problem information and action taken: The individual responsible for monitoring the performance information and taking action can issue reports on the status of what is being monitored. These reports would be issued to more senior management, and would show what the indicator was, whether action was warranted and, if so, what action was taken.
>
> *Process 2.* Set up an audit process to review the decision-making process: Through the use of audits by auditors, or senior managerial review, the decision-making process used to take action should be periodically evaluated to judge whether or not action is being taken at the appropriate points.

The end product of this four-step process is problem identification and correction. If problems occur that are not identified, new analyses should be established. On the other hand, if problems are identified and no action taken, then the means must be put into place to ensure that action is taken at the appropriate point. Note that after action is taken, the objectives and measures may need to be changed to reflect the changing business conditions and processes.

RECOMMENDED ACCOUNTING AND AUDITING PRINCIPLE FOR THE DATA PROCESSING MANAGER
A good measure identifies the potential problem; and a good manager takes action on that problem as soon as the measure indicates that action is warranted.

ACCOUNTING ANALYSIS SELF-ASSESSMENT CHECKLIST

One of the questions many people ask about auditors is: Who audits the auditors? An equally important question to ask about measurement is: Who determines whether the measures are good? The answer to that second question is that data processing management should periodically evaluate the effectiveness of the measurement program and the actions taken on those measures.

A self-assessment checklist for accounting measures is provided as Figure 42. This checklist is designed for use by data processing management. Yes responses are indicative of good accounting measurement processes, while no responses indicate potential measurement weaknesses and warrant analysis to determine whether that measure or decision-making process associated with the measure should be changed.

Item	Response			
	Yes	No	N/A	Comments
1. Does data processing management use accounting as a measurement tool? (Note that if this question is answered no, the remaining questions can be skipped.)				
2. Does management understand that measurement can cause change in behavior to enable individuals to score positively on the measure?				
3. Is accounting used to measure business activities or events?				
4. Is accounting used to measure technical activities or events?				
5. Are the measures used to evaluate behavior and are not used as numerical goals for accomplishment?				
6. Does data processing management add new accounts to the chart of accounts if necessary for measurement purposes?				
7. Is the activity or event to be controlled identified prior to determining how to measure that event?				
8. Is the method of measurement determined before the information needed for measurement is determined?				
9. Have the following measurement methods been considered for identifying potential problems:				
(a) Financial statements				
(b) Comparison against other like accounting entities				
(c) Ranking of costs				
(d) Stratification				
(e) Measures of central tendency				
(f) Return on investment				
(g) Trend analysis				

Figure 42. Accounting Analysis Self-Assessment Checklist.

Item	Response			
	Yes	No	N/A	Comments
(h) Comparison against a standard or goal				
(i) Comparison against other organizations				
(j) Development of ratios				
10. Are available sources of information analyzed to determine if the needed measurement information is already available?				
11. Are existing data collection methods expanded to collect new information rather than to establish new data collection methods?				
12. Is the needed information collected through automated processes wherever possible?				
13. Have the levels at which action should be taken been determined for each measure?				
14. Is a single individual accountable to take action on each measure?				
15. Is action taken when warranted on each measure?				
16. Are review methods, such as audits, undertaken regularly to ensure that appropriate action is taken on the measures?				
17. Are the measures adjusted as necessary to reflect changing business conditions?				

Figure 42. Accounting Analysis Self-Assessment Checklist (continued).

Chapter Twelve

Communicating with Management in the Accounting Language

Management's mastery of the language of computerese is minimal. The probability of senior management's improving its computer language skills is also minimal. The only language available to data processing management for communication with senior management is accountingese. Since senior management will probably not learn computerese, the only viable solution appears to be for data processing management to learn accountingese.

Surveys have shown that few data processing managers move into the rank of senior management. One of the major reasons for this lack of upward mobility is a language barrier. Data processing managers are frequently viewed as technicians who have excluded themselves from promotion. The solution to this technical dilemma is to communicate in the language of accounting.

The previous chapters in this book have provided the accounting basics necessary for survival. This chapter could have been titled "Beyond Survival." The objective is to explain how to use the language of accounting as a positive means of communication. It is designed to explain conversational accounting. There is no self-assessment in this chapter; the assessment is one's ability to effectively communicate with management—and one's acceptance into the senior management ranks.

THE STATE OF THE ART IN COMMUNICATING WITH SENIOR MANAGEMENT

A discussion with the data processing manager of a major U.S. corporation indicated that he rarely ever met with his boss or other members of senior management. In the 20 years that he had been data processing manager, the meetings were very few. He recalled that when he was given the position of data processing manager his boss told him that he didn't want to hear any complaints from users. The senior manager went on to tell him to do his job and, if there were no complaints, the senior manager would be very happy and there would be no need to get together. The data processing manager kept users happy for 20 years and he and his boss never got together.

This story may be an exaggerated example of what is happening, but it is all too typical. There are the annual rituals of planning and budgeting, which require some contact with senior management. With that exception, contact is frequently limited to problem resolution. Data processing managers are rarely "one of the good old boys" who are involved in general counseling, planning, and idea sessions.

The reasons for this lack of contact with senior management are twofold. First, few senior managers recognize that we are in an information society, and the importance of information to organizations. Second, many data processing managers are more concerned with the technical solutions to problems than the business solutions. Let's look at the impact of these two impediments individually.

Many organizations are already in the business of information processing, while others are moving there rapidly. Fifteen years ago, banks were in the business of banking. Five years ago, banks moved into the business of being a full-service financial institution. Today, banks are in the information processing business. Most of the work performed by a bank is information processing and transfer. If organizations fail to recognize the business they are in, the consequences can be dire. For example, the railroads in the United States kept insisting they were in the railroad business, when their business was actually changing to the transportation business. The failure to recognize the business they were in limited them to railroads and excluded them from the newer forms of transportation, such as buses, taxicabs, and airplanes. The failure to recognize the importance of information in business sytems has not only resulted in excluding data processing management from high-level business planning but may negatively impact the long-range success of the organization.

Data processing management tends to view everything as a technical problem. If users are unhappy with data processing services, the solutions tend to be technical. For example, in order to improve satisfaction with data processing applications, data processing managers have introduced a large volume of technical forms to be completed. Access control is viewed primarily as a technical problem.

Data processing managers must learn that technical problems can be solved with business solutions, but business problems can rarely ever be solved with technical solutions. Business problems involve the three M's of business, which are men, money, and materials. The three M's can be described in accounting terminology, but are difficult to describe in technical terminology. For example, the problem with user satisfaction is frequently an inability to get users to properly communicate their needs. While an additional set of forms may be helpful, it does not attack the core problem. The problem is communication, which requires business solutions. The companies that have been most successful in this area have found ways to get users to express their needs in business terms; then data processing's understanding of that terminology can translate those business needs into technical terms.

Data processing managers can improve their communication skills with management by doing the following:

Reading what management reads.

Talking the way management talks.

Thinking the way management thinks.

Learning the way management learns.

Anticipating what management wants.

We will discuss each of these individually and offer suggestions on how to use the guidelines to improve discussion in the accounting language.

READING WHAT MANAGEMENT READS

As previously explained, the two documents read by every member of senior management are the balance sheet and statement of income and expense. Obviously, senior managers read a lot more, but these are the documents on which they concentrate their analysis. Statements read like a novel to senior managers, and they draw great insight from the two documents. In many organizations, they also draw their bonuses on the story presented in these documents.

The balance sheet tells the story of the status of the organization. It explains how much inventory is on hand, how much cash is available, how much money is owed to creditors both long term and short term, as well as the ability of the organization to survive some difficult economic conditions. It is this information that helps the manager develop workable plans. Without the ability to fund, plans seldom get off the drawing board.

The statement of income and expense tells how the organization performed during the statement period. The statement could be retitled "how are we doing?" This statement shows all of the sources of income and all of the expenses. It explains to senior management the type of actions it needs to take in order to improve bottom-line profitability. For example, if revenues are holding steady, but data processing costs are increasing, then a logical action by management would be to limit or reduce the amount of funds going into data processing. Many of the day-to-day actions taken by senior management are dictated by their reading and interpretation of the statement of income and expense.

Few data processing managers read and study these documents. Of course, they are interested in the bottom-line profitability, but rarely study these statements in depth. On the other hand, data processing can offer solutions to the problems presented by these statements.

If data processing management reads these two statements, they will know the areas of concern to senior management. Reading does not mean glancing through the statements but, rather, obtaining the detailed statements and studying them intensively. Data processing management should use many of the accounting analytical methods described in Chapter 11 in this study process. Again, accounting is a measurement tool. Financial statements provide the basic information, but the full story requires an analysis using the analytical accounting methods.

In studying the financial statements, it is important to have:

Comparisons to last year or the last period

Trends over extended periods

Plans and other documents indicating financial expectations

Statements of other companies within the same industry

When one reads what senior management reads, one is prepared to talk like senior management talks. Conversation is always improved when people share the same interests. Reading what senior management reads enables this sharing and conversing to occur.

TALKING THE WAY MANAGEMENT TALKS

The major item of interest to senior management is the bottom-line profitability of the organization. Of course, their interests are varied and include a range of organizational activities. However, the underlying interest and concern of senior management remains bottom-line profitability. If the organization cannot remain profitable, it will not remain in business. It is great to be benevolent, but benevolence only comes out of riches, and riches are tied to bottom-line profitability.

Data processing management must learn to directly or indirectly relate all conversation to bottom-line profitability. This does not mean that profitability will enter into all conversations, but conversations that appear counter or ignore bottom-line profitability are not the language of senior management.

The emphasis in many data processing conversations is on improving technical capability: Going to new versions of operating systems, upgrading the hardware, acquiring software packages. "MIPS" is a wonderful technical term and certainly describes internal processing capabilities, but it is absolutely worthless to senior management. Processing information faster is difficult to translate into more orders, increased customer satisfaction, and increased bottom-line profitability. It may have an impact, but if it does most data processing managers fail to make the appropriate connection for senior management.

Bottom-line profitability can be expressed in two topics of conversation. The first is increasing revenue, and the second is reducing expenses. Both of these topics translate directly to bottom-line profitability.

Data processing management must talk in these terms, or their conversation will be of little interest to management. For example, software maintenance is viewed strictly as an expense. It appears in the statement of income and expense as an expense and, although senior management recognizes it is necessary, they frequently consider it a necessary evil. If data processing management could translate that expense into extending the life of an application system asset, providing new services to users that enable them to generate more revenue, and improving efficiency in performing maintenance, which can be translated into reduced expenses, the topic of maintenance would be translated into the accounting language of senior management.

Talking like senior management talks means translating technical conversations into bottom-line profitability. This only occurs when data processing managers think like senior managers. As long as data processing managers think in technical terms, they will have difficulty talking in business terms. In order to become a senior manager, one must think like a senior manager.

THINKING THE WAY MANAGEMENT THINKS

If senior managers read financial statements and talk bottom-lime profitability, they must also think in these same terms. One cannot talk about software maintenance in terms of bottom-line profitability unless one thinks in terms of bottom-line profitability. Conversation, both oral and written, is a product of one's experiences.

Thinking in accounting terms is a difficult transition for a technician. An individual trained in technical skills tends to think in terms of technical problems and solutions. On the other hand, individuals trained in business and accounting skills are more apt to think in those terms. While senior managers can come from all disciplines, their success in reaching the senior ranks are frequently tied closely to their abilities to think in accounting terms.

Let us examine a few of the thought processes of senior management as they view situations:

Budgeting as a Control

Budgeting involves both general and specific authorization from senior management to lower-level management outlining its financial responsibility for the budgetary period. However, on the expenditure side this does not authorize managers to spend money, which comes from specific authorization. For example, a budget may include funds to acquire a new computer, but that expenditure must still have specific authorization.

The senior manager views the budget as the primary control mechanism. Compliance to and effective use of budgeting funds is important to the senior manager. Many senior management commands relate to budgetary accounts. They will either request increased revenue or changes in the use of expenditures, and monitor closely over and under variances from budgeted amounts. When viewing the operation of a function like data processing, they frequently see it more in terms of budgets than work performed by the organization. While senior managers assume that lower-level managers will do the correct work, their concern is whether or not it can be done within the budgeted allocation.

Return on Investment

Senior managers view most situations as positive or negative return on investment situations. When a junior manager presents a proposal to a senior manager, it is viewed in terms of return on investment. If the proposal does not include a return on investment, then the senior manager must mentally make that calculation. If the senior manager's calculation shows a negative return on investment, there is a high probability that the proposal will be rejected. The failure to include this valuable piece of information has resulted in many proposals being rejected.

The anti-return-on-investment argument is that the numbers are meaningless. This is because junior managers do not think in the same way as senior managers think. Return on investment does not have to be a high-precision calculation. For example, if the return on investment was 20 percent or 200 percent, the decision would probably be go.

Current Value of Money

Money is worth something. Its worth is considered the current value of money. As previously indicated, a rule of thumb for the current value of money is the prime rate charged by banks to their big customers. Some organizations assume that money is worth slightly more than the prime rate. For example, if the prime rate is 12 percent, the current value of money to an organization may be 15 percent, because they could invest their money and get a 15 percent return.

The current value of money has two impacts on management thinking. The first is that if internal projects do not provide a return equal to the current value of money, the organization would be better off investing the money in the money market than to undertake the project. Second, the current value of money concept demonstrates that future dollars are not worth as much as current dollars. Therefore, projects that show large benefits but with benefits years away are not nearly as attractive as projects that have an immediate return on investment. Unfortunately, many data processing projects fall into the long-range category and, thus, have a negative impact on the current value of money thinking.

What Are Our Competitors Doing?

Many senior managers are very curious over the types of activities being undertaken by their competitors. While this may not sound like basic accounting thinking, it is. Organizations must be equal to or better than their competitors to survive in the marketplace.

Therefore, what one's competitors are doing is an important criterion in evaluating a situation. For example, if one's industry was going to data base technology, that would be an important criterion in selling data base to senior management. Just as senior managers watch the financial statements of their competitors, so do they like to watch the internal activities of their competitors.

This thinking does not mean that senior management wants to do exactly what their competitors are doing. Their interest is what their competitors are doing and why. Having this information, they are in a better position to assess and make decisions on internal proposals. On the other hand, if senior management finds that their industry is all going in one particular direction, and that data processing within their organization is proposing a solution that goes in an opposite direction, they become very concerned. Part of this thinking, too, is related to the fact that senior management may not understand the intricacies of technical proposals, and want an external yardstick against which to measure them. That yardstick is partially what other organizations in the same industry are doing.

Scoring as a Decision Tool

Scoring is a numerical method used for decision making. Senior management spends much of their time making decision and needs a basis on which to make decisions. In many instances, return on investment provides that basis, but not always. For example, return on investment from two or more proposals may be approximately equal, or the decision may be one that cannot be based solely on return on investment, for example, deciding who to promote or where to locate a warehouse.

Scoring involves the following four steps:

Step 1. Select the Criteria to Be Used in Making the Decision. For example, if the decision is where to locate a warehouse, the criteria might be availability of cheap labor, good transportation, low rental, and proximity to customers.

Step 2. Determine the Importance of Each Criterion. This is usually done by assigning a weight to each criterion. In our warehouse location example, it might be decided that location close to customers is twice as important as the other three criteria. Thus, location would be given a weight of two, while all other criteria would be given a weight of one.

Step 3. Score Each Item Being Evaluated on Its Ability to Satisfy the Criteria. All items being considered must be evaluated by the criteria established in Step 1, up to the maximum weight or score determined in Step 2. In our warehouse example, if we assumed the weight was the maximum score, then each warehouse location considered would be scored a maximum of two points for location, and a maximum of one point for each of the other three criteria. Thus, the perfect warehouse location would have five points and a totally unsatisfactory location would have zero points. Each criterion would be evaluated by management and a score developed.

Step 4. Total the Score and Compare Against Other Considered Items. The item with the highest score would be the one that management would decide upon. Note that this may not be a high-precision method and, therefore, very close scores may be considered a tie. For example, if one warehouse location got 4.8 and another 4.7, this might be considered a tie and then managerial judgment would be needed to break the tie. On the other hand, a location scoring 4.8 would be a definite winner over one scoring 3.2.

This four-step process implies a formalization that might not exist in decision-making criteria. The entire four steps can be performed as a mental thought process. Although in major decisions senior managers may want to formalize the scoring process, in minor decisions it is part of the thought process of managers in deciding what to do. In many instances, it is done almost by instinct, rather than in a formal step-by-step manner.

The ability of the data processing manager to think like senior managers means that the data processing manager has equivalent experience. In most instances, this is not true. Therefore, the senior manager must through education acquire at least some of the experience and thought processes used by senior managers.

LEARNING THE WAY MANAGEMENT LEARNS

Studies of the skills possessed by data processing managers indicate that many data processing managers do not possess business-oriented skills. These are the accounting, statistics, and management theory skills. Most senior managers possess these skills, while many data processing managers do not.

It is generally impossible for the data processing manager to possess the breadth of business experience possessed by the senior manager. This is true in any field. The new computer science graduate does not have nearly the same understanding and feel for system design and implementation as possessed by the senior systems analyst. On the other hand, that new computer science graduate possesses the same skills, although has not mastered them nearly as well as the senior systems analyst.

The starting point for data processing managers in thinking and communicating like a senior manager is to possess the basic skills. This is not an overwhelming task, but one that will take time and effort on the part of the data processing manager.

A highly desirable method to accomplish this is to return to one of the universities that offers an executive MBA program. These are the programs in which the manager goes to school one day a week and works the other four. However, individuals are usually chosen for this program, and data processing managers requesting it may not be granted admission to the MBA program.

The three other options that are available to the data processing manager to improve basic managerial skills are: on-the-job training, self-study courses, and formal education.

On-the-Job Training. Many data processing managers do not personally perform many of the managerial functions of their department. For example, data processing managers who do not like budgeting may have a member on their staff prepare the budget, accounting reports, etc. Data processing managers can improve their accounting type of skills by becoming more personally involved in the accounting activities of their department. This means a better understanding of the organization's chart of accounts, the financial statements produced, and the types of analyses that are performed on those statements.

Self-Study Courses. Many educational opportunities to learn new skills are available to an individual. Some of these are formal and some are informal. The formal training courses are published by executive and accounting associations, universities, professional education organizations, and profit-making groups. The courses can be in video format, audio format, or narrative study format. In many instances, the data processing manager will have to take and pass an examination to show mastery of the skills.

The informal self-study learning experiences involve reading books and technical publications. Many organizations have a business library that includes numerous books on accounting, statistics, and management theory. In addition, it is advisable for data processing managers to read the business press and technical publications. For example, publications such as the *Wall Street Journal*, and technical magazines such as the *Financial Executive* and *Journal of Accountancy*, are good primers on day-to-day trends and activities of senior financial managers. It may even be good practice to leave some of these publications on one's desk so that visiting senior executives can observe the types of materials that the data processing manager is reading in order to properly fulfill the business mission of data processing.

Formal Education. Local schools and universities offer formal courses in accounting and management skills. In most instances, it is not necessary for the data processing manager to enroll in a degree program. The manager should be looking for select courses, such as basic, intermediate, and advanced accounting. These frequently can be taken without prerequisites if the manager is not enrolled in a degree program. Also, it is not even necessary for the manager to take examinations as courses can be monitored for no credit. Because the data processing manager's interest is in understanding the skills, as opposed to being proficient at them, even the time and effort required to take the course can be significantly reduced. For example, the data processing manager may choose not to do a lot of the homework and study assign ments but, rather, gain as much as possible from the classroom and discussion experiences.

The one skill that is the most difficult to learn is the skill of knowing what is important. It is frequently said that nothing is older than yesterday's newspaper. The data processing manager must address current topics of senior management interest and not yesterday's topics.

ANTICIPATING WHAT MANAGEMENT WANTS

The trends in the book *Megatrends** were determined by analyzing newspapers. The authors studied the amount of space that newspapers allocated to specific topics, for example, the amount of space allocated to people in organizations moving to the Sun Belt. The authors reasoned that newspapers printed what people wanted to read. The topics that people were interested in were indicative of what is going on in society.

*John Naisbitt, *Megatrends* (New York; Warner 1982).

By identifying the amount of space allocated to topics and the space trend, the authors were able to identify national trends. For example, they found that a significant amount of space in newspapers discussed people in organizations moving to the Sun Belt. They also found that the amount of space allocated to this topic was increasing. The conclusion, then, was that there was a trend within the United State of movement to the Sun Belt.

This simple but powerful concept in identifying trends can be applied to business situations. Data processing managers should treat senior managers as the equivalent of newspapers. The topics that they are discussing, and the frequency and time allocated to those topics, are indicative of managerial trends. For example, if senior management discusses more frequently cost savings, that is most likely a managerial trend within that organization. The DP manager should pick up and keep track of topics and the time allocated to them.

The topics that senior management is discussing less frequently should be regarded as yesterday's newspaper. Data processing management should avoid those topics in their conversation. On the other hand, the topics that are growing in frequency of discussion are the trendy topics. These are the managerial hot buttons. Data processing managers that focus their attention and proposals on those topics have a much greater probability of successful communication with senior management, than those that are discussing yesterday's topics or topics not yet on management trend lists.

Conversations that couple the trend topics with an accounting orientation result in serious senior management conversations. It has frequently been stated that a good conversationalist is one who talks about the interests of the other member(s) of the conversation. Trend topics in an accounting orientation are those topics of interest to senior managers.

PUTTING THE ART OF CONVERSATION TOGETHER

This chapter has addressed reading, talking, thinking, learning, and anticipating in a senior management perspective. Each topic has been discussed and suggestions presented on how to improve one's self in that area. However, mastery of these individual topics is not enough.

The materials presented in this chapter are not meant to be presented in shopping-basket format. In other words, the data processing manager cannot pick one or two of the topics, master them, and then expect to act like senior managers and converse freely with them.

The topics in this chapter are presented as a package. They should be used in total or not at all. For example, it is difficult to think like a manager without learning managerial skills, or anticipating management's current topics unless one reads what management is reading so that the topics can be put into the proper perspective.

One does not want to be created in the same image or mold as one's boss.

The objective of this chapter is not to remake the data processing managers into something that these individuals are not and may not want to be. The objective of this chapter has been to show data processing managers the skills and attributes that they need to supplement their data processing skills. It is the combination of the two that will make tomorrow's manager.

The best way to get senior managers knowledgeable in information systems is to promote data processing management to senior management. In order for this to happen, data processing managers will need the managerial skills of accounting. It is generally easier for a data processing manager to acquire the accounting and business skills than it is for a senior manager to acquire information processing skills.

RECOMMENDED ACCOUNTING AND AUDITING PRINCIPLE FOR THE DATA PROCESSING MANAGER
The ability to communicate is limited by language. Because accountingese is the language of senior management, it must be learned in order to permit more effective conversations to occur between data processing managers and senior management.

Part Five

EVALUATING THE INTEGRITY OF ACCOUNTING SYSTEMS

The integrity of the accounting information will be partially based on verifying the integrity of the accounting system. In most organizations, this is performed by an independent group—commonly called auditors. This part briefly describes the methods for verifying the integrity of accounting systems and then explains how to survive an EDP audit.

Chapter Thirteen

How to Survive an EDP Audit

An audit is an independent appraisal activity. To audit means to review the work performed by others. The key concepts of audit are that it is performed by individuals independent of the area being audited and that it is designed to apprise someone of the conditions of the area under audit.

In the early days of data processing, auditors avoided reviewing the computer field because of the technical complexity of computers. They developed a process called auditing "around the computer." Unfortunately, a massive computer-related fraud at the Equity Funding Corporation in about 1970 thrust the auditors onto the EDP scene. Equity Funding created an entirely new profession called EDP auditors, and a new field of auditing called EDP auditing. Since that time, data processing has been fair game for audits.

This chapter offers a strategy to survive EDP audits. Auditing need not be a life-threatening situation evoking fear into the heart of the data processing manager. Not only are audits survivable, but they can be beneficial. This chapter explains the audit process and then recommends strategies for working with auditors and addressing audit findings and recommendations.

WHO WILL AUDIT DATA PROCESSING?

There are three general categories of auditors that might become involved with data processing. These are independent, regulatory, and internal. Any or all three groups of auditors may become involved in evaluating the data processing function.

Independent auditors review entire organizations and issue opinions on the adequacy of their financial statements and system of internal control. Independent auditors work for a firm other than the organization in which they audit. They are normally certified public accountants or chartered accountants.

Independent auditors are subject to standards established by their own profession. They are bound to evaluate their clients in accordance with auditing standards or are personally liable for damages due to improper audits.

United States corporations covered under the Securities and Exchange Act of 1934 are required to be audited by independent auditors. So are corporations traded on recognized stock exchanges, and many banks require organizations to be audited by independent auditors prior to lending those organizations funds. The end product of an audit by an independent auditor is an opinion that most companies append to their financial statement as part of their annual report.

Regulatory auditors are employees of a regulatory agency. This grouping of auditors are concerned that the requirements of their agency are satisfied by the organization required to comply with the regulations. The more common regulatory auditors are associated with regulated industries such as banking and insurance, but there are other auditors involved with special programs such as sales tax, equal employment opportunity, and the Occupational Safety and Health Act.

The end product of a regulatory audit will be an assessment of compliance to the regulatory requirements. If the organization, or data processing department if it is being reviewed, fails to comply with the appropriate legislation, civil and/or criminal damages may evolve. Some legislation requires that triple or more damages be paid where regulations were not complied with.

Many organizations have their own internal auditors who may be the most common auditor reviewing the data processing function. Internal auditors are employees of the organizations that they audit. While they have a professional association that has issued standards for the professional conduct of internal auditing, most internal auditors are not bound by those standards. Many times, internal auditing is used as a training ground, so that the internal auditors may not be highly skilled in the performance of the audit function. The mission and responsibility of internal auditing varies significantly from organization to organization. In some organizations, the internal auditors are merely clerks verifying the correctness of financial documents, while in other organizations they are internal consultants.

Internal auditors like to believe that they are the "eyes and ears" of management. Many internal auditors believe they are performing functions that senior management would perform if senior management had adequate time, Thus, any aspect of data processing that would be of interest to senior management is also of interest to internal auditing.

THREE TYPES OF AUDITING

The three types of auditing are compliance, operational, and program auditing. Compliance auditing is concerned with whether or not a department has complied with all of the policies, procedures, and standards of an organization in doing its work. It has strong financial connotations. Operational auditing evaluates the effectiveness, economy, and efficiency of operations. The third category of auditing is program auditing. These audits are designed to determine whether or not what an organization is doing is reasonable and proper.

Compliance auditing evaluates whether a department is following the rules of the organization. Operational auditing determines whether they are following the rules in an efficient, effective, and economical manner. Program auditing challenges whether the rules are right.

Independent auditors are primarily concerned with compliance auditing. Internal auditors were established by organizations to assist their independent auditors so that the effort and fees of independent auditors could be reduced. Thus, the initial work of internal auditors was also compliance auditing. However, over time, internal auditors became more involved in evaluating the operation of the organization. Depending on the mission of internal audit, they might also evaluate the propriety of the program. Note that the independent auditors frequently have a management advisory staff as part of their firm that will perform the operational and program reviews for their clients.

HOW DO AUDITORS KNOW WHAT TO LOOK FOR?

Auditing is a negative process. Its objective is to determine what's wrong, and not to determine what's right. The fact that something is not noted to be wrong implies that it is functioning correctly, but audit reports are not designed to report on what is working correctly.

Auditing is a process of probing and sampling. It is designed to provide management with the highest probability of assurance that there are no major problems, except those reported, with minimal effort. The average staffing for internal auditors is one internal auditor per 1,000 employees. The staffing ratio alone indicates that a single auditor cannot review many transactions.

Auditors have developed methodologies that help lead them to problem areas. Data processing managers can use these same strategies to help identify problems prior to audit and, thus, survive.

The primary strategy used by auditors is risk analysis. The auditors identify the high-risk areas, and then concentrate their audit effort in areas in which problems are most likely to occur.

High-risk areas are identified in one of two manners. The first is audit experience. Much of this experience is embodied into audit checklists and programs that lead auditors to look at the high-risk activities and transactions within an organization. The second risk identification approach is in auditing called a preliminary survey. This is a quick overview and probing exercise that the auditor uses to identify specific high-risk areas.

Risk analysis, then, subjects an organization to two risk exercises. The first is general risk that occurs in activities of the type being reviewed, and the second is specific risk that is associated with the way an organization performs its work. For example, auditors will always look at the access to the computer room because this is a general high risk in all data processing, but through probing may find specific risks such as failure to properly safeguard computer room passes. Both of these situations would then be evaluated during the audit process.

HOW DO AUDITORS UNDERSTAND THE TECHNICAL ASPECTS OF DATA PROCESSING?

Auditors are generalists, not specialists. Even those auditors that specialize in data processing are primarily generalists in the data processing field, as opposed to specialists. Auditors do not hold themselves out to be detailed experts in any area, but do profess to have enough understanding of the area being audited that they can identify major problems.

Since data processing is a highly technical area, being audited by generalists poses some potential audit problems. First, the auditors may overlook some significant risk areas because of lack of experience. Second, the auditor may make recommendations that cannot be implemented because of the general nature of the recommendation.

The auditor's ability to evaluate the data processing area is built around three auditing traits. The first is that the auditor is taught how to review and investigate an area. While the auditor may not know data processing in depth, the auditor does know how to perform the audit process. Second, auditors familiarize themselves with the area under review. Auditors build up a file explaining the functions and methods used in the area under audit. They also talk to knowledgeable people about the area, tour and talk to people in the area under review, and frequently take courses or study about the area being reviewed. Note that while no one auditor may understand data processing fully, the audit team as a whole may possess the needed skills. Third, auditors use a methodology for audit. It is the methodology that helps them perform a successful audit. For example, most people could build a television set if they were provided with detailed instructions on how to put it together such as Heath Company provides its customers. Likewise, auditors with minimal data processing skills may be able to perform a successful data processing audit given a good methodology.

WHAT AUDIT METHODOLOGIES DO AUDITORS USE?

The audit process is divided into three general areas: planning, doing, and reviewing. Auditors plan what and how they will audit; auditors conduct or do the audit; and then audit management reviews the work to ensure that the audit was performed properly. Each step of the audit process must be documented and, thus, the review permits the more senior people to ensure that the less experienced people have performed their work properly.

The detailed audit processes are as numerous and as varied as system development methodologies. An oversimplification is that a development methodology consists of planning, doing, and testing (i.e., reviewing). The methodology is broken down into steps, but there is less agreement on what these specific steps are.

The following seven-step audit process is representative of most audit processes. However, it needs to be recognized that different audit groups will follow slightly different audit processes.

Step 1. Develop Annual Audit Plan

The first risk analysis process performed by auditing is determining what will be audited during the year. The high-risk activities are selected in the audit plan. Lower-risk activities may not be audited or may be audited less than annually.

The audit plan includes all of the major audits. If data processing is to be audited, or individual data processing activities audited, such as computer security, then that audit will be described in the annual audit plan. In some organizations, that is a public document and the data processing manager could determine what data processing activities will be audited and when.

The annual audit plan also includes time for special audits. In other words, events during the year may lead auditors to conduct audits that are not included in the plan. Time is normally allotted for these special audits. In addition, nondata processing audits may involve data processing because the applications involve data processing. For example, an audit of the organization's payroll department may lead to evaluating the automated payroll programs. The audits in the plan will be initiated one by one, with the following six steps repeated for each audit.

Step 2. Perform Preliminary Survey

The detailed audit planning is performed during the survey step. During this step, the audit team has been assigned and is putting together the programs that will be followed during the conduct of the audit. The annual audit plan normally allocates a predetermined number of man-weeks for the audit. During the survey phase, the auditor in charge determines how best to use the allotted resources.

The activities common during the survey phase include:

Interviewing users of data processing services

Interviewing senior management having jurisdiction over data processing

Reviewing results of previous audits

Talking to individuals involved in previous audits

Reading data processing policies, procedures, and standards

Tour of the data processing area (if auditors are in close proximity)

Interview with key data processing managers

The end product of the survey is a list of tasks to be performed during the audit. The survey will enable the auditor in charge to estimate the high-risk areas, and then build a program to address those risks. Note that in many instances the audit program available in the audit department will identify the general risk areas. An audit program is a work program describing the individual steps to be performed during the conduct of the audit.

Step 3. Hold an Entrance Conference

The entrance conference is the formal start of the audit fieldwork. While the auditors may have taken a tour of the data processing area and may have interviewed some key personnel, the real fieldwork does not commence until after the entrance conference.

The conference is a formality in which the auditors explain the audit process and what they hope to accomplish, and provide the data processing staff with the opportunity to question the performance of the audit. The entrance conference is part information and part marketing on behalf of the auditing personnel.

Auditors know that they need the cooperation of the auditee in order to perform their job correctly. It is during the entrance conference that they hope to establish the right atmosphere or mood for auditing. The entrance conference also provides the auditee with an opportunity to indicate areas of concern that they would like the auditor to investigate.

If there are any special needs that the auditors will ask the auditee to satisfy, they are usually expressed at the entrance conference. Generally, the auditors will need space to work, access to the computer, documentation, and access to data processing documents. Note that in most organizations auditors have the right to see any document they want, but out of courtesy normally ask permission.

Step 4. Conduct Fieldwork

Audits tend to be divided into the three parts described earlier. Each part takes about one-third of the total audit time. Appropriate planning and surveying consume about one-third of the audit effort, conducting the audit another third (this step), and the reviewing and report writing the remaining one-third of the effort.

During the fieldwork, the auditors will execute the audit program developed during the survey step. While the audit program allows a certain amount of leeway in what the auditors do, it generally guides them to perform certain predetermined tasks. However, should the auditor suspect problems, the audit team normally has authority to take the time to probe those areas.

It is during the fieldwork that the auditors will use automated tools and techniques. Many auditors acquire generalized audit software packages for this purpose. These have the same characteristics as many of the analysis and report-writing packages available to data processing. For example, Pansophic's EASYTRIEVE, which is a data processing retrieval report-writing package, has been redesigned as PANAUDIT and provided to auditors. The primary difference is that audit software has statistical sampling capabilities, while the data processing analysis and retrieval systems do not.

At the end of the fieldwork, all of the detailed analyses of the data processing department will have been completed. At this point, the auditors will have collected all of the factual information that they need. From this factual information, they will develop findings and recommendations. Findings are differences between what is and what should be, and recommendations are the auditors' suggestions to correct the findings.

Step 5. Conduct Exit Conference

The exit conference is designed to permit the auditee to see and discuss the audit findings and recommendations prior to any other area of the organization seeing that information. During the exit conference, the auditor wants to verify that the findings are correct. They should be correct because this is the factual part of the audit report. The auditor also wants to gain acceptance from the auditee for any recommendations.

During the exit conference, the auditee is normally provided with a draft copy of the audit report. At this point, the auditee can challenge the findings, recommendations, or the way that the information is presented. Most auditors are willing to compromise on presentation, are willing to reevaluate if the facts appear incorrect, and are willing to consider alternative recommendations if they accomplish the desired objectives. This is not to imply that the auditors will readily make changes to please the auditee but, rather, that auditors recognize that findings and recommendations which the auditee agrees to implement are more valuable than those that must be fought for throughout the organization hierarchy.

Step 6. ***Issue Audit Report***

The audit report will be finalized, prepared, and issued to all interested parties. The action copy of the audit report will go to the auditee—in this case, the data processing manager. Other copies of the audit report may go to:

- Members of senior management (at a minimum, the individual to whom the data processing manager reports)
- The chief executive officer of the organization
- The audit committee of the board of directors
- The organization's firm of independent public accountants

The auditee is requested to respond to the audit report. The response normally indicates whether the recommendation will be accepted as is, will be accepted with modification, or will be rejected and, if so, why.

If the auditors agree with the response, the audit is concluded. If the auditors disagree, they will attempt to negotiate an acceptable solution with the auditee. If the auditors and auditee cannot agree, then the findings and recommendations must be resolved by senior management. Since this is generally an unpopular conclusion to an audit, it is better to resolve audit differences at the auditor/auditee level if possible.

Step 7. ***Follow Up on Audit Reports Where Necessary***

If the auditee fails to respond in a reasonable period of time, the auditors will follow up to obtain the response. In many instances, the auditors indicate in the audit report by what date they expect the response. Note that it is generally important to the auditors, senior management, and the audit committee of the board of directors that auditees make timely responses to audit findings and recommendations. If the auditee fails to respond, senior management will usually step in and take whatever action is necessary to ensure that a response is made.

STRATEGIES FOR SURVIVING THE AUDIT PROCESS

One definition of auditors are those individuals that go on the battlefield after the battle is over—and shoot the wounded! Everyone has their auditor joke. On the other hand, auditors need to be recognized as a force that will be around for a long time and should be dealt with professionally.

In talking about surviving audits, one must define what is meant by survival. Three different definitions of survival can be established:

Survival Definition 1. No Problems Identified by Auditors:

Under this definition, the auditee wants to implement a strategy to prevent the auditors from identifying any significant problems in the auditee area.

Survival Definition 2. Auditors Identify All Significant Problems:
Under this strategy, the auditee is looking for the auditors to help in identifying problems before they become serious. This strategy assumes the auditor to be an ally so that any problem uncovered by the auditor may prevent disastrous situations from happening at a later point in time.

Survival Definition 3. The Audit Findings and Recommendations Do Not Have a Negative Impact on the Auditee:
Under this strategy, it is unimportant what the auditors uncover as long as what is found is not deemed to be negative from the perspective of senior management. The strategy is one of assuring the continual credibility of the auditee in the eyes of management.

The survival strategy selected by the auditee will determine the actions that need to be taken. The strategy aimed at preventing auditors from identifying significant problems requires action prior to the audit. The auditor is an ally. This strategy involves working closely with the auditors during the audit; and the strategy to avoid being hurt by audit findings and recommendations is an after-the-fact audit strategy. We will examine these before-, during-, and after-audit strategies individually.

Before the Audit Strategy

This strategy is preventative. It is frequently used when senior management uses the auditors to assess the performance of their subordinates. This management philosophy is easy to detect through comments by senior managers and comments during performance appraisal sessions.

The preaudit strategies are designed primarily to identify problems before auditors identify them. This requires auditor-type thinking on the part of the auditee. There are three actions that an auditor can take to minimize the probability of problems being uncovered by auditors:

Action 1. Perform Risk Analysis
A risk analysis exercise requires the auditee to attempt to identify the risks present in the auditee area. A risk is the probability that an unfavorable event may occur. The auditee attempts to identify all the unfavorable events, and then estimate the potential magnitude of those events. The end product is a ranking of risks in the auditee area from high to low.

The risk analysis is usually performed by a team of senior people. The process that they use is called greenlighting. This permits every individual to suggest potential risks; through a synergistic effect the group agrees upon what are the most probable risks and the ranking of those risks.

Once the risks have been identified and ranked, the auditee personnel then attempt to determine whether or not there are adequate controls to reduce those risks to an acceptable level. If not, controls should be strengthened. The data processing staff may also want to investigate to determine whether in fact the risks have turned into losses. If so, remedial action should be taken where appropriate, and controls strengthened to ensure that these type of losses do not occur in the future.

Action 2. Conduct Data Processing Audits

Data processing audit programs are readily available from internal auditors, independent auditors, auditing associations, and educational organizations. The programs are also available in many books (e.g., *Auditing Computer Applications* by Keagle W. Davis and William E. Perry, published by John Wiley & Sons, offers such audit programs).

This action requires data procesing personnel to actually perform audits on their own function. The data processing staff will execute the steps outlined in the audit program. Any findings uncovered during the audit need to be addressed by data processing management so that the problems have been handled long before actual audits occur.

Action 3. Direct Auditors to Areas of Known Problems

Auditors can be used to achieve the desired objectives. For example, if data processing wants a data dictionary, but is having difficulty in getting management approval, it may want to direct the auditors to investigate the problems associated with inadequate data documentation. Obviously, the desired solution is not disclosed, nor is the purpose of the audit suggestion. Auditors normally ask auditees if there are areas of concern, and at that time the data processing manager can suggest that auditors make certain types of investigations. The more time auditors take to investigate concerns of the data processing manager, the less time auditors will have for their own concerns.

During the Audit Strategy

The audit commences in the auditee area with the entrance conference. The audit proceeds during the fieldwork step and concludes during the exit conference. Between the entrance and the exit conference, the auditee has the opportunity to influence the audit process.

The actions that the auditee can take to ensure that the problems identified by the auditors are valid problems requiring action include:

Action 1. Confirm the Validity of Auditor-Identified Findings

Findings are factual information. Both the auditor and the auditee should agree on the validity of the findings. If the auditee disagrees with the auditor's findings, it is primarily the auditee's responsibility to prove to the auditor what the true facts are. Time expended in clarifying findings is normally a good investment of resources.

Action 2. Ensure That the Reported Findings Are Significant

Reporting findings that are insignificant is annoying to most auditees. One data processing manager described insignificant findings as spending large amounts of effort to "give birth to a mouse." If the audit reports do not indicate the significance or magnitude of the finding, the auditee should request that the auditors attach a magnitude to each finding. If the auditors do not state the magnitude of a finding, then the auditee should attach their own magnitude. It is unrealistic for senior management to discuss problems until it has been apprised of the probable magnitude of those problems.

Action 3. Monitor the Work of Auditors and Make Recommendations

One data processing manager said that audits were too important to leave to the auditors. The manager qualified it by saying that anything that affected that individual's performance was something he wanted to control. The more the auditee knows about the audit process, the easier it is for the auditee to direct the auditors to the appropriate area, transactions, and events.

Some auditors are very willing to discuss with auditees their audit programs and the actions and tasks they are undertaking. Other auditors are very secretive about their process and do not want to disclose either their intent or their procedures. However, it is not difficult to identify what the auditors are doing by monitoring their activities. Once the auditee knows the objectives and methodology that the auditors are following, recommendations can be made to assist the auditors in performing their function more effectively.

Action 4. Ensure That Recommendations Show the Potential Return on Investment

Recommendations are auditors' suggestions on how to address problems identified by auditors. Recommendations are made because when auditors report problems senior management's first question normally is "What should be done to correct the situation?"

Auditors tend to spend large amounts of time developing and supporting findings. On the other hand, recommendations may not receive the same time and attention. Therefore, it is important that the cost and benefits of recommendations be clearly identified. Knowing the estimated return on investment from a recommendation is important in determining whether or not to adopt it. Also, requiring auditors to perform this calculation should improve the type of audit recommendations that are made. If the auditors fail to develop a return on investment, then the auditee should make that calculation.

After the Audit Strategy

The auditee may or may not be able to convince the auditor to change findings and recommendations. The audit report is the report of the auditors. What they choose to report, they will report.

The type of actions that the auditee can take to minimize any negative impact of audit findings and recommendations include the following four actions:

Action 1. Make Rapid Responses to Audit Reports

Timely reports indicate auditee interest in remedying unfavorable situations. Both the auditors and senior management may view this positive action as indicating a strong desire on the part of the auditee to run an efficient and effective operation. It is often how one deals with the problem, rather than the problem itself, that is the overriding factor in attitudes about auditee performance.

Action 2. Attach the Auditee Response to the Audit Report

Many auditors offer auditees the option to attach their reaction to the audit findings and recommendations to the audit report. Some auditors automatically provide space and request the auditee to make such responses. If the auditors do not offer the opportunity, the auditee may suggest that it would like to write a response and attach it to the audit report.

The objective of the auditee response is to provide senior management with the information it needs to dispose of the audit report. If senior management knows that the auditee agrees with the audit report, or that it has a plan of action to address the auditor's findings and recommendations, senior management may read and automatically dispose of the audit report. On the other hand, if there are items open, management may hold the audit report in abeyance until it hears that the problems have been resolved. Normally, the quicker the report is disposed of, the more favorable senior management will view the auditee area and the actions taken by the auditee.

Action 3. Propose Alternatives to Auditor Recommendations

Auditees do not have to accept auditor recommendations. They do have to respond to them. It is perfectly acceptable to respond with an alternative recommendation. The alternative can be a completely new recommendation, or a modified recommendation. If the auditor agrees with the auditee's new or modified recommendation, then the audit report is finished and the audit concluded. From an auditee perspective, the objective should be to obtain the most favorable recommendation that solves the finding uncovered by the auditors.

Action 4. Attack the Validity of the Audit Recommendation

A less desirable, but frequently effective, approach is for the auditee to challenge the validity of the recommendation. Auditees do not have to accept recommendations. They can reject auditor recommendations outright as impractical and unworkable. The premise can be that it is more economical to live with a problem than to implement the solution. Frequently, the cure is more painful than the illness. However, auditees should carefully select those cases where they challenge the auditors. Auditees always want to be sure that they do not win a battle and lose a war.

SENIOR MANAGEMENT UNDERSTANDS THE LANGUAGE OF AUDITORS

Auditors, like accounting, are the tools of management. Auditors are the representatives of senior management. They help senior management fulfill their control responsibilities. Therefore, it would be impractical for data processing management to reject the audit concept. Auditing is important to management and, therefore, it should be important to the data processing manager.

The bottom line of surviving accounting and auditing is to put oneself in a position of a senior manager. An old proverb states that one cannot understand another person's position until one has walked in that other person's shoes. Surviving accounting and auditing requires the data processing manager to stand in the senior manager's shoes. Once the data processing manager can view the organization from senior management's perspective, survival becomes easy.

RECOMMENDED ACCOUNTING AND AUDITING PRINCIPLE FOR THE DATA PROCESSING MANAGER
A data processing manager must act like a senior manager before becoming a senior manager. The shoes of senior management are accounting and auditing.

Guidelines for Developing and Implementing a Charging System

This appendix is a discussion of the recommended steps for developing and implementing a charging system outlined in Chapter 9. The steps are grouped into four phases and should be followed in sequence to the extent that they are relevant to a particular DP environment.

PLANNING PHASE

The planning phase consists of preparing the organization's developmental plans for the charging system. The preparation of the developmental plans consists of establishing the project structure, determining the charging system characteristics, and preparing the project plan. This phase is the most important of the four phases because (1) the organization will be establishing the general structure of the charging system and (2) the decisions made will guide the work during the remaining three phases. Representatives of the charging team and senior organization management should be responsible for the work during this phase. The three steps of the planning phase are discussed below.

Step 1. Establish the Project Structure

The objectives of the tasks performed during this step are to establish the management structure for the charging system project and to select the charging team.

This appendix has been adapted from Federal Information Processing Standards Publication, FIPS PUB 96, U.S. Department of Commerce, National Bureau of Standards, December 1982.

A. Establish the Management Structure

The management structure refers to the relationship between the individuals who must perform, manage, and oversee the charging system project. Senior organization management should start the charging system project by appointing a Project Manager and an Oversight Official. The Project Manager should come from either the DP or accounting departments and the Oversight Official should be a member of senior management. The Project Manager of the charging system should be responsible for performing the following functions:

The Project Manager will need to interface with senior management (Oversight Official) on a regular basis. This interface is important since senior management will be one of the primary users and beneficiaries of the charging system and the charging system project may need the authority of senior management to implement certain aspects of the charging system.

The Project Manager will need to review all of the relevant literature on charging systems in order to make the many decisions that will be required when developing the charging system.

The Project Manager will be responsible for the overall management of the project. Such management will include dealing with the day-to-day problems that normally arise during projects of this magnitude.

The Project Manager should be somewhat familiar with the groups that will be most affected by charging systems; that is, senior management, data processing, accounting, budgeting, and the users.

B. Establish the Charging Team

The second task that must be performed for Step 1 is for the Project Manager to establish a Charging Team. The purposes of the Charging Team are to (1) design, develop, and implement the charging system and (2) provide a forum whereby problems that arise can be resolved, and information and decisions from the involved groups can be easily requested and obtained. The Charging Team should consist of at least one representative from each of the organization's major groups that will be most affected by a charging system. Typically, the Charging Team members should come from the following groups: management, data processing, accounting, budgeting, and the users. The Charging Team's work will be made less complicated if the accounting member has a strong background in cost accounting. The Project Manager should be included as a member of the Charging Team. For organizations with small DP facilities, costs can be conserved by limiting the Charging Team to one or two part-time members from one or two of the groups. When this situation arises, the members should be from data processing and accounting.

As a group, the Charging Team is responsible for designing the charging system, for organizing the charging system project to satisfy the design, and for determining the organizational approach to be used to develop the charging system. When work is assigned to individual Charging Team members, the DP and accounting representative typically will receive responsibility for most of the work. The Charging Team collectively should have the authority, expertise, and experience to plan and execute the design, development, implementation, and operation of the charging system.

Step 2. Determine Charging System Characteristics

This step of the planning phase sets the direction of the work that will be performed during the subsequent steps of the project. During this step, the first attempt at determining the desired mixture of charging system characteristics will be performed. Use of the term "first attempt" implies the continuing modification throughout the project of the degree that each characteristic will influence the charging system. The proper mixture of the charging system characteristics can only be determined after study of certain DP facility characteristics, related to charging systems, and after study of the reasons the organization is charging for DP services.

This step will also indicate how the charging system can provide senior management with some of the potential benefits expected. For example, the allocation of scarce resources, a potential benefit of charging systems, can only be obtained if the proper mixture of charging system characteristics is selected.

A. Clarify DP Facility Characteristics

The first task of Step 2 is to clarify the DP facility characteristics. The major DP facility characteristics that relate to charging systems are the stage of maturity that the DP facility has achieved, the role of the DP facility in the organization, and the degree of decentralization of the DP budgeting and funding processes. Each of these characteristics is briefly discussed below.

1. *DP Facility Stage of Maturity.* DP facilities can be viewed as being in one of four stages of maturity: initiation, contagion, control, or integration. The stage that a DP facility is in and is moving toward will dictate a certain mixture of characteristics that should be selected for the charging system. For example, a DP facility at the contagion level of maturity would be viewed as a minor part of an organization and, therefore, may not need a highly sophisticated charging system. Conversely, a DP facility at the integration level of maturity would be viewed as a major part of an organization and, therefore, would need a highly sophisticated charging system.

2. *Role of the DP Facility in the Organization.* The DP facility's role in an organization is that of either providing support, providing service, or making a profit. The role of the DP facility will dictate a certain mixture of

characteristics that should be selected for the charging system. A support center provides services free of charge and is not directly related to any specific department. A service center operates on the concept that those who use computer services should pay for them and should, subsequently, be charged on a cost reimbursable basis. A profit center operates as an independent business, and the user is charged at the market rate for the computer services supplied.

3. *Degree of Decentralization of DP Budgeting and Funding.* Most organizations currently have a centralized approach for DP budgeting and funding. This centralization is accomplished by senior management's approval of DP usage through the DP facility's budget. DP budgeting and funding can be decentralized by approving DP usage via the users' budgets. The degree of decentralization that the organization currently has, or plans to have, will dictate a certain mixture of characteristics that should be selected for the charging system.

B. CLARIFY REASONS FOR CHARGING

Since the organization's reasons for developing and implementing a charging system are primarily the responsibility of senior management, they should be clarified by both the Charging Team and senior management. Aside from company regulations, there are many interrelated reasons why an organization would want to charge for DP services. Some of the major reasons are briefly discussed below.

1. *Encourage Efficiency.* An organization may wish to charge for DP services in order to encourage its users to utilize the DP facility more efficiently. Users can utilize the DP facility more efficiently if they are able to determine, in a timely manner, the volume and cost of each specific service they utilize and, thereby, can modify their use of those services. Additionally, the organization can charge for DP services to encourage DP managers to be more efficient and accountable in managing the DP facility. A charging system can lead to more efficient and accountable DP management because the system often increases dramatically the visibility of many DP managers' decisions.

2. *Allocate Scarce Resources.* An organization may wish to charge for DP services in order to allocate services according to organizational priorities. This influence can entail the use of premiums or discounts to either balance the workload, encourage or discourage the use of particular services at a particular time, or control system performance. Any charging system will implicitly, if not explicitly, influence user behavior; therefore, care must be taken to avoid any presumptuous or inappropriate control over resource allocation which may result in a net loss to the organization as a whole.

3. *Recover Costs.* An organization may wish to charge for DP services

in order to recover the costs of operating the facility. Decisions will eventually have to be made concerning from which users to recover costs, which costs are to be recovered, the method used to account for costs, and the method used to recover the costs.

4. *Report Usage and Costs.* An organization may wish to charge for DP services in order to report only DP usage and the costs of operating the facility. The charges that are reported to the users are never recovered.

5. *Encourage Competition.* An organization may wish to charge for DP services in order to provide its users with the opportunity to compare its billing rates with those of other DP facilities. This enables the users to obtain the most economical price available to support their applications. An additional benefit is that competition encourages the DP facility to operate as efficiently as it can in order to retain its users.

C. Determine Mixture of Charging System Characteristics

The third task of Step 2 is to determine the desired mixture of the major charging system characteristics. Charging system characteristics deal primarily with the particular features that the charging system should have. It is important that a first attempt at determining the desired mixture of characteristics be performed prior to designing the charging system, because attempting to completely redesign a charging system to satisfy a completely different mixture of characteristics is costly and time consuming. When determining characteristics for the charging system, the following should be considered:

Characteristics can be emphasized in the charging system to varying degrees.

Some of the characteristics may conflict; thus, trade-offs between conflicting characteristics must be considered.

Whenever possible, it is best to minimize the complexity of the charging system; that is, "keep it simple."

Twelve major charging system characteristics need to be determined. Each is briefly discussed below.

1. *Repeatability.* When a given DP service is utilized more than once without changes being made either to the number of service units or to the billing rate, then the usage charge should be the same. The charging system should be able to keep track of the service units utilized by each user, regardless of the number of other users currently utilizing the same service. Repeatable charges enable users to make better plans and increase their trust in the functionality of the charging system.

2. *Understandability.* Whenever possible, reports of service usage and charges that are supplied to the users should be in terms that they under-

stand. If the users cannot understand the information, they will not be able to improve their efficiency or make adequate plans/budgets concerning future use. The type of information that is supplied to the users on usage reports should conform to their background and level of DP knowledge.

3. *Equitability.* Users should be charged only for the services they actually receive. The techniques selected to measure the use of services should provide accurate and consistent data. Equitable charges will help prevent users from becoming disgruntled at having to pay more than their fair share.

4. *Auditability.* An audit trail should be available to determine the type and quantity of the services which generated the charges. An audit trail enables the user, the DP facility, and senior management to evaluate the charging system and determine if it is calculating accurate charges.

5. *Adaptability.* The charging system must be flexible enough to respond to the constant changes typical of the environments of most DP facilities. Changes often occur in most DP facilities due to hardware, software, and other technical advances. To minimize problems when changes do occur, the charging system should be capable of responding to these changes.

6. *Cost to Operate.* Because the charging system is an important and potentially costly activity for the DP facility, the Charging Team should attempt to keep the cost of efficiently operating the charging system in line with the overall cost of operating the DP facility.

7. *Implementation.* Whenever possible and despite their complexity, charging systems should be designed and developed so that their implementation, operation, and maintenance are relatively simple. This characteristic is closely related to characteristic (6) above, since the more difficult a charging system is to implement and maintain, the more expensive its operation is likely to be.

8. *Controllability.* Controllability refers to the charging system producing charges that can be controlled by the user. If users attempt to make a program or application more efficient, then their charges should reflect their actions in a predictable manner. Variations in charges over which users have no control soon lead to frustration and prevent effective planning.

9. *Stability.* The procedures and billing rates of the charging system should be changed as infrequently as possible. When users budget for DP services, they do so based on the projected billing rates provided by the DP facility. If the DP facility changes its rates after the users' budgets have been approved, the users may not be able to complete their work within their prescribed budget limits. One approach for preventing unexpected rate changes is to set the billing rates only once during the users' budgeting period; that is, the rate period should match the budgeting period. The rates

should be kept stable during this period, unless there is a major and unexpected change in resources or services of the DP facility. Users should be adequately forewarned and encouraged to participate in decisions regarding the charging system and procedural changes via a steering committee.

10. *Simplicity.* Complexity in the method of calculating charges can confuse users, thereby causing frustration and an unwillingness to use the charging system as an aid to planning or achieving efficiency. A simple method of calculating charges will also enable the charging system to be more flexible to changes in resources and services.

11. *Easy to Use.* The charging system should be easy enough to use so that extensive training and technical knowledge are not required. A charging system that is easy to use will encourage users to participate in decisions regarding modifications and enhancements to the charging system.

12. *Provide Valuable Information.* The reports provided by the charging system should be sufficiently informative to enable users to improve their efficiency, control their costs, and determine the status of their accounts in a timely manner.

D. RECONCILE THE CHARGING SYSTEM CHARACTERISTICS

The fourth task of Step 2 is to reconcile the charging system characteristics with the DP facility characteristics and the organization's reasons for charging. The purpose of this reconciliation is to identify conflicting characteristics, characteristics that will be too expensive to incorporate, and any additional characteristics that should have been determined but were overlooked.

Step 3. Prepare the Project Plan

The final step of the planning phase is the preparation of a formal Project Plan to guide the design, development, and implementation of the charging system. Special attention should be given to the Project Plan by the Charging Team. The Plan should include (a) the decisions made on the project structure in Step 1, (b) the characteristics that were determined in Step 2, and (c) budget and work schedules for each phase, step, and task described in this appendix, and for any additional tasks added by the Charging Team.

After the Charging Team has completed the Planning Phase, senior management should review the Charging Team's results. This is the first of several major checkpoints that should be utilized by senior management to make certain that the charging system project is progressing satisfactorily.

DESIGN PHASE

During the design phase, the work performed during the planning phase is used to direct the conceptual development and general design of the charging system. The objectives of the design phase are to begin developing/modifying a DP cost accounting system to complement the charging system; establish cost distribution matrices (i.e., matrices to be used to proportion the costs of the resources to the services); and to prepare the functional requirements, data requirements, and general design documents for the charging system. These documents, along with the DP cost accounting system and the cost distribution matrices, will be used during subsequent phases to guide the detailed design, development, implementation, and operation of the rate-setting and billing subsystems. The Charging Team should perform the work during this phase. The three steps of the design phase are discussed below.

Step 4. Initiate a Data Processing Cost Accounting Project

The objective of this step is to initiate a project that will develop a new DP cost accounting system or modify the existing DP cost accounting system to provide the charging system with appropriate DP cost data. It is important for the Charging Team to understand that unless there is a good DP cost accounting system in place, it will have difficulty obtaining the cost data needed for the charging system. In many organizations the cost data, mechanisms to obtain the cost data, or both just do not exist. Therefore, without a DP cost accounting system designed specifically to collect the cost data for a charging system, the Charging Team could have great difficulty obtaining any sort of useful cost data. Consequently, the DP cost accounting system should be developed/improved prior to, or in parallel, with the charging system. This step consists of one task, to initiate a project that will design and develop a new or improved DP cost accounting system.

A. Fundamental Concepts

Before initiating the project to develop or modify a DP cost accounting system, the Charging Team should understand some general concepts about DP cost accounting and related design and developmental issues.

1. *DP Cost Accounting.* Cost accounting is that method of accounting that provides for the assembling and recording of all the elements of cost incurred to accomplish a purpose, to carry on an activity or operation, or to complete a unit of work or a specific job. A DP cost accounting system is a system by which the costs incurred by a DP facility for providing its services are monitored and recorded. When the DP facility is using a charging system, the DP cost accounting system is typically the source of the historical cost data used to forecast DP costs. The cost data forecasted for the rate period are used to determine the billing rates for the services

provided by the DP facility. Figures A-1 through A-3 provide examples of some of the data that might be kept by a DP cost accounting system. Cost accounting and accounting techniques are not necessarily as straightforward and simple as might be assumed from reading this publication. There are a variety of accounting techniques that could be used when accounting for DP costs. For more information on cost accounting, accounting techniques, and DP cost accounting systems, the Charging Team should obtain the help of a cost accountant and read the documents listed in the following section.

2. *Design and Developmental Issues for a DP Cost Accounting System.* First, since the DP cost accounting system needs to be developed prior to or in parallel with the charging system, the Charging Team should read this entire publication in detail prior to designing the DP cost accounting system. This will enable the Charging Team to determine more easily the exact data that the DP cost accounting system will have to provide for the charging system.

Second, the Charging Team should read the following documents prior to designing the DP cost accounting system: "Guidelines for Accounting for Automated Data Processing Costs;" "Guidelines for Cost Accounting Practices for Data Processing;" and "Management Guidelines for Cost Accounting and Costs Control for Automatic Data Processing Activities and Systems."

These documents and the assistance of a cost accountant should more than adequately help the Charging Team determine the specifications for the design of the DP cost accounting system.

Third, DP cost accounting systems can be designed to maintain cost data at varying levels of detail. The Charging Team needs to make certain that the DP cost accounting system maintains data at the level of detail needed by the charging system. This means that the Charging Team will need to anticipate the level of detail of charging system cost data.

Fourth, the Charging Team should survey the organization's current cost accounting capabilities and budget submission process. Most organizations have a cost accounting system that can probably be used by the DP facility with minor modifications. All possibilities should be explored prior to designing and developing a new DP cost accounting system.

Fifth, the Charging Team should strongly consider an evolutionary approach to its DP cost accounting system design, because the charging system will need accurate cost data with which to forecast costs before it can be implemented. It will probably take several years before the DP cost accounting system will be able to provide cost data with the desired accuracy. Therefore, the DP cost accounting system should be designed to provide the best data currently available. This will enable the charging system to be implemented earlier, although the charges and data provided

COST ELEMENTS / PERSONNEL	TOTAL ANNUAL COST ESTIMATE						TOTALS		
	FUNDED COSTS					UNFUNDED COSTS			
	DIRECT		INDIRECT						
	REGULAR WAGES	OVERTIME WAGES	OTHER EXPENSES (TRAINING, TRAVEL, ETC.)	FRINGE BENEFITS	MISC. COSTS	RETIREMENT ETC.	FUNDED	UNFUNDED	TOTAL
MIS OFFICE									
DATA CENTER PERSONNEL									
SYSTEMS ANALYSIS AND PROGRAMMING BRANCH									
TOTAL									

Figure A-1. Sample Cost Accounting Data for the Personnel Category.

COST ELEMENTS / EQUIPMENT AND SOFTWARE	FUNDED COSTS				UNFUNDED COSTS (DEPRECIATION)	TOTAL
	LEASE	RENTAL	MAINTENANCE	TOTAL		
EQUIPMENT						
1. PROCESSORS						
2. CORE MEMORY						
3. I/O MULTIPLEXOR						
4. DATA COMMUNICATIONS GEAR						
5. DISK DRIVES						
6. TAPE DRIVES						
7. UNIT RECORD CONT.						
8. PRINTER						
9. CARD READER/PUNCH						
10. TERMINALS						
EQUIPMENT SUBTOTAL						
SOFTWARE						
1. OPERATING SYSTEM, LANGUAGE PROCESSORS, UTILITIES, ETC.						
2. DATA BASE SOFTWARE						
3. APPLICATIONS SOFTWARE						
SOFTWARE SUBTOTAL						
TOTAL						

Figure A-2. Sample Cost Accounting Data for the Equipment and Software Categories.

COST ELEMENTS / OTHER	FUNDED			UNFUNDED (DEPRECIATION)	TOTAL
	LEASE	RENT	MAINTENANCE		
<u>SUPPLIES</u>					
1. OFFICE SUPPLIES					
2. DATA PROCESSING SUPPLIES					
3. MISCELLANEOUS EXPENSES					
<u>CONTRACTED SERVICES</u>					
1. TECHNICAL AND CONSULTING SERVICES					
2. EQUIPMENT MAINTENANCE					
3. OPERATIONS SUPPORT					
4. TELECOMMUNICATIONS NETWORK SERVICES					
<u>SPACE OCCUPANCY</u>					
1. MIS FLOOR SPACE					
2. MIS OFFICE FURNITURE					
3. UTILITIES AND MAINTENANCE					
<u>INTRA-COMPANY SERVICES AND OVERHEAD</u>					
TOTAL					

Figure A-3. Sample Cost Accounting Data for the Other Resource Categories.

by the charging system will only be as accurate as those provided by the DP cost accounting system.

Finally, one area of cost forecasting that often proves to be cumbersome is calculating the depreciation costs. Depreciation costs for both hardware and software must be incorporated into the costs to be charged out to the users. There are a number of different ways to calculate depreciation for hardware and software. *Straight-line depreciation over the management-defined useful life of the original investment is recommended.*

B. INITIATE PROJECT TO DESIGN AND DEVELOP A DP COST ACCOUNTING SYSTEM

The purpose of this task is for the Charging Team to begin a separate project to design and develop a DP cost accounting system. This project should be managed by an accountant with some DP cost accounting experience, possibly the accounting representative on the Charging Team. It is important that there be a constant flow of information between the cost accounting and charging system projects because data from the DP cost accounting system will be needed for the charging system.

It is not within the scope of this publication to provide detailed direction concerning the design and development of the DP cost accounting system. The Charging Team should obtain the direction that they need from the documentation cited earlier in this step and from the accounting department.

Step 5. Establish the Distribution Matrices

The objective of the tasks performed during this step is to develop the cost distribution matrices. The distribution matrices, which can be viewed as the nuclei of the rate-setting subsystem, are the mechanisms by which the costs of the resources are proportioned to the services. Depending on the level of detail desired, establishing the distribution matrices can be an extremely complex and time-consuming process because of the variety and number of decisions that must be made. Consequently, it is important for the Charging Team to expend considerable effort on the tasks in this step. This step consists of the following four tasks:

Define the services, service units, and service centers for the DP facility.

Define the areas of management responsibility, work functions, subfunctions, and work units.

Itemize resources and define the resource units.

Test and adjust the distribution matrices.

A. FUNDAMENTAL CONCEPTS

Before attempting to establish the distribution matrices, it is important for the Charging Team to understand

The concepts of full and partial cost allocation.
Billing rates based on expected usage.
The purposes and content of the distribution matrices.

A discussion of each of these concepts follows.

1. *Full and Partial Cost Allocation.* Full cost allocation means that all of the DP facility's costs are incorporated into the distribution matrices and charged out to the users of the DP facility. Partial cost allocation means that only a predetermined subset of the DP facility's total costs are incorporated into the distribution matrices, such as only the costs for hardware, software, and personnel. It is important that the Charging Team understand the difference between full and partial cost allocation. Organizations must account for and allocate the full cost of operation. The only reason partial cost allocation might be justifiable may be the difficulty, due to a lack of data, of using full cost allocation during the first several times the billing rates are calculated. Thus, organizations could begin with partial cost allocation in order to speed up the implementation of the charging system. As more complete data become available, organizations could begin to use full cost allocation.

2. *Billing Rates Based on Usage.* It is possible to base service billing rates on either expected service usage or service capacity. Expected usage refers to the total number of service units, for a particular service, that the Charging Team expects to be used during the rate period. Capacity refers to the total number of service units, for a particular service, available during the rate period. *It is recommended that the Charging Team base its billing rates on expected usage.*

3. *Distribution Matrices.* The purposes of the distribution matrices are to provide a mechanism that can be used (a) to proportion the costs of the resources to the subfunctions, (b) to proportion the costs of the subfunctions to the service centers, and (c) to develop a billing rate for each service of the service centers. The use of a series of matrices, instead of some other allocating mechanism, is recommended because matrices provide the clearest, easiest technique for tracking the large volume of information required to calculate the billing rate. Figures A-4 through A-6 are examples of the distribution matrices and show the major categories of information needed. Completing the three matrices is the major objective of the work that will be performed during the rate-setting phase.

The resource, subfunction, and billing rate distribution matrices contain 19 categories of information. A brief discussion of each type of information is presented below.

Area of Management Responsibility (AMR). Name of a DP facility department, managed by one individual, with responsibility for one or more work areas.

AREA OF MANAGEMENT RESPONSIBILITY	AMR1	AMR2									AMR3				
WORK FUNCTION	WF1	WF2			WF3			WF4			WF5				WF6
SUB-FUNCTION RESOURCE COST	SF1		SF2	SF3		SF4	SF5		SF6	SF7		SF8	SF9	SF10	SF11
R1 C1															
R2 C2															
R3 C3															
R4 C4															
R5 C5						$RP_{5,4}$ $RPC_{5,4}$									
R6 C6															
R7 C7															
R8 C8															
R9 C9															
R10 C10															
R11 C11															
SUBTOTAL															
WORK FUNCTION COSTS															
TOTAL	TC1		TC2	TC3		TC4	TC5		TC6	TC7		TC8	TC9	TC10	TC11

Figure A-4. Sample Resource Distribution Matrix.

SERVICE CENTER / SUBFUNCTION TOTAL COST	SC1	SC2	SC3	SC4	SC5	SC6
SF1 TC1						
SF2 TC2						
SF3 TC3		$SP_{3,2}$ $SPC_{3,2}$				
SF4 TC4						
SF5 TC5						
SF6 TC6						
SF7 TC7						
SF8 TC8						
SF9 TC9						
SF10 TC10						
SF11 TC11						
TOTAL	CSC1	CSC2	CSC3	CSC4	CSC5	CSC6

Figure A-5. Sample Subfunction Distribution Matrix.

SERVICE CENTER	SC1						SC2		SC3				SC4		SC5	SC6
SERVICE	S1	S2	S3	S4	S5	S6	S7	S8	S9	S10	S11	S12	S13	S14	S15	S16
SERVICE UNIT	SU1	SU2	SU3	SU4	SU5	SU6	SU7	SU8	SU9	SU10	SU11	SU12	SU13	SU14	SU15	SU16
COST OF SERVICE CENTER	CSC1						CSC2		CSC3				CSC4		CSC5	CSC6
SERVICE FORECAST	SF1	SF2	SF3	SF4	SF5	SF6	SF7	SF8	SF9	SF10	SF11	SF12	SF13	SF14	SF15	SF16
STANDARD-IZATION FACTORS	F1	F2	F3	F4	F5	F6	F7	F8	F9	F10	F11	F12	F13	F14	F15	F16
STANDARDIZED FORECAST	STF1						STF2		STF3				STF4		STF5	STF6
BASE RATE	B1						B2		B3				B4		B5	B6
BILLING RATE	BR1	BR2	BR3	BR4	BR5	BR6	BR7	BR8	BR9	BR10	BR11	BR12	BR13	BR14	BR15	BR16

Figure A-6. Sample Billing Rate Distribution Matrix.

Work Function (WF). The name of a work area performed by the DP facility. The work function consists of one or more subfunctions.

Subfunction (SF). The name of an area of work that is more specific than that characterized by its corresponding work function.

Resource (R). The name of the resource that will be used as the lowest level of detail to collect cost data.

Cost (C). The dollar value that the organization incurs for each itemized resource.

Resource Proportion (RP). The proportion of a resource used to support a particular subfunction.

Resource Proportion Cost (RPC). The proportionate cost of a resource used to support a particular subfunction. The resource proportion cost is calculated by multiplying the cost of a particular resource by the resource proportion for a particular subfunction; for example,

$$RPC_{N,M} = C_N * RP_{N,M}$$

where N = a particular resource
M = a particular subfunction.

Total Cost of Subfunction (TC). The total cost of performing a subfunction, calculated by summing all of the resource proportion costs; for example,

$$TC_1 = \sum_{i=1}^{N} RPC_{i,1}$$

where N = number of resources.

Service Center (SC). The name of a group of services that have been grouped for a particular purpose.

Subfunction Proportion (SP). The proportion of a subfunction used to support a particular service center.

Subfunction Proportion Cost (SPC). The proportionate cost of a subfunction used to support a particular service center. The subfunction proportion cost is calculated by multiplying the cost of a particular subfunction by the subfunction proportion for a particular service; for example,

$$SPC_{M,L} = TC_M * SP_{M,L}$$

where M = a particular subfunction.
L = a particular service center.

Cost of Service Center (CSC). The cost of providing a service center, calculated by summing all of the subfunction proportion costs; for example,

$$CSC_1 = \sum_{i=1}^{M} SPC_1$$

where M = number of subfunctions.

Service (S). Commonly used name for each service that will be offered by the DP facility.

Service Unit (SU). The name of the unit that will be used to report and bill users for utilizing a given service.

Service Forecast (SF). The number of service units projected to be used for the planning period.

Standardization Factor (F). A number chosen for a particular service such that, when it is multiplied by the service forecast, the result is a forecast expressed in standardized units.

Standardized Forecast (STF). For each Service Center, the standardized forecast is the sum of the service forecasts multiplied by their respective standardization factors; for example,

$$STF_1 = \sum_{i=1}^{N} SF_i^* F_i$$

where N = number of services in Service Center 1.

Base Rate (B). The amount that represents the cost of providing each unit of the standardized forecast. The base rate for a service center is calculated by dividing the cost of a service center by its standardized forecast; for example,

$$B_1 = \frac{CSC_1}{STF_1}$$

Billing Rate (BR). The dollar amount charged to the users for each service unit. The billing rate for a service is calculated by multiplying the base rate of its service center by its standardized factor; for example,

$$BR_1 = B_1{}^*F_1$$

To illustrate the manner in which distributions matrices should be completed, sample distribution matrices will be completed in succeeding sections of this appendix to provide the Charging Team with concrete examples of the approaches recommended in the text. As direction is provided on how to complete a specific section of the distribution matrices, the corresponding completed section of the sample distribution matrices will be illustrated. Sample distribution matrices are intended for *illustrative purposes only*; they are not recommendations for using particular resources, areas of management responsibility, work functions, subfunctions, service centers or services.

B. Determine Services, Service Units, and Service Centers

The first task in Step 5 is to determine the services and service units that the DP facility will provide to its users. The Charging Team should then group the services into service centers.

1. *Determine Services.* Determining the DP facility's services will probably be one of the most difficult tasks for the Charging Team to perform; it is also among the most important tasks, since the services form the foundation of the entire charging system. The Charging Team should remember the following principles when determining the DP facility's services.

It is best to have only one measure, one service unit, for each service.

Services and service units should be easily understood by the users.

The services should represent a significant portion of the DP facility's work.

The services should not be limited only to hardware services. Other DP services, especially personnel-based services, are often very costly and should be explicitly charged for whenever possible.

Whenever possible, services that are transaction or output based should be selected. A transaction or output based service is one which has a service unit that users can easily understand and that is closely related to the work that the user is performing. Examples of transaction or output based services are payroll, with the service unit being the number of checks printed; catalogue orders, with the service unit being the number of orders processed; and literature search, with the service unit being the number of documents searched.

The services chosen will be the basis for charging the users and are the most visible aspects of the charging system to users; therefore, they should be chosen with care. Examples of typical services are presented in the sample distribution matrices presented later in this section.

2. *Determine Service Units.* The Charging Team should consider the following when determining the service unit for each service.

There should be no more than one service unit per service. Having only one unit per service facilitates cost distribution and billing rate calculation and helps keep the charging system simple.

The service unit, like the service it measures, should be selected so that it can be easily understood by the users.

The service unit should be a good measure of the work that is supplied by the service.

The service unit should be as easy to measure accurately as possible. If the number of units consumed cannot be easily and accurately measured, then the utility of that particular unit is significantly decreased.

3. *Group Services into Service Centers.* After determining the services and service units, the Charging Team should then group the services into service centers to facilitate the distribution of costs and the calculation of

billing rates. Costs are distributed only to the level of the service center, not the service, in the distribution matrices. Consequently, revenues should be required only to balance at the service center level, not at the service level.

The Charging Team should consider the following concepts when grouping the services into service centers.

> The purpose of grouping services into service centers is (a) to permit greater management flexibility in calculating the services' billing rates and (b) to balance costs and revenues at a level more general than services. This greater management flexibility allows the Charging Team to more easily incorporate such features as priorities, normalization factors, surcharges, and discounts. Balancing costs at a higher level allows senior management to more easily manage the DP facility.
>
> The services grouped within one service center should be related in some reasonable manner. The relationship can be logical or physical. An example of a physical relationship is grouping CPU services with different priorities into a service center. These services are physically related in that they have the same type of service unit, CPU seconds. An example of a logical relationship is grouping a microfiche service and a printing service into a service center. These services are logically related in that they are both output devices, but there is no direct relationship.
>
> The relationship between services should not be forced; there should be a rational reason for grouping them. For example, it is rational for the Charging Team to group two services, place a surcharge on one and a discount on the other, in order to encourage the users to use more of one than the other. But it is not rational for the Charging Team to group two services because neither can be grouped under any other service center. If services cannot be grouped rationally under any other service center, they should be treated as a service center with one service.
>
> The magnitude of the service's billing rates can be adjusted from service to service within the same service center. But company policies require that the Charging Team must have a rational, defendable reason for doing so, and the total cost of the service center should not be over- or under-charged.
>
> The grouping of services into service centers is one area of the charging system where management can exert significant influence over the allocation of scarce resources.

4. *Review Selections.* Upon completing this task, the Charging Team should review all of the services identified in order to ensure that no services have been inadvertently omitted or unnecessarily included. The service units should also be reviewed to ensure that they satisfy all of the suggestions set forth in this document. Finally, the groupings of the services into service centers should be reviewed and validated. After reviewing the

services, service units, and service centers, the Charging Team should complete the corresponding parts of the subfunction and billing rate distribution matrices.

5. *Sample Distribution Matrices.* Sixteen sample services have been chosen and grouped into six service centers for inclusion in the sample distribution matrices. The services, their respective service units, and service centers are listed in Figure A-7. The services, service units, and service centers have been included in the sample subfunction and billing rate distribution matrices and are presented in Figures A-8 and A-9.

C. DETERMINE AREAS OF MANAGEMENT RESPONSIBILITY, WORK FUNCTIONS, SUBFUNCTIONS, AND WORK UNITS

The second task of Step 5 is to determine the areas of management responsibility (AMRs) within the DP facility, the distinct work functions within each AMR, the various subfunctions within each work function, and the work unit that is the measure of work for each subfunction.

The AMRs work functions, and subfunctions are incorporated into a charging system in order to provide senior and DP management with more

Service Center	Service	Service Unit
Processing A		
	CPU prime shift high priority	CPU second
	CPU prime shift normal priority	CPU second
	CPU prime shift low priorty	CPU second
	CPU nonprime shift high priority	CPU second
	CPU nonprime shift normal priority	CPU second
	CPU nonprime shift low priority	CPU second
Processing B		
	High-speed CPU	CPU second
	Low-speed CPU	CPU second
Application Programming		
	Senior Analyst Support	Analyst Hour
	Analyst Support	Analyst Hour
	Junior Analyst Support	Analyst Hour
	Apprentice Analyst Support	Analyst Hour
Reporting		
	Microfiche	Fiche
	Printing	Lines
DBMS		
	DBMS	Users
Payroll		
	Payroll	Checks

Figure A-7. Service centers, services, and service units for the sample distribution matrices.

SERVICE CENTER / SUBFUNCTION TOTAL COST	PROCESSING A	PROCESSING B	APPLICATIONS PROGRAMMING	REPORTING	DBMS	PAYROLL
TOTAL						

Figure A-8. Sample Subfunction Distribution Matrix with Service Centers Added.

SERVICE CENTER	PROCESSING A						PROCESSING B		APPLICATIONS PROGRAMMING				REPORTING		DBMS	PAY-ROLL
SERVICE	PRIME HIGH	PRIME NORMAL	PRIME LOW	NON-PRIME HIGH	NON-PRIME NORMAL	NON-PRIME LOW	HIGH SPEED	LOW SPEED	SENIOR ANALYST	ANALYST	JUNIOR ANALYST	APPREN. ANALYST	MICRO-FICHE	PRINT-ING		
SERVICE UNIT	SECONDS	SECONDS	SECONDS	SECONDS	SECONDS	SECONDS	SECONDS	SECONDS	HOUR	HOUR	HOUR	HOUR	FICHE	1000 LINES	USERS	CHECKS
COST OF SERVICE CENTER																
SERVICE FORECAST																
STANDARD-IZATION FACTORS																
STANDARDIZED FORECAST																
BASE RATE																
BILLING RATE																

Figure A-9. Sample Billing Rate Distribution Matrix with Service Centers, Services, and Service Units Added.

information on the costs and revenues of the DP facility so that they can better manage. Therefore, it is extremely important that the Charging Team include these three work categories as part of the charging system. Senior and DP management should take an active role in determining the AMRs work function, and the subfunctions in order to obtain the types of information that they need.

1. *Determine Areas of Management Responsibility.* The Charging Team should consider the following concepts when determining the areas of management responsibility for the charging system.

An AMR should be an area of work in the DP facility that is managed by one individual.

To ensure that the individual in charge of an AMR is conscious of and responsible for the costs incurred within his/her area of control, costs should be accounted for and reported by the AMR.

The individual in charge of an AMR will need to be provided with information for planning and control, so that costs can, where possible, be related to decisions.

Revenue from billing for service usage may be calculated for each AMR and compared to the AMRs cost in order to help evaluate management performance.

Whenever possible, AMRs should be selected to correspond to the existing management structure within the DP facility.

2. *Determine Work Functions.* After determining the AMRs for the charging system, the Charging Team should determine the work functions performed by the DP facility in each AMR. Several reasons require that costs be grouped by work functions.

To permit an evaluation of the efficiency of performing specific operations and comparison of the costs of functions that can be accomplished in more than one way or by more than one source.

To provide a means of isolating costs for similar activities and work processes which have a common unit for measuring resource consumption.

To segregate the costs of the DP facility into different work functions for effective management of the DP facility.

The Charging Team should consider the following when determining work functions.

Work functions can be either product-oriented or support-oriented. Product-oriented work functions are those for which the output can be traced directly to the services offered to the DP facility's users. Support-oriented work functions are those upon which product-oriented work functions rely for certain services and skills. For example, I/O is a product-oriented work function if the DP facility provides various I/O services to its users, while administration is a support-oriented work function.

Work functions should be established both for computer processing and for software activities. Software work functions should include maintenance and development activities.

A work function should not be spread between two AMRs. If the Charging Team determines that one or more work functions are spread between two AMRs and cannot be logically separated into two work functions, then the Charging Team should consider restructuring the AMRs to encompass distinct work functions.

3. *Determine Subfunctions.* Once the Charging Team has determined the work functions of the charging system, it should next determine whether or not each work function can be further divided into subfunctions. The reasons for dividing work functions into subfunctions are:

To provide an additional level of cost information to senior and DP management.

To facilitate distribution of the costs of the work functions to the services provided by the DP facility.

The Charging Team should consider the following concepts when dividing the work functions into subfunctions.

Each subfunction should be chosen so that a single measure can be used to represent the work of the subfunction.

There should be a rational reason for dividing the work functions into subfunctions.

If a work function cannot be divided into two or more subfunctions, it should be treated as having only one subfunction.

4. *Determine Work Units.* The last thing that the Charging Team should do in this task is to determine a work unit for each subfunction. These work units will be used by the Charging Team to facilitate distribution of the costs of the subfunctions to the service centers in the distribution matrices. The Charging Team should consider the following concepts when determining the work units.

Each subfunction should have only one work unit.

The work unit should be a good measure of the major type of work performed in the subfunction.

The work unit should be easy to measure accurately. If the number of work units performed cannot be easily and accurately measured, the utility of that particular unit is significantly decreased.

5. *Review Selections.* Upon completing this task, the Charging Team should review all of the AMRs work functions, and subfunctions previously determined in order to ensure that no work area has been inadvertently omitted or unnecessarily included. The work units should also be reviewed to ensure that they satisfy all of the suggestions set forth in this appendix. After reviewing the AMRs work functions, subfunctions and work units, the Charging Team should complete the corresponding parts of the resource and subfunction distribution matrices.

6. *Sample Distribution Matrices.* For illustrative purposes, three AMRs, six work functions, and 11 subfunctions have been chosen and are listed in Figure A-10. The sample resource and subfunction distribution matrices have been completed with these AMRs work functions, and subfunctions and are presented in Figures A-11 and A-12.

D. ITEMIZE RESOURCES AND DETERMINE RESOURCE UNITS

The third task of Step 5 is to list in detail the resources that the DP facility uses to provide its services and to determine the resource units that can be used to facilitate distribution of the costs of the resources to the work functions and subfunctions.

Area of Management Responsibility	Work Function	Subfunction
Administration	DP Administration	DP Administration
Computer Processing Operations	Computer Operations	CPU Storage Devices
	Reporting	Microfiche Printing
	Technical Support	Data Base Management Equipment Management
Software Development Maintenance	Software Development	Applications Software Analysis and Design Coding and Testing
	User Liaison	User Liaison

***Figure A-10.** Areas of management responsibility, work functions, and subfunctions for the sample distribution matrices.*

AREA OF MANAGEMENT RESPONSIBILITY / WORK FUNCTION / SUB-FUNCTION / RESOURCE COST	ADMIN.	COMPUTER PROCESSING OPERATIONS									SOFTWARE DEVELOPMENT AND MAINTENANCE				
	DP ADMIN.	COMPUTER OPERATIONS			REPORTING			TECHNICAL SUPPORT			SOFTWARE DEVELOPMENT				USER LIAISON
			C. P. U.	STORAGE DEVICES		MICROFICHE	PRINTING		DATA BASE MANAGEMENT	EQUIPMENT MAINTENANCE		APPLICATIONS SOFTWARE	ANALYSIS AND DESIGN	CODING AND TESTING	
SUBTOTAL															
WORK FUNCTION COSTS															
TOTAL															

Figure A-11. Sample Resource Distribution Matrix with Areas of Management Reponsibility, Work Functions, and Subfunctions Added.

SERVICE CENTER / SUBFUNCTION TOTAL COST	PROCESSING A	PROCESSING B	APPLICATIONS PROGRAMMING	REPORTING	DBMS	PAYROLL
ADMINISTRATION						
C. P. U.						
STORAGE DEVICES						
MICROFICHE						
PRINTING						
DATA BASE MANAGEMENT						
EQUIPMENT MAINTENANCE						
APPLICATIONS SOFTWARE						
ANALYSIS AND DESIGN						
CODING AND TESTING						
USER LIAISON						
TOTAL						

Figure A-12. Sample Subfunction Distribution Matrix with Subfunctions Added.

1. *Itemize Resources.* The Charging Team should consider the following concepts when itemizing the resources.

The resources should be listed by specific categories.

The resources should be as detailed as possible, since a cost will have to be forecast for each resource listed. For example, when a computer system is leased, the various components (e.g., tape and disk drives) should be listed separately if the cost for each can be forecasted. If the costs for the various components cannot be forecasted separately, the computer system should be listed as one resource.

For every resource listed, a corresponding entry should appear in the new/modified DP cost accounting system discussed in Step 4.

2. *Determine Resource Units.* After the Charging Team has itemized the resources of the DP facility, it should determine a resource unit for each resource. These resource units will be used by the Charging Team to facilitate distribution of the costs of the resources to the work functions and subfunctions. The Charging Team should consider the following concepts when determining the resource units.

Each resource should have only one unit associated with it.

The resource unit should be a good measure of the work performed by the resource.

The resource unit should be easy to measure accurately. If the number of resource units consumed cannot be easily and accurately measured, the utility of that unit is significantly decreased.

3. *Review Selections.* Upon completing this task, the Charging Team should review all of the resources that have been listed to ensure that all resources have been included at the appropriate level of detail. After completing this review, the Charging Team should list the resources in the resource distribution matrix.

4. *Sample Distribution Matrices.* Eleven resources have been selected for illustration and included in the sample resource distribution matrix, as shown in Figure A-13.

E. TEST AND ADJUST THE DISTRIBUTION MATRICES.

The fourth task of Step 5 is to test and adjust the distribution matrices. When the actual resource and subfunction proportions are determined during the rate-setting phase, the Charging Team's work will be facilitated if the resources have a clear relationship to the subfunctions and the subfunctions have a clear relationship to the service centers. These relationships consist of being able to identify how much of each resource is used to support each subfunction and how much of each subfunction is used to provide each service center. The purposes of this task are (1) to identify any vague relationships between the resources and subfunctions or the subfunctions and service centers and (2) to attempt to clarify the relationship, if possible.

The best technique to use in identifying vague relationships is to estimate (1) the resource proportions for each resource across subfunctions and (2) subfunctions proportions for each subfunction across service centers. These estimates should be performed mentally with the objective of identifying obvious vague relationships. Once the vague relationships have been identified, they should be clarified by redefining the particular resources or subfunctions. Resources can be bundled together or unbundled into more detailed resources. Subfunctions can be grouped back into work functions or separated.

The testing and adjusting of the distribution matrices should not be a time-consuming process but should serve as a checkpoint for the Charging Team to identify and correct potential problems. The Charging Team should view this task as such and realize that problems that are missed now can be corrected later.

Step 6. Design the Charging System

The distribution matrices established in Step 5 provide the framework for designing the charging system. During Step 6, the distribution matrices are used to define the charging system's functional and data requirements, to explore alternative techniques for satisfying these requirements, and to prepare the charging system's general design. The tasks in Step 6 may result in the need to reevaluate and revise the distribution matrices and the characteristics and objectives established in earlier tasks.

Three documents are produced during Step 6: the Functional Requirements, the Data Requirements, and the General System Design. Most organizations have guidelines or standards which prescribe the format, content, and approach to be used. Additional guidance is contained in FIPS Publications (FIPS PUBS) 38 and 64 as well as in numerous other industry publications. Because of the availability of guidance in these areas, the discussion in this step will focus on the underlying charging system concepts that the Charging Team should address.

The documents that will be produced during this step should be viewed as undergoing an evolutionary process of refinement during subsequent steps. The Charging Team should produce the documents after considering the needs and expertise of the intended audiences and the flexibility needed for revisions. These documents will provide the blueprint for the detailed design and development of the charging system. This step consists of four tasks:

Define functional requirements.

Define data requirements.

AREA OF MANAGEMENT RESPONSIBILITY	ADMIN.	COMPUTER PROCESSING OPERATIONS									SOFTWARE DEVELOPMENT AND MAINTENANCE				
WORK FUNCTION	DP ADMIN.	COMPUTER OPERATIONS			REPORTING			TECHNICAL SUPPORT			SOFTWARE DEVELOPMENT				USER LIAISON
SUB-FUNCTION / RESOURCE / COST			C. P. U.	STORAGE DEVICES		MICROFICHE	PRINTING		DATA BASE MANAGEMENT	EQUIPMENT MAINTENANCE		APPLICATIONS SOFTWARE	ANALYSIS AND DESIGN	CODING AND TESTING	
MANAGEMENT $300,000															
ANALYSTS $600,000															
COMPUTER A $150,000															
COMPUTER B $100,000															
PRINTERS $40,000															
MICROFICHE CAMERA $10,000															
DBMS $15,000															
PAYROLL SOFTWARE $10,000															
MICROFICHE $20,000															
COMPUTER PAPER $25,000															
SPACE OCCUPANCY $150,000															
SUBTOTAL															
WORK FUNCTION COSTS															
TOTAL															

Figure A-13. Sample Resource Distribution Matrix with Resources Added.

Explore alternative techniques for satisfying the requirements.

Prepare the charging system's general design.

A. FUNDAMENTAL CONCEPTS

Prior to producing the design documents, the Charging Team needs to understand the difference between the methods of actual and standard cost distribution and to incorporate one of the two into the charging system's general design.

1. *Actual Cost Distribution.* The actual cost distribution method attempts to reduce the chance of over- or underdistributing costs to users by periodically adjusting billing rates. This periodic adjustment is performed as often as necessary to reflect both the actual cost of providing services and the actual usage levels. When the recalculations are performed, they are based upon the last rate period's usage and costs, as well as on the projected usage and costs for the upcoming rate period. These adjustments allow the DP facility to report (i.e., bill) all of its actual costs. Since this method provides billing rates that more accurately reflect costs, it can supply valuable information for accurate project costing, cost-benefit analyses, and management/project efficiency evaluation.

The major disadvantage to the actual cost method is that the billing rates change frequently. This constant fluctuation in the billing rates can cause budgeting problems for users. Another disadvantage is the tendency for underutilization of the DP facility. If utilization falls off, billing rates will increase to compensate. As the billing rates increase, utilization often may decrease further, precipitating a vicious circle of decreasing utilization and increasing billing rates. Still another disadvantage is the problem of implementing new resources. For example, initial usage of new hardware is typically low, necessitating high billing rates. High billing rates may prevent increased utilization. When utilization does increase, the billing rates decrease, resulting in higher demand when least needed. One solution to these disadvantages is to increase the time between billing rate adjustments. When billing rates are held constant for a long period of time, the distribution method is referred to as standard cost distribution.

2. *Standard Cost Distribution.* Standard cost distribution calls for the development of a set of billing rates for a fixed (reasonably long) period of time (rate period). During this period, billing rates do not fluctuate unless there is a major, unexpected change in the DP facility and/or the level of service utilization. The major advantages of the standard cost distribution are that:

Variances between actual and recovered costs can be analyzed at the end of the rate period.

Rates will not rise during short periods of low utilization.

The fixed billing rates enable users to plan better and adhere to their DP budgets.

The disadvantages are that:

Billing rates will not always reflect the current cost of providing service.

Fewer opportunities exist to effect resource utilization via the billing rates, especially if demand exceeds available capacity.

Users of the DP facility may be over- or undercharged.

The Charging Team's decision on which allocation method to use will have the primary effect of determining the frequency with which billing rates will be recalculated. *The Charging Team should select the standard cost, versus the actual cost, distribution method unless extenuating circumstances dictate otherwise.* The primary reason for this recommendation is that standard cost distribution will make the charging system easier to operate and more helpful to both management and users. It is important that the Charging Team make its final decision before completing the design documents discussed in this step.

B. DEFINE THE FUNCTIONAL REQUIREMENTS

The first task in Step 6 is to define the functional requirements of the charging system. The definition of the charging system's functional requirements began in Step 4 and 5 with the establishment of the DP cost accounting system and the distribution matrices. The functional requirements document is a description of proposed methods for operating the charging system. The requirements that must be analyzed and specified include:

The desired performance criteria of the subsystem procedures.

The inputs, processes, and outputs for each procedure.

The operating environment.

Steps 7 through 14 describe many of the performance criteria, inputs, processes, and outputs for each procedure of the rate-setting and billing subsystems. The operating environment, the DP facility's organizational and operational structure, should be described by listing such things as the administrative structure, security and privacy requirements, and backup and operational controls.

C. DEFINE THE DATA REQUIREMENTS

The second task in Step 6 is to define the data requirements of the charging system. There are two categories of data in any system, static data and dynamic data. Static data refers to data used during the operation of the system but updated or maintained independently of the system's operation schedule. Dynamic data refers to data which are updated during the system's normal operation. The Charging Team should identify all of the static and dynamic data of the charging system and list them in the Data Requirements document.

Static data are important to the charging system in that they form the basis upon which the dynamic data are monitored, collected, and used to operate the charging system. Examples of static data in a charging system are the lists of user identifiers and the accounting codes that are used to track costs.

It is important for the Charging Team to consider all types of dynamic data when defining the data requirements of the charging system, because the charging system's operation revolves around the monitoring and collection of the different types of data. There are four main types of dynamic data for a charging system: cost, resource unit, work unit, and service unit data.

The Charging Team should attempt to "look ahead" in the developmental process, as well as "look behind," when producing the Data Requirements document, since existing technical and operational constraints can limit the ability to collect certain types of data. These constraints need to be identified so that the techniques requiring the respective data can be modified. For example, if the Charging Team desired to charge users based on the length of time their programs were in real memory, but that data could not presently be monitored and collected, a different service unit would have to be selected or new monitoring techniques established.

D. Explore Alternative Techniques for Satisfying Requirements

The third task of Step 6 is to explore alternative techniques for satisfying the functional and data requirements of the charging system. The general design of the charging system should be based on an analysis of alternative techniques for satisfying these requirements. The four major decisions that the Charging Team will have to make during this task are whether to:

Use existing techniques or new techniques.

Centralize or decentralize the charging system.

Use manual techniques or automated techniques.

Purchase needed software or develop it in-house.

The Charging Team will have to make these four decisions for each procedure in the rate-setting and billing subsystems.

The discussion below provides examples of the issues that must be considered for each of the four decisions. Evaluation of which decision is best should include brief feasibility and cost-benefit analyses. The choices made while exploring the alternatives of each decision may affect the requirements and objectives defined earlier. The Project Plan, the Functional Requirements document, and the Data Requirements document should be modified or refined, as appropriate, to reflect the choices made for each decision. Also, the choices made for each decision will seldom be limited to the extremes presented below; instead, most requirements will probably be satisfied by using a combination of the alternatives.

1. *Existing Versus New Techniques.* Most organizations have existing techniques capable of satisfying many requirements for the charging system. Even if the DP facility has never charged for its services, many data requirements could be satisfied by using existing cost accounting systems, usage accounting techniques, and historical data routinely collected for accounting, budgeting, and capacity planning purposes. Most computers have measurements software which can be used for monitoring machine-based resource, subfunction, and service usage. Existing techniques and data should be used when appropriate, although many procedures will require that new techniques be developed. For example, usage accounting systems are frequently inadequate for personnel-based systems if the DP facility has not previously charged for its services. Time sheets may have to be modified to allow personnel to associate the work they do with a particular user, user account, or project.

2. *Centralized Versus Decentralized Charging System.* The second decision the Charging Team should make is the choice between a centralized or decentralized charging system. An organization may operate numerous DP facilities or have remote processing or job entry stations that are linked to a central facility. For example, an organization may operate two DP facilities and permit users in many locations to employ either facility via remote job entry. The organization may prefer to centralize the rate-setting procedures of the charging system by establishing an organization-wide billing rate schedule that is applied to the DP services at both facilities. In this example, usage accounting could be decentralized and all other procedures centralized. If the two DP facilities operate different types of computer equipment, billing rates may have to be normalized so that charges for a job run at either facility would be equal. Conversely, the organization may prefer to use different charging systems and billing rates for each DP facility and decentralize all of the procedures. The choices between centralized and decentralized procedures and subsystems are heavily influenced by the DP facility's mode of operations and management policies.

3. *Manual Versus Automated Techniques.* The procedures of the charging system can be manual, automated, or a combination of both. Typically, the rate-setting procedures are manual and the billing procedures (except cost recovery) are automated. For example, the usage forecasting procedure may incorporate manual user surveys and data from automated

systems, such as measurement software, both of which can be analyzed using an automated statisical package. Each procedure should be evaluated to determine the degree of automation required to satisfy the objectives and requirements established earlier.

4. *Purchased Software Versus In-House Developed.* The fourth decision to be made is whether to develop needed software in-house or to purchase the software from commercial sources. Most organizations will find it feasible to adapt software provided by vendors or other DP facilities, if available, to avoid the costs and risks of in-house development. Usage accounting for machine-based resources, subfunctions, or services is the best example of the potential risks, complexity, and expense of in-house development. Most computer operating systems have measurement software that is used for capacity planning and performance measurement. These capabilities are difficult to develop in-house because of the need to modify operating systems. Another example is the reporting procedure, which requires software that is typically available from vendors or other sources.

E. PREPARE THE GENERAL DESIGN DOCUMENT FOR THE CHARGING SYSTEM

The fourth task of Step 6 is to prepare the charging system's general design. Once the alternative techniques have been explored and the choices for the four decisions selected, the charging system requirements should be refined. The refined requirements are then used to prepare the charging system General Design document.

The general design should include a description of the flow of information among procedures and a definition of the individual who is reponsible for each procedure. The General Design document is used as a blueprint by the Charging Team for the detailed design, development, and implemetation of each procedure during subsequent phases.

The General Design document should be used as a second major checkpoint by senior management to determine the progress of the charging system development project. It is important that senior management ensure that their objectives for the charging system are satisfied before permitting the project to proceed to the next phase.

RATE-SETTING PHASE

The next four steps focus on developing and implementing the procedures of the rate-setting subsystem. These procedures will need to be performed each time the billing rates are (re)set; that is, at the end of every rate period. The Charging Team should remember the following points as it develops the four steps of this phase.

This assumes that most of the techniques developed in this phase are not new to the Charging Team; however, it may be the first time that the Charging Team has encountered these techniques in the context of DP charging.

Many of the techniques may already be in place.

Each organization should expand or modify the steps and tasks in this phase in order to meet its own particular charging system objectives and requirements.

Step 7. Forecast Usage

This step discusses usage forecasting techniques as they relate to the charging system and is concerned with the usage of services, subfunctions, and resources. The Charging Team will need to forecast the usage of services, subfunctions, and resources in order to calculate the billing rates. The tasks in this step will show the Charging Team how to develop and implement the usage forecasting procedure. Each task is structured around the following four assumptions:

The Charging Team is familiar with the DP facility's current forecasting techniques and has access to historical usage forecasts and data.

Expertise in usage forecasting techniques is available or can be acquired.

The expertise is available to translate the forecasted service usage into forecasted subfunction and resource usage.

The values for the resource units, work units, and service units that are needed throughout the rate-setting phase are typically obtained from the usage accounting procedure. When developing the charging system for the first time the Charging Team should obtain the values from whatever data it has available.

This step consists of three tasks:

Collecting and analyzing usage forecasting data for services, subfunctions, and resources.

Determining and resolving discrepancies between the forecasted service usage and the current resource capacity.

Reevaluating the distribution matrices.

A. Collect and Analyze Usage Forecasting Data

The first task in Step 7 is to collect and analyze service, subfunction, and resource usage data. Collecting the data entails surveying the users, validating the users' responses, collecting the current rate period's usage accounting data, retrieving all pertinent historical usage accounting data, and readying the data for analysis. Whenever possible, the data should be collected in terms of the service, work, and resource units defined in the distribution matrices. After the Charging Team has collected the data, the data should be analyzed using regression and trend analysis techniques, and the results described in terms of service, work, and resource units. The results should provide a projection of the amount of usage for each service in the distribution matrices, the data needed to determine the resource proportions for each subfunction, and the data needed to determine the subfunction proportions for each service center. It is not within the scope of this paper to present a thorough description of workload forecasting techniques; therefore, the reader is encouraged to consult the relevant literature, organization capacity planners, and/or outside experts, as appropriate, to obtain an understanding of how to forecast and how to use the forecasts once they are available.

B. Determine and Resolve Discrepancies Between Capacity and Usage

The second task in Step 7 is to determine and resolve discrepancies between available capacity and forecasted usage. After the Charging Team has analyzed the usage data, it should work with the DP facility's capacity planner(s) to compare forecasted usage with available service and resource capacity. It is possible that the usage forecasts will have to be reanalyzed or translated into units that can be used to plan capacity. Discrepancies occur if the forecasted usage exceeds available service, subfunction, or resource capacity.

If the Charging Team determines that there are discrepancies between the forecasted usage and available capacity, then it must resolve the discrepancies. There are three possible resolutions if the forecasted usage exceeds the capacity:

More resources can be acquired to increase the capacity of the DP facility.

The extra work can be sent to another DP facility.

The projected usage can be cut back.

If projected usage is below available capacity, there are three possible resolutions:

Reduce capacity of the services and resources for which usage is unacceptably low. This should only be done if a trend of declining usage has continued for a long period and if the DP facility is incurring a substantial cost for the excess capacity.

Assume that usage has temporarily declined and will pick up later, and leave capacity unchanged.

Share the excess capacity with other organizations.

Regardless of the actions taken, declining usage should be monitored very closely, because it could indicate an operating deficiency in the DP facility. Operating deficiencies can range from not offering competitive rates to providing unacceptable levels of services. The decisions required to resolve discrepancies may require extensive interaction with, and compromises among, all of the DP facility's users. The Charging Team should be responsible for organizing meetings where the proper interactions can take place.

C. REEVALUATE THE DISTRIBUTION MATRIX

The third task in Step 7 is to reevaluate the distribution matrices. The Charging Team should reevaluate the distribution matrices at this point if services, subfunctions, or resources are to be added or removed as a result of the capacity planning and resolution efforts. If new services are to be offered, new subfunctions created, or new resources acquired, they will have to be incorporated into the distribution matrices, necessitating a restructuring of the matrices. If any of the three are added, it is very likely that additional usage forecasting will be needed. The removal or elimination of existing services, subfunctions, or resources could also necessitate a similar restructuring. If service, subfunctions, or resources are removed from the distribution matrices, usage forecasts may need to be modified to reflect both the loss of the services, subfunctions, or resources as well as any resulting increase in other services, subfunctions, or resources.

Once the Charging Team has reevaluated the distribution matrices, it should complete the row for service forecasts of the billing rate distribution matrix.

D. SAMPLE DISTRIBUTION MATRICES

The service forecast row has been completed for the sample billing rate distribution matrix and is presented in Figure A-14.

Step 8. Forecast Costs

This step discusses cost forecasting techniques as they relate to the charging system and involves projecting the costs of the resources for the rate period. The Charging Team will be developing and implementing the cost forecasting procedure of the rate-setting subsystem in this step. It is important that the Charging Team forecast the costs of the resources for the same time period for which usage was forecast; otherwise, the base rates will be inequitable. Cost forecasts are used in conjunction with usage forecasts to calculate the base rates. The discussion in this step assumes that the DP cost accounting system discussed in Step 4 has been designed and developed.

Prior to performing the tasks in this step, the Charging Team must determine whether or not salaries should be included as part of the costs of operating the DP facility. There are certain limitations on the transferral of salaries and the Charging Team should determine what its organization's policies are. This step consists of three tasks:

SERVICE CENTER	PROCESSING A						PROCESSING B		APPLICATIONS PROGRAMMING				REPORTING		DBMS	PAY-ROLL
SERVICE	PRIME HIGH	PRIME NORMAL	PRIME LOW	NON-PRIME HIGH	NON-PRIME NORMAL	NON-PRIME LOW	HIGH SPEED	LOW SPEED	SENIOR ANALYST	ANALYST	JUNIOR ANALYST	APPREN. ANALYST	MICRO-FICHE	PRINT-ING		
SERVICE UNIT	SECONDS	SECONDS	SECONDS	SECONDS	SECONDS	SECONDS	SECONDS	SECONDS	HOUR	HOUR	HOUR	HOUR	FICHE	1000 LINES	USERS	CHECKS
COST OF SERVICE CENTER																
SERVICE FORECAST	500,000	6,000,000	2,500,000	1,500,000	1,000,000	500,000	4,000,000	4,000,000	9,000	15,000	3,000	3,000	80,000	30,000	100	70,000
STANDARD-IZATION FACTORS																
STANDARDIZED FORECAST																
BASE RATE																
BILLING RATE																

Figure A-14. Sample Billing Rate Distribution Matrix with Service Forecasts Added.

Obtain or establish a trial budget for the DP facility.

Collect and analyze the cost forecasting data.

Reevaluate and update the distribution matrices.

A. Obtain or Establish a Trial Budget

The first task in Step 8 is to obtain or establish a trial budget for the DP facility. The trial budget is generally available and can be used to offset deficiencies in the DP cost data when first calculating the billing rates. As a basis for forecasting costs, the Charging Team can obtain estimates of resource costs for the rate period from the trial budget and can use these estimates to supplement the data from the DP cost accounting system. The data obtained from the trial budget will have to be adjusted to reflect any changes resulting from resolving the discrepancies between capacity and usage in Step 7. The adjusted data should form the basis for both the DP facility's budget request and for cost forecasting. It is very important for senior management and the budget representative of the Charging Team to be involved if a trial budget needs to be established.

B. Collect and Analyze Cost Forecasting Data

The second task in Step 8 is to collect and analyze cost forecasting data. The Charging Team should collect the data needed for cost forecasting, including the trial budget, the usage forecasts, and the DP cost accounting system data. Whenever possible, the data should be collected at the same level of detail as used in the distribution matrices and for the same rate period for which usage forecasts were prepared. After the Charging Team has collected the cost data, it must analyze the data either manually or by using automated statistical analysis techniques. The analysis should include itemizing and categorizing the data for the appropriate resources. The results of the analysis should provide estimates of the costs for each resource listed in the distribution matrices. The next task will discuss what the Charging Team should do if costs cannot be calculated for some of the resources.

C. Reevaluate and Update the Distribution Matrices

The third task in Step 8 is to reevaluate and update the distribution matrices. Once the Charging Team has analyzed the cost data, the resources for which costs could not be calculated must be reevaluated or removed from the distribution matrices. A problem that typically occurs is the inability to reduce the cost data to the appropriate level of detail. When this occurs, the distribution matrices should be restructured by grouping the resources, whose costs are difficult to itemize, with other related resources.

Once the Charging Team has reevaluated the distribution matrices, it should complete the section for resource costs in the resource distribution matrix.

D. Sample Distribution Matrices

The resource cost section has been completed for the sample resource distribution matrix and is presented in Figure A-15.

Step 9. Calculate Billing Rates

This step discusses calculating the billing rates for the charging system. Billing rates are one of the most visible parts of the charging system to the users and can have a profound influence on them. Thus, the Charging Team should ensure that all of the information obtained from prior steps is as accurate as possible before beginning this step. The objective of the tasks in this step is to calculate the billing rates by using the cost and usage forecasts collected in Steps 7 and 8. This step consists of four tasks.

Determine the resource proportions and resource proportion costs.

Determine the subfunction proportions and proportion costs.

Calculate the base rates.

Calculate the billing rates.

A. Determine the Resource Proportions and Proportion Costs

A resource proportion is the percentage of a resource that is used to support a particular subfunction. A resource proportion cost is that cost that the DP facility incurs for utilizing a resource to support a particular subfunction. The resource proportion cost is calculated by multiplying the cost of the resource by the resource proportion. It is important that the Charging Team use care in determining the resource proportions, since they will form the basis for distributing the cost of each resource to each subfunction and, ultimately, to each service center. To determine the resource proportions and proportion costs, the Charging Team must:

Separate the resources into three categories: direct, indirect, and overhead.

Use the resource usage data to determine the proportions and proportion costs for the resources in the direct category.

Determine the proportions and proportion costs for the resources in the indirect category.

Determine the proportions and proportion costs for the resources in the overhead category.

Determine the subfunction costs.

1. *Separate the Resources into Direct, Indirect, and Overhead Categories.* The differentiation between direct, indirect, and overhead resources is an important distinction that the Charging Team must make. A direct resource is one that is associated with one or more subfunctions

AREA OF MANAGEMENT RESPONSIBILITY	ADMIN.	COMPUTER PROCESSING OPERATIONS									SOFTWARE DEVELOPMENT AND MAINTENANCE				
WORK FUNCTION	DP ADMIN.	COMPUTER OPERATIONS			REPORTING			TECHNICAL SUPPORT			SOFTWARE DEVELOPMENT				USER LIAISON
SUB-FUNCTION / RESOURCE COST			C. P. U.	STORAGE DEVICES		MICROFICHE	PRINTING		DATA BASE MANAGEMENT	EQUIPMENT MAINTENANCE		APPLICATIONS SOFTWARE	ANALYSIS AND DESIGN	CODING AND TESTING	
MANAGEMENT															
ANALYSTS															
COMPUTER A															
COMPUTER B															
PRINTERS															
MICROFICHE CAMERA															
DBMS															
PAYROLL SOFTWARE															
MICROFICHE															
COMPUTER PAPER															
SPACE OCCUPANCY															
SUBTOTAL															
WORK FUNCTION COSTS															
TOTAL															

Figure A-15. Sample Resource Distribution Matrix with Costs of Resources Added.

because of a distinct logical and measurable relationship between them. Computer equipment and application programmers are typically categorized as direct resources. An indirect resource is one that is associated with one or more subfunctions because there is a logical, but not readily measurable, relationship between them. Space is typically categorized as an indirect resource. An overhead resource is one that is associated with all of the subfunctions by management fiat because there is neither a logical nor measurable relationship between them. Management personnel are typically categorized as overhead resources. The Charging Team should categorize every resource as either direct, indirect, or overhead. This process is not as easy as it may seem at first glance, so the Charging Team should proceed with caution and allow sufficient time to perform it.

2. *Determine the Resource Proportions for the Direct Resources.* The Charging Team should determine the proportions and proportion costs of the resources in the direct category prior to those in the indirect and overhead categories.

To determine the resource proportions, the Charging Team should use the resource usage data forecast in Step 7 and its own experience and judgment. The value of resource proportions can vary from 0.00 to 1.00, but the sum of the proportions across subfunctions should never exceed 1.00. For example, consider the Computer A resource in the sample distribution matrices. Assume that the resource usage data and the Charging Team's experience indicates that this resource is used approximately 80 percent of the time to support the CPU subfunction, approximately 10 percent of the time to support the Storage Device subfunction, approximately 10 percent of the time to support the Microfiche subfunction, and is never used to support any of the other subfunctions. Then the resource proportions for this resource would be 0.80, 0.10, and 0.10 for the three subfunctions mentioned, and 0.00 for the rest of the subfunctions.

The above example illustrates an important concept that the Charging Team should remember when determining the resource proportions: when a resource is used to support more than one subfunction, excessive cost and time should not be expended trying to determine the exact value of the resource proportion. If the data are available to determine the proportions exactly, then the Charging Team should calculate them. But, if the data are not available, then the Charging Team must use its experience and judgment to determine the proportions. The Charging Team should take steps to collect additional resource usage data, for calculating the resource proportions more exactly, only if it feels the added information is worth the cost of collecting the data.

After determining the resource proportions, the Charging Team should next calculate the resource proportion costs. Continuing with the above example, the Charging Team should multiply each resource proportion by the cost of the Computer A resource, $150,000, to find its proportionate cost. This calculation would yield $120,000, $15,000, and $15,000 for the CPU, Storgage Device, and Microfiche subfunctions, respectively.

After determining all of the resource proportions and calculating the resource proportion costs for the resources in the direct category, the Charging Team should complete the appropriate parts of the resource distribution matrix.

The sample resource distribution matrix with the above example completed is presented in Figure A-16, while Figure A-17 illustrates the sample resource distribution matrix with all of the resource proportions and proportion costs completed for the direct resources.

3. *Determine the Resource Proportions for the Indirect Resources.* The Charging Team should next determine the proportions and proportion costs for the resources in the indirect category. When determining the resource proportions for the indirect category, the Charging Team should use whatever resource usage data are available and its experience and judgment to assist in the process. One problem that the Charging Team may have in this process is that it is often difficult to determine a resource proportion value for a small subfunction. *When this situation arises, the Charging Team should group appropriate cost under the parent work function.* The work function's costs can then be distributed to its subfunctions later, after all of the resource costs have been distributed.

The following example from the sample distribution matrices should help clarify the above process. Of the 11 resources in the sample distribution matrices, only Space Occupancy has been categorized as an indirect resource. It has been determined, based on square foot measurements, that the space is used by the work functions and subfunctions according to the following percentages:

5 percent by the DP Administration work function.

30 percent by the CPU subfunction.

10 percent by the Storage Devices subfunction.

10 percent by the Microfiche and Printing subfunctions. The actual breakdown could not be determined, therefore the percentage was grouped under the Reporting work function.

5 percent by the Equipment Maintenance subfunction.

5 percent by the Technical Support work function. The proportion could not be divided between the Data Base Management and Equipment Maintenance subfunction.

30 percent by the Software Development work function. The proportion could not be divided between the Application Software, Analysis and Design, and Coding and Testing subfunctions.

5 percent by the User Liaison work function.

AREA OF MANAGEMENT RESPONSIBILITY	ADMIN.	COMPUTER PROCESSING OPERATIONS									SOFTWARE DEVELOPMENT AND MAINTENANCE				
WORK FUNCTION	DP ADMIN.	COMPUTER OPERATIONS			REPORTING			TECHNICAL SUPPORT			SOFTWARE DEVELOPMENT				USER LIAISON
SUB-FUNCTION / RESOURCE COST			C. P. U.	STORAGE DEVICES		MICROFICHE	PRINTING		DATA BASE MANAGEMENT	EQUIPMENT MAINTENANCE		APPLICATIONS SOFTWARE	ANALYSIS AND DESIGN	CODING AND TESTING	
MANAGEMENT $300,000															
ANALYSTS $600,000															
COMPUTER A $150,000			.80 120,000	.10 15,000		.10 15,000									
COMPUTER B $100,000															
PRINTERS $40,000															
MICROFICHE CAMERA $10,000															
DBMS $15,000															
PAYROLL SOFTWARE $10,000															
MICROFICHE $20,000															
COMPUTER PAPER $25,000															
SPACE OCCUPANCY $150,000															
SUBTOTAL															
WORK FUNCTION COSTS															
TOTAL															

Figure A-16. *Sample Resource Distribution Matrix with Proportions and Proportion Costs for the Computer A Resource Added.*

AREA OF MANAGEMENT RESPONSIBILITY	ADMIN.	COMPUTER PROCESSING OPERATIONS									SOFTWARE DEVELOPMENT AND MAINTENANCE				
WORK FUNCTION	DP ADMIN.	COMPUTER OPERATIONS			REPORTING			TECHNICAL SUPPORT			SOFTWARE DEVELOPMENT				USER LIAISON
SUB-FUNCTION / RESOURCE COST			C. P. U.	STORAGE DEVICES		MICROFICHE	PRINTING		DATA BASE MANAGEMENT	EQUIPMENT MAINTENANCE		APPLICATIONS SOFTWARE	ANALYSIS AND DESIGN	CODING AND TESTING	
MANAGEMENT $300,000															
ANALYSTS $600,000									.10 60,000	.10 60,000		.25 150,000	.25 150,000	.20 120,000	.10 60,000
COMPUTER A $150,000			.80 120,000	.10 15,000		.10 15,000									
COMPUTER B $100,000			.90 90,000	.04 4,000		.03 3,000	.03 3,000								
PRINTERS $40,000							1.00 40,000								
MICROFICHE CAMERA $10,000						1.00 10,000									
DBMS $15,000									1.00 15,000						
PAYROLL SOFTWARE $10,000												1.00 10,000			
MICROFICHE $20,000						1.00 20,000									
COMPUTER PAPER $25,000							1.00 25,000								
SPACE OCCUPANCY $150,000															
SUBTOTAL															
WORK FUNCTION COSTS															
TOTAL															

Figure A-17. Sample Resource Distribution Matrix with Proportions and Proportion Costs for the Direct Resources Added.

The resource proportion costs have been calculated for the Space Occupancy resource proportions and both are listed in the sample resource distribution matrix in Figure A-18. The distribution of the work function costs to their subfunctions will be discussed after the overhead resource proportions have been calculated.

4. *Determine the Resource Proportions for the Overhead Resources.* The next part of determining the resource proportions is for the Charging Team to determine the proportions and proportion costs for the resources in the overhead category. The Charging Team should use the same techniques for the overhead resources as it used for the indirect resources.

Of the resources in the sample distribution matrices, only the Management resource has been categorized as overhead. The sample resource distribution matrix in Figure A-19 shows the resource proportions and resource proportion costs for the Management resource.

5. *Determine the Subfunction Costs.* The last part of determining the resource proportions is for the Charging Team to calculate the subfunction costs. To do this, the Charging Team should first begin to distribute the work function costs to their subfunctions by summing all of the resource proportion costs for each work function and subfunction. Figure A-20 shows what the totals are for the sample distribution matrices.

Second, for every work function that meets the following criteria, its undivided cost should be distributed to its subfunctions.

The work function has more than two subfunctions.

The work function has an undivided cost greater than zero.

It is recommended to distribute the work function cost based on the percentage of each subfunction's costs to the total of all of the subfunction costs of that particular work function. Working through an example from the sample distribution matrices should help clarify this process. The Reporting work function has a $15,000 cost and has two subfunctions, so it meets both criteria. The total of both subfunction costs is $116,000 and the percentage of each subfunction cost to this total is 41 percent and 59 percent for the Microfiche and Printing subfunctions, respectively. Thus, 41 percent ($6,200) of the Reporting work function cost is distributed to the Microfiche subfunction and 59 percent ($8,800) of the cost is distributed to the Printing subfunction.

Third, the new totals for all of the affected work functions and subfunctions should be calculated. Figure A-21 shows the results of the above calculations for the work functions and subfunctions of the sample distribution matrices.

AREA OF MANAGEMENT RESPONSIBILITY	ADMIN.	COMPUTER PROCESSING OPERATIONS									SOFTWARE DEVELOPMENT AND MAINTENANCE				
WORK FUNCTION	DP ADMIN.	COMPUTER OPERATIONS			REPORTING			TECHNICAL SUPPORT			SOFTWARE DEVELOPMENT				USER LIAISON
SUB-FUNCTION / RESOURCE COST			C. P. U.	STORAGE DEVICES		MICROFICHE	PRINTING		DATA BASE MANAGEMENT	EQUIPMENT MAINTENANCE		APPLICATIONS SOFTWARE	ANALYSIS AND DESIGN	CODING AND TESTING	
MANAGEMENT $300,000															
ANALYSTS $600,000									.10 60,000	.10 60,000		.25 150,000	.25 150,000	.20 120,000	.10 60,000
COMPUTER A $150,000			.80 120,000	.10 15,000		.10 15,000									
COMPUTER B $100,000			.90 90,000	.04 4,000		.03 3,000	.03 3,000								
PRINTERS $40,000							1.00 40,000								
MICROFICHE CAMERA $10,000						1.00 10,000									
DBMS $15,000									1.00 15,000						
PAYROLL SOFTWARE $10,000												1.00 10,000			
MICROFICHE $20,000						1.00 20,000									
COMPUTER PAPER $25,000							1.00 25,000								
SPACE OCCUPANCY $150,000	.05 7,500		.30 45,000	.10 15,000	.10 15,000			.05 7,500		.05 7,500	.30 45,000				.05 7,500
SUBTOTAL															
WORK FUNCTION COSTS															
TOTAL															

Figure A-18. Sample Resource Distribution Matrix with Proportions and Proportion Costs for the Space Occupancy Indirect Resource Added.

AREA OF MANAGEMENT RESPONSIBILITY	ADMIN.	COMPUTER PROCESSING OPERATIONS									SOFTWARE DEVELOPMENT AND MAINTENANCE				
WORK FUNCTION	DP ADMIN.	COMPUTER OPERATIONS			REPORTING			TECHNICAL SUPPORT			SOFTWARE DEVELOPMENT				USER LIAISON
SUB-FUNCTION / RESOURCE / COST			C. P. U.	STORAGE DEVICES		MICROFICHE	PRINTING		DATA BASE MANAGEMENT	EQUIPMENT MAINTENANCE		APPLICATIONS SOFTWARE	ANALYSIS AND DESIGN	CODING AND TESTING	
MANAGEMENT $300,000	1.00 300,000														
ANALYSTS $600,000									.10 60,000	.10 60,000		.25 150,000	.25 150,000	.20 120,000	.10 60,000
COMPUTER A $150,000			.80 120,000	.10 15,000		.10 15,000									
COMPUTER B $100,000			.90 90,000	.04 4,000		.03 3,000	.03 3,000								
PRINTERS $40,000							1.00 40,000								
MICROFICHE CAMERA $10,000						1.00 10,000									
DBMS $15,000									1.00 15,000						
PAYROLL SOFTWARE $10,000												1.00 10,000			
MICROFICHE $20,000						1.00 20,000									
COMPUTER PAPER $25,000							1.00 25,000								
SPACE OCCUPANCY $150,000	.05 7,500		.30 45,000	.10 15,000	.10 15,000			.05 7,500		.05 7,500	.30 45,000				.05 7,500
SUBTOTAL															
WORK FUNCTION COSTS															
TOTAL															

Figure A-19. Sample Resource Distribution Matrix with Proportions and Proportion Costs for the Management Overhead Resource Added.

AREA OF MANAGEMENT RESPONSIBILITY / WORK FUNCTION / SUB-FUNCTION / RESOURCE COST	ADMIN.	COMPUTER PROCESSING OPERATIONS									SOFTWARE DEVELOPMENT AND MAINTENANCE				
	DP ADMIN.	COMPUTER OPERATIONS			REPORTING			TECHNICAL SUPPORT			SOFTWARE DEVELOPMENT				USER LIAISON
			C. P. U.	STORAGE DEVICES		MICROFICHE	PRINTING		DATA BASE MANAGEMENT	EQUIPMENT MAINTENANCE		APPLICATIONS SOFTWARE	ANALYSIS AND DESIGN	CODING AND TESTING	
MANAGEMENT $300,000	1.00 300,000														
ANALYSTS $600,000									.10 60,000	.10 60,000		.25 150,000	.25 150,000	.20 120,000	.10 60,000
COMPUTER A $150,000			.80 120,000	.10 15,000		.10 15,000									
COMPUTER B $100,000			.90 90,000	.04 4,000		.03 3,000	.03 3,000								
PRINTERS $40,000							1.00 40,000								
MICROFICHE CAMERA $10,000						1.00 10,000									
DBMS $15,000									1.00 15,000						
PAYROLL SOFTWARE $10,000												1.00 10,000			
MICROFICHE $20,000						1.00 20,000									
COMPUTER PAPER $25,000							1.00 25,000								
SPACE OCCUPANCY $150,000	.05 7,500		.30 45,000	.10 15,000	.10 15,000			.05 7,500		.05 7,500	.30 45,000				.05 7,500
SUBTOTAL	307,500	0	255,000	34,000	15,000	48,000	68,000	7,500	75,000	67,500	45,000	160,000	150,000	120,000	67,500
WORK FUNCTION COSTS															
TOTAL															

Figure A-20. Sample Resource Distribution Matrix with Subtotals for the Work Functions and Subfunctions Added.

AREA OF MANAGEMENT RESPONSIBILITY	ADMIN.	COMPUTER PROCESSING OPERATIONS									SOFTWARE DEVELOPMENT AND MAINTENANCE				
WORK FUNCTION	DP ADMIN.	COMPUTER OPERATIONS			REPORTING			TECHNICAL SUPPORT			SOFTWARE DEVELOPMENT				USER LIAISON
SUB-FUNCTION / RESOURCE COST			C. P. U.	STORAGE DEVICES		MICROFICHE	PRINTING		DATA BASE MANAGEMENT	EQUIPMENT MAINTENANCE		APPLICATIONS SOFTWARE	ANALYSIS AND DESIGN	CODING AND TESTING	
MANAGEMENT $300,000	1.00 300,000														
ANALYSTS $600,000									.10 60,000	.10 60,000		.25 150,000	.25 150,000	.20 120,000	.10 60,000
COMPUTER A $150,000			.80 120,000	.10 15,000		.10 15,000									
COMPUTER B $100,000			.90 90,000	.04 4,000		.03 3,000	.03 3,000								
PRINTERS $40,000							1.00 40,000								
MICROFICHE CAMERA $10,000						1.00 10,000									
DBMS $15,000									1.00 15,000						
PAYROLL SOFTWARE $10,000												1.00 10,000			
MICROFICHE $20,000						1.00 20,000									
COMPUTER PAPER $25,000							1.00 25,000								
SPACE OCCUPANCY $150,000	.05 7,500		.30 45,000	.10 15,000	.10 15,000			.05 7,500		.05 7,500	.30 45,000				.05 7,500
SUBTOTAL	307,500	0	255,000	34,000	15,000	48,000	68,000	7,500	75,000	67,500	45,000	160,000	150,000	120,000	67,500
WORK FUNCTION COSTS	0		0	0		6,200	8,800		3,900	3,600		16,700	15,700	12,600	0
TOTAL	307,500		255,000	34,000		54,200	76,800		78,900	71,100		176,700	165,700	132,600	67,500

Figure A-21. *Sample Resource Distribution Matrix with Work Function Costs Distributed and Total Subfunction Costs Added.*

B. DETERMINE THE SUBFUNCTION PROPORTIONS AND PROPORTION COSTS

The second task of Step 9 is to determine the subfunction proportions and proportion costs. A subfunction proportion is the percentage of a subfunction that is used to support a particular service center. A subfunction proportion cost is that cost that the DP facility incurs for performing that subfunction in support of a particular service center. The subfunction proportion cost is calculated by multiplying the cost of the subfunction by the subfunction proportion. It is important that the Charging Team uses care in determining the subfunction proportions, because they will form the basis for distributing the cost of each subfunction to each service center. To determine the subfunction proportions and subfunction proportion costs, the Charging Team must:

Determine the proportions and proportion costs for the subfunctions of the product-oriented work functions.

Determine the proportions and proportion costs for the subfunctions of the suppport-oriented work functions.

Calculate the service center costs.

1. *Determine the Proportions and Proportion Costs for the Product-Oriented Subfunctions.* The Charging Team should determine the proportions and proportion costs for the subfunctions of the product-oriented work functions prior to those of the support-oriented work functions. To determine the subfunction proportions, the Charging Team should use the work usage data forecast in Step 7 and its own experience and judgment. The same principles and techniques that were used to determine the resource proportions should be used to determine the subfunction proportions.

It is important that the Charging Team not be overly constrained by the distribution matrices. Instead, it should lean to use the matrices to accomplish certain objectives. For example, Figure A-22 shows the sample subfunction distribution matrix with the proportions and proportion costs for the subfunctions of the product-oriented work functions. The Charging Team should note how the cost of the Payroll Software resource was passed to the service center Payroll via the subfunction Application Software. The main point for the Charging Team to remember is that is has a certain degree of flexibility in working with the matrices, as long as the decisions made are defendable.

2. *Determine the Proportions and Proportion Costs for the Support-Oriented Subfunctions.* The Charging Team should next determine the proportions and proportion costs for the subfunctions of the support-oriented work functions. There are two methods that the Charging Team can use to determine the proportions for the support-oriented subfunctions:

SERVICE CENTER / SUBFUNCTION TOTAL COST	PROCESSING A	PROCESSING B	APPLICATIONS PROGRAMMING	REPORTING	DBMS	PAYROLL
ADMINISTRATION $307,500						
C. P. U. $255,000	.40 102,000	.30 76,500		.10 25,500	.05 12,750	.15 38,250
STORAGE DEVICES $34,000	.45 15,300	.35 11,900			.10 3,400	.10 3,400
MICROFICHE $54,200				1.00 54,200		
PRINTING $76,800				.90 69,120		.10 7,680
DATA BASE MANAGEMENT $78,900					1.00 78,900	
EQUIPMENT MAINTENANCE $71,100	.50 35,550	.40 28,440		.10 7,110		
APPLICATIONS SOFTWARE $176,700			.85 150,195			.15 26,505
ANALYSIS AND DESIGN $165,700			1.00 165,700			
CODING AND TESTING $132,600			.85 112,710		.10 13,260	.05 6,630
USER LIAISON $67,500						
TOTAL						

Figure A-22. Sample Subfunction Distribution Matrix with Proportions and Proportion Costs for the Product-Oriented Subfunctions Added.

By management fiat, or, in other words, a reasonable proportion in the considered judgment of the Charging Team.

By a function of the costs of the product-oriented subfunctions that have already been distributed.

The latter method is recommended, since it can be more easily justified. To determine the proportion for the support-oriented subfunctions as a function of the costs of the product-oriented subfunctions, the Charging Team should do the following:

Sum all of the product-oriented subfunction proportion costs for each service center. (Figure A-23 shows the results of this summation for the sample distribution matrices.)

Calculate the ratio for the cost of each service center to the cost of all service centers.

Use these ratios as the proportions for the support-oriented subfunctions.

The proportion costs for the support-oriented subfunctions can now be easily calculated. Figure A-24 shows the proportions and proportion costs for both the support-oriented and product-oriented subfunctions for the sample distribution matrices.

3. *Calculate the Service Center Costs.* The last part of this task is for the Charging Team to calculate the costs of the service centers. This calculation can be easily performed by summing the subfunction proportion costs for each service center. Figure A-25 shows the service center costs for the sample distribution matrices.

C. CALCULATE THE BASE RATES

The third task of Step 9 is to calculate the base rates. To do this, the Charging Team must:

Determine the standardization factors for each service.

Calculate the standardized forecasts for each service center.

Divide the total cost of each service center by the standardized forecast for that service center.

Processing A	*Processing B*	*Applications Programming*	*Reporting*	*DBMS*	*Payroll*
152,850	116,840	428,605	155,930	108,310	82,465
		TOTAL 1,045,000			

Figure A-23. Subtotals of the Product-Oriented Subfunction Proportion Costs.

SERVICE CENTER / SUBFUNCTION TOTAL COST	PROCESSING A	PROCESSING B	APPLICATIONS PROGRAMMING	REPORTING	DBMS	PAYROLL
ADMINISTRATION $307,500	.15 46,125	.11 33,825	.41 126,075	.15 46,125	.10 30,750	.08 24,600
C. P. U. $255,000	.40 102,000	.30 76,500		.10 25,500	.05 12,750	.15 38,250
STORAGE DEVICES $34,000	.45 15,300	.35 11,900			.10 3,400	.10 3,400
MICROFICHE $54,200				1.00 54,200		
PRINTING $76,800				.90 69,120		.10 7,680
DATA BASE MANAGEMENT $78,900					1.00 78,900	
EQUIPMENT MAINTENANCE $71,100	.50 35,550	.40 28,440		.10 7,110		
APPLICATIONS SOFTWARE $176,700			.85 150,195			.15 26,505
ANALYSIS AND DESIGN $165,700			1.00 165,700			
CODING AND TESTING $132,600			.85 112,710		.10 13,260	.05 6,630
USER LIAISON $67,500	.15 10,125	.11 7,425	.41 27,675	.15 10,125	.10 6,750	.08 5,400
TOTAL						

Figure A-24. Sample Subfunction Distribution Matrix with Proportions and Proportion Costs for the Support-Oriented Subfunctions Added.

SERVICE CENTER / SUBFUNCTION TOTAL COST	PROCESSING A	PROCESSING B	APPLICATIONS PROGRAMMING	REPORTING	DBMS	PAYROLL
ADMINISTRATION $307,500	.15 46,125	.11 33,825	.41 126,075	.15 46,125	.10 30,750	.08 24,600
C. P. U. $255,000	.40 102,000	.30 76,500		.10 25,500	.05 12,750	.15 38,250
STORAGE DEVICES $34,000	.45 15,300	.35 11,900			.10 3,400	.10 3,400
MICROFICHE $54,200				1.00 54,200		
PRINTING $76,800				.90 69,120		.10 7,680
DATA BASE MANAGEMENT $78,900					1.00 78,900	
EQUIPMENT MAINTENANCE $71,100	.50 35,550	.40 28,440		.10 7,110		
APPLICATIONS SOFTWARE $176,700			.85 150,195			.15 26,505
ANALYSIS AND DESIGN $165,700			1.00 165,700			
CODING AND TESTING $132,600			.85 112,710		.10 13,260	.05 6,630
USER LIAISON $67,500	.15 10,125	.11 7,425	.41 27,675	.15 10,125	.10 6,750	.08 5,400
TOTAL	209,100	158,090	582,355	212,180	145,810	112,465

Figure A-25. Sample Subfunction Distribution Matrix with Service Center Costs Added.

1. *Determine the Standardization Factors.* The first thing that the Charging Team must do to calculate the base rates is to determine the standardization factors. Standardization factors are important parts of the rate-setting process, and the Charging Team should spend considerable time and effort in determining them. The importance of standardization factors can be more easily comprehended once their function is understood. Standardization factors are used to convert to a common unit the service units of the services within one service center, the common unit is then used to calculate the standardized forecast. The standardized forecast, in turn, is used to calculate the base rates, which are subsequently multiplied by the standardization factors to calculate the billing rates.

Although no set procedures exist for determining the standardization factors, there are a number of concepts that the Charging Team should remember.

Determining the standardization factors can be either a quantitative or a subjective process. The process can be quantitative because the standardization factors are often based on numerical measures of the service units, the cost of the services, or measures of the resources that are used to provide the services. The process can be subjective because the standardization factors are often based on particular management objectives that the Charging Team and/or senior management want to achieve with the charging system. Priority charging and the use of surcharges and discounts to allocate scarce resources are examples of approaches to achieve management objectives. Typically, the Charging Team will use both quantitative and subjective bases in determining the standardization factors for services within the same service center.

Whichever basis (i.e., quantitative or subjective) is used in determining the standardization factors, the Charging Team should be able to justify the values determined. The Charging Team must have clear and defendable reasons for each factor chosen. Essentially, the Charging Team must leave an audit trail so that the rationale for calculating the value of each standardization factor can be determined.

The total amount charged out for each service center should equal the cost of the service center. Therefore, the standardization factor must always be 1.0 for a service in a service center that contains just the one service. Otherwise, the amount charged out will not equal the cost of the service center.

The use of standardization factors is the mechanism by which the Charging Team can incorporate the concepts of priority charging and shift differentials. Priority charging and/or shift differentials should be incorporated by (a) determining the number of priorities and/or shifts, letting each priority and/or shift equal a unique service, and then grouping these services under one service center; (b) determining the relative values of a unit of each priority and/or shift (e.g., high priority might be twice as expensive as normal priority); and (c) assigning the relative values of the priorities and/or shifts as the standardization factors.

Working through an example from the sample distribution matrices should help clarify this process. The Processing A service center contains six services, each representing a different priority for one of two shifts. There are high, normal, and low priorities for prime and nonprime shifts. It has been determined, based on judgment and past experience with processing usage, that the relative values of the high, normal, and low priorities for both prime and nonprime shifts should be 2.0, 1.0, 0.75, 0.60, 0.50 and 0.25, respectively. These values have been used as the standardization factors for the Processing A service center in the sample distribution matrices.

Two things should be noted at this point. First, when determining the standardization factors for priority services, the proper value of the factors should be whatever it will take to shift users from using one priority to another. Second, many DP facilities have eliminated priority charging because it had not leveled out the workload as desired and caused user animosity toward the DP facility. This animosity was developed because the users tried to use the highest priority all of the time; this resulted in the high priority providing no better turn around than normal priority but at a higher cost. The user of priority charging as an example is for illustrative purposes only and should not be construed as a recommendation for its use.

The use of standardization factors is the mechanism by which the Charging Team can incorporate the concept of normalization between two or more services. In the context of charging systems, normalization between services refers to charging the same price for performing a quantity of work, regardless of which service performs the work. The concept of normalization is most often seen used with two computers of different speeds so that a job costs the same when run on either computer. Normalization can be accomplished by (a) determining the services that are to be normalized, then grouping them under one service center; (b) determining the relative weight of a unit of each service (e.g., processing on the high-speed computer is twice as fast as processing on the low-speed computer); and (c) assigning the relative weights of the service units as the standardization factors.

An example from the sample distribution matrices should help clarify this process. The Processing B service center contains two CPU services. One service is provided by a computer significantly faster than the computer that provides the second service. It has been determined, based on performance measures of the two computers, that the high-speed computer is twice as fast as the low-speed computer. The values of 2.0 and 1.0 have been used as the standardization factors for the high-speed and low-speed services, respectively.

Standardization factors are also the mechanism by which the Charging

Team can incorporate the concept of surcharges and discounts. This can be accomplished in a manner similar to that used for the concepts of priorities and normalization; (a) determining the services to which the surcharges and discounts will be applied and grouping them under one service center; (b) determining the relative weight of a unit of each service (e.g., it should cost three times as much to use a unit of a Printing service than it does to use a unit of a Microfiche service); and (c) assigning the relative weight of the service units as the standardization factors.

Again, an example from the sample distribution matrices should help clarify the above. The Reporting service center contains two services, Printing and Microfiche. Management desired to place a surcharge on the Printing service and a discount on the Microfiche service in order to encourage users to use the Microfiche service. It has been determined, based on experience and judgment, that if the printing unit is three times more expensive than the microfiche unit, then the users will use the Microfiche service more often. The values of 1.0 and 3.0 have been used as the standardization factors for the Microfiche and Printing services, respectively.

Figure A-26 shows the standardization factors for the services in the sample distribution matrices. The standardization factors for the four services in the Application Programming service center were based on the salary levels of the four categories of analysts.

2. *Calculate the Standardized Forecasts.* After the Charging Team has calculated the standardization factors, it should next calculate the standardized forecasts for each service center. A standardized forecast represents the projected number of standardized service units to be used for an entire service center. Determining the standard forecast is relatively easy and is calculated by multiplying each service forecast by its standardization factor and summing the result for all services within one service center. Figure A-27 shows the standardized forecasts for the service centers in the sample distribution matrices.

3. *Calculate the Base Rates.* The last part of this task is for the Charging Team to calculate the base rate of each service center. A base rate is the amount that must be charged by the DP facility in order to recover the projected cost of providing a standardized service unit. A service center's base rate may or may not be the same as its service's billing rates. The base rate are easily calculated by dividing the cost of the service center by the standardized forecast. Figure A-28 shows the base rates for the service centers in the sample distribution matrices.

D. CALCULATE THE BILLING RATES

The last task in Step 9 is to calculate the billing rates. To do this, the Charging Team need only multiply the base rate of a service center by the standardization factor for each service in that service center. At this time, the Charging Team should ensure that within each service center, the sum

SERVICE CENTER	PROCESSING A						PROCESSING B		APPLICATIONS PROGRAMMING				REPORTING		DBMS	PAY-ROLL
SERVICE	PRIME HIGH	PRIME NORMAL	PRIME LOW	NON-PRIME HIGH	NON-PRIME NORMAL	NON-PRIME LOW	HIGH SPEED	LOW SPEED	SENIOR ANALYST	ANALYST	JUNIOR ANALYST	APPREN. ANALYST	MICRO-FICHE	PRINT-ING		
SERVICE UNIT	SECONDS	SECONDS	SECONDS	SECONDS	SECONDS	SECONDS	SECONDS	SECONDS	HOUR	HOUR	HOUR	HOUR	FICHE	1000 LINES	USERS	CHECKS
COST OF SERVICE CENTER	209,100						158,090		582,355				212,180		145,810	112,465
SERVICE FORECAST	500,000	6,000,000	2,500,000	1,500,000	1,000,000	500,000	4,000,000	4,000,000	9,000	15,000	3,000	3,000	80,000	30,000	100	70,000
STANDARD-IZATION FACTORS	2.0	1.0	.75	.60	.50	.25	2.0	1.0	1.2	1.0	.75	.50	1.0	3.0	1.0	1.0
STANDARDIZED FORECAST																
BASE RATE																
BILLING RATE																

Figure A-26. Sample Billing Rate Distribution Matrix with Standardization Factors Added.

SERVICE CENTER	PROCESSING A						PROCESSING B		APPLICATIONS PROGRAMMING				REPORTING		DBMS	PAY-ROLL
SERVICE	PRIME HIGH	PRIME NORMAL	PRIME LOW	NON-PRIME HIGH	NON-PRIME NORMAL	NON-PRIME LOW	HIGH SPEED	LOW SPEED	SENIOR ANALYST	ANALYST	JUNIOR ANALYST	APPREN. ANALYST	MICRO-FICHE	PRINT-ING		
SERVICE UNIT	SECONDS	SECONDS	SECONDS	SECONDS	SECONDS	SECONDS	SECONDS	SECONDS	HOUR	HOUR	HOUR	HOUR	FICHE	1000 LINES	USERS	CHECKS
COST OF SERVICE CENTER	209,100						158,090		582,355				212,180		145,810	112,465
SERVICE FORECAST	500,000	6,000,000	2,500,000	1,500,000	1,000,000	500,000	4,000,000	4,000,000	9,000	15,000	3,000	3,000	80,000	30,000	100	70,000
STANDARD-IZATION FACTORS	2.0	1.0	.75	.60	.50	.25	2.0	1.0	1.2	1.0	.75	.50	1.0	3.0	1.0	1.0
STANDARDIZED FORECAST	10,400,000						12,000,000		29,550				170,000		100	70,000
BASE RATE																
BILLING RATE																

Figure A-27. Sample Billing Rate Distribution Matrix with Standardized Forecasts Added.

SERVICE CENTER	PROCESSING A						PROCESSING B		APPLICATIONS PROGRAMMING				REPORTING		DBMS	PAY-ROLL
SERVICE	PRIME HIGH	PRIME NORMAL	PRIME LOW	NON-PRIME HIGH	NON-PRIME NORMAL	NON-PRIME LOW	HIGH SPEED	LOW SPEED	SENIOR ANALYST	ANALYST	JUNIOR ANALYST	APPREN. ANALYST	MICRO-FICHE	PRINT-ING		
SERVICE UNIT	SECONDS	SECONDS	SECONDS	SECONDS	SECONDS	SECONDS	SECONDS	SECONDS	HOUR	HOUR	HOUR	HOUR	FICHE	1000 LINES	USERS	CHECKS
COST OF SERVICE CENTER	209,100						158,090		582,355				212,180		145,810	112,465
SERVICE FORECAST	500,000	6,000,000	2,500,000	1,500,000	1,000,000	500,000	4,000,000	4,000,000	9,000	15,000	3,000	3,000	80,000	30,000	100	70,000
STANDARD-IZATION FACTORS	2.0	1.0	.75	.60	.50	.25	2.0	1.0	1.2	1.0	.75	.50	1.0	3.0	1.0	1.0
STANDARDIZED FORECAST	10,400,000						12,000,000		29,550				170,000		100	70,000
BASE RATE	.0201						.0131		19.70				1.25		1458	1.61
BILLING RATE																

Figure A-28. Sample Billing Rate Distribution Matrix with Base Rates Added.

of the products of each service's forecast and billing rate is equal to, with error allowed for rounding, the cost of the service center. Figure A-29 shows the billing rates for the services in the sample distribution matrices.

Step 10. Assist with DP Budgeting

This step discusses areas in the DP budgeting process where information obtained from the charging system can be of assistance to the organization's budgeting process. Certain data need to flow between the DP facility and the organization's budgeting groups; providing this data is a tertiary objective of the charging system.

The three tasks in this step consist of developing techniques to:

Assist users in generating their DP budgets.

Provide input to the DP facility budgeting process.

Provide input to the organization's budgeting process.

A. Assist Users in Generating Their DP Budgets

Once implemented, the charging system will provide users with the data needed to forecast their DP budgets. The first task in Step 10 is for the Charging Team to develop techniques that will instruct the users in how to employ the data from the charging system to forecast their DP budgets. Users will probably need assistance in understanding how to better forecast their own usage, how to utilize the rate schedule, and how to budget for their DP funds. Such assistance to users can result in an added benefit for the DP facility: once users become more proficient and accurate in forecasting their usage, the Charging Team's work during the rate-setting phase will become simpler.

B. Provide Input to the DP Facility Budgeting Process

Certain data from the charging system may be used by the DP facility to develop its budget requests. These data include, but are not limited to:

Forecasted cost of service centers and subfunctions.

Funds charged out.

Funds recovered.

Prior year costs.

The second task in Step 10 is for the Charging Team to develop techniques that will provide the necessary data to the DP facility to facilitate its budgeting process.

C. Provide Input to the Organization's Budgeting Process

Certain data from the charging system may also be used by the organization in its budget process. Examples include:

SERVICE CENTER	PROCESSING A						PROCESSING B		APPLICATIONS PROGRAMMING				REPORTING		DBMS	PAY-ROLL
SERVICE	PRIME HIGH	PRIME NORMAL	PRIME LOW	NON-PRIME HIGH	NON-PRIME NORMAL	NON-PRIME LOW	HIGH SPEED	LOW SPEED	SENIOR ANALYST	ANALYST	JUNIOR ANALYST	APPREN. ANALYST	MICRO-FICHE	PRINT-ING		
SERVICE UNIT	SECONDS	SECONDS	SECONDS	SECONDS	SECONDS	SECONDS	SECONDS	SECONDS	HOUR	HOUR	HOUR	HOUR	FICHE	1000 LINES	USERS	CHECKS
COST OF SERVICE CENTER	209,100						158,090		582,355				212,180		145,810	112,465
SERVICE FORECAST	500,000	6,000,000	2,500,000	1,500,000	1,000,000	500,000	4,000,000	4,000,000	9,000	15,000	3,000	3,000	80,000	30,000	100	70,000
STANDARD-IZATION FACTORS	2.0	1.0	.75	.60	.50	.25	2.0	1.0	1.2	1.0	.75	.50	1.0	3.0	1.0	1.0
STANDARDIZED FORECAST	10,400,000						12,000,000		29,550				170,000		100	70,000
BASE RATE	.0201						.0131		19.70				1.25		1458	1.61
BILLING RATE	.0402	.0201	.015	.012	.01	.005	.0263	.0131	23.64	19.70	14.78	9.85	1.25	3.75	1458	1.61

Figure A-29. Sample Billing Rate Distribution Matrix with Billing Rates Added.

Forecasted cost of the DP facility, obtained by summing the costs of the subfunctions.

Funds charged out.

Funds recovered.

Prior year costs.

The third task of Step 10 is for the Charging Team to develop techniques that will provide the necessary data to the organization to facilitate its budgeting process.

The completion of this step should be used as the third major checkpoint by senior management to evaluate the progress of the Charging Team. It is important for senior management to ensure that their objective for the charging system are being met.

BILLING PHASE

The last four steps of this appendix will focus on developing and implementing the procedures of the billing subsystem. When developing these procedures, the Charging Team must remember that the billing subsystem will be used almost continuously. Thus, each of the procedures must be well designed and, where applicable, developed according to standard systems development methodology. After completing the four steps in this phase, the Charging Team will have incorporated all of the work completed during the planning, design, and rate-setting phases and will have developed any automated parts of the charging system.

Step 11. Assist with DP Accounting

During this step, the Charging Team will be developing and implementing the procedure that will assist with the accounting activities related to the charging system. This step discusses techniques that provide the interface between (a) the organization's accounting department and the charging system and (b) the various types of accounting activities, internal to the DP facility, required because of the charging system.

The four tasks in this step consist of developing techniques for:

Establishing and maintaining user accounts.

Providing data to the organization's accounting department.

Assisting in the maintenance of accounting information.

Handling charges for aborted work.

If additional guidance for any of the tasks is needed, the Charging Team can consult its organization policies and guidelines, its organization accounting group, and the accounting literature.

A. ESTABLISHING AND MAINTAINING USER ACCOUNTS

User accounts are the records used to keep track of authorized DP funds and actual expenditures for each user. Information that is usually kept on a user account includes past and current service usage and charges itemized by service. An effective set of techniques for handling user accounts is important to the efficient operation of a charging system. The first task of Step 11 is for the Charging Team to determine the types of data to be maintained in the user accounts and to establish the techniques established prior to implementation of the charging system.

B. PROVIDING DATA TO THE ORGANIZATION'S ACCOUNTING DEPARTMENT

The organization's accounting department will need certain information from the charging system. Typically, the accounting department will need at least the following information:

The amount of funds that users wish to authorize for their accounts.

The amounts billed to the users.

Invoices for resources currently in use.

The extent to which the accounting department will be involved with the charging system will vary from organization to organization. The second task of Step 11 is for the Charging Team to determine exactly which data will need to be exchanged between the accounting department and the charging system and to develop the techniques for exchanging the information.

C. ASSISTING IN THE MAINTENANCE OF ACCOUNTING INFORMATION

Some DP facilities maintain accounting information for their organization's accounting departments. The third task of Step 11 is for the Charging Team to develop techniques for:

Maintaining the accounting information.

Determining how to charge for the maintenance.

Determining how to transfer the pertinent data from the charging system to the accounting files.

D. HANDLING ABORTED WORK

A problem that exists with every new implementation of a charging system is how to handle the charges for aborted work when it is not the fault of the user. There are several possible ways of handling aborted work. *Providing free reruns for the users or giving the users credit for the cost of the aborted work is recommended.* The DP facility thus absorbs the cost of the aborted work as a cost of operation and eliminates a source of confrontation with its users. After a number of years of collecting data on the cost of aborted work, the costs can be projected and incorporated into the billing rates. The fourth task of Step 11 is for the Charging Team to determine and develop techniques for handling aborted work.

Step 12. Account for Usage

The Charging Team will develop and implement the usage accounting procedure of the billing subsystem during this step. Usage accounting refers to the monitoring and recording of the utilization of services, subfunctions, and resources. Detailed data on the utilization of services are needed to determine user charges. Data on the utilization of subfunctions and resources are needed to help determine the subfunction and resource proportions for the distribution matrices. When accounting for the utilization of services, the number of service units utilized by each user needs to be monitored. When accounting for the utilization of subfunctions, the number of work units for each particular subfunction will be needed. Typically, utilization data will be needed for only those subfunctions for which the Charging Team has difficulty determining subfunction proportions. When accounting for the utilization of resources, the number of resource units for each particular resource will be needed. As with the subfunctions, utilization data will be needed for only those resources for which the Charging Team has difficulty determining resource proportions.

The work of the Charging Team in this step assumes that the DP facility has some service, subfunction, or resource usage accounting capability and that any additional capabilities needed can be purchased or developed. This step consists of two tasks:

Designing the usage accounting procedure.

Developing and implementing the usage accounting procedure.

A. FUNDAMENTAL CONCEPTS

Before attempting to design and develop the usage accounting procedure, it is important for the Charging Team to understand measurement software and usage accounting data. A discussion of each concept follows:

1. *Measurement Software.* Measurement software is used to monitor and record the computer services received by users and the computer resources used to provide those services. Typically, this software is available from computer vendors or other commercial sources for most of the large computers currently on the market. Service and resource utilization information is collected by the measurement software and stored in a log for later analysis. The content and accuracy of the information collected and stored by this software varies from computer to computer. Measurement software is often not even available for smaller computers. To determine if measurement software is available for its computer, the Charging Team should start by contacting the computer's vendor. Measurement soft-

ware is usually too complex to be developed in-house and, thus, should be purchased whenever possible.

Measurement software usually accounts for the usage of computer-related services, subfunctions, and resources. Examples of the other services, subfunctions, and resources for which usage must also be accounted are personnel, data entry machines, and CRT displays. If the costs of these services are to be charged to the users, then their usage must also be monitored. Most DP facilities monitor the use of these types of services with manual techniques that have been developed in-house. For example, personnel data can be collected on timesheets and then entered into an automated usage accounting system. It is important that the Charging Team develop techniques that will collect sufficient data to make these charges equitable. But the Charging Team must remember that as it tries to make charges more equitable, it also increases the quantity of utilization data that will need to be collected. Also, increasing the equitability can result in complex and costly monitoring techniques. The Charging Team must determine the proper trade-offs between equitability and costs that will be needed in its charging system.

2. *Usage Accounting Data.* The decisions that the Charging Team made during earlier steps should be used to help determine the data that will need to be collected with the usage accounting procedure.

The distribution matrices should help to further define the exact service, subfunction, and resource data elements that will need to be collected.

The billing rates should help define the eventual format of the service usage accounting data.

The Charging Team should contact computer hardware and software vendors to determine the type of data collected by its measurement software.

All of this information will be used by the Charging Team while performing the next two tasks.

B. DESIGN THE USAGE ACCOUNTING PROCEDURE

The first task in Step 12 is to design the usage accounting procedure, which should be designed in two stages. The first stage is to design automated techniques to monitor service, subfunction, and resource utilization; the second stage is to design the manual techniques.

The Charging Team must remember that some of the techniques used to monitor the utilization of subfunctions and resources will need to be of a more temporary or intermittent nature, since some subfunction and resource usage data will not need to be collectecd on a continual basis. For example, determining how much time an operator spends performing data entry each day may only need to be performed for one month due to the repetitive nature of the operator's work. Similar examples could be given for other resources and subfunctions.

When designing the automated techniques, the Charging Team should remember that there will be very little to design unless it chooses to develop the techniques in-house. *The Charging Team should not attempt to develop measurement software in-house, since such development is usually extremely complex, sophisticated, and requires a great deal of time and expense.*

Since only a limited quantity of measurement software is usually available for any particular computer, the Charging Team, when selecting measurement software, should determine whether or not the selected software will need to be modified. The extent of modification will depend on the number of services, subfunctions, and resources that the measurement software will need to monitor. The Charging Team should determine the exact parts of the measurement software that will need to be modified and design what the new parts will look like. If, for some reason, a service's utilization cannot be monitored by the modified measurement software and there is no other way to monitor it, then that service should be dropped from the charging system.

Manual usage accounting techniques are too numerous and varied to recommend specific techniques. Basically, the techniques should be tailored to fit the charging system. The techniques the Charging Team selects should be coordinated to meet the objectives and criteria set forth for the charging system and to monitor all of the services, subfunctions, and resources that the automated techniques do not monitor.

C. Develop and Implement the Usage Accounting Procedure

The second task of this step is to develop and implement the usage accounting procedure. This development effort can be fairly simple and straightforward if measurement software can be purchased and the manual techniques are not complicated. On the other hand, the developmental effort can be complex and expensive if the software must be developed in-house and the manual techniques are complicated. *It is recommended that the Charging Team use a balanced, cost-effective approach.*

Step 13. Report Usage

The Charging Team should develop and implement the reporting procedure of the billing subsystem during this step. The reporting procedure consists of the techniques for reducing the service usage accounting data, calculating the user charges, and preparing and distributing reports on service usage and charges to the users. If the DP facility is recovering costs, then the reports can be considered bills or invoices. The reporting procedure is typically performed using automated packages. Such packages are commercially available and can be modified to handle the specific type of service data collected by a DP facility's usage accounting procedure. The tasks discussed in this step are based on the following assumptions:

The usage accounting procedure has been designed, and the data to be collected have been determined.

All the work in the planning, design, and rate-setting phases has been completed to the point that the types of data needed for the reporting procedure are known.

This step consists of two tasks:

Design the reporting procedure.

Develop and implement the reporting procedure.

A. Fundamental Concepts

Before attempting to design and develop the reporting procedure, it is important for the Charging Team to understand automated and manual reporting techniques, and reporting data. A discussion of each concept follows:

1. *Automated and Manual Reporting Techniques.* The major decision that the Charging Team will have to make during this step is to determine which, if any, of the reporting techniques should be automated. *Whenever any of the following situations occur, the Charging Team should choose to automate most, if not all, of the reporting techniques.*

A large volume of usage accounting data will have to be reduced and analyzed.

A large number of users will receive reports.

Several different types of reports will need to be prepared.

The reports will need to be prepared frequently.

The cost of acquiring or developing the automated techniques is not excessive.

In-house personnel are available to develop the automated techniques that cannot be purchased.

2. *Reporting Data.* Data from the design phase should be used to determine the requirements for the reporting procedure, such as the recipients of the reports, the content and format of reports, and the frequency of report preparation. Data from the "Assist with DP Accounting" procedure should be used to provide a description of the report recipients and the type of information that should be reported to the accounting department.

B. Design the Reporting Procedure

The first task of Step 13 is to design the techniques of the reporting procedure. These techniques will be used:

To reduce the service usage accounting data for services.

To calculate charges.

To prepare and distribute the reports on service usage to the users and other pertinent groups.

The main feature that should be designed into all of the reporting techniques is flexibility. Charging systems tend to change frequently, which results in the usage accounting data changing often. Therefore, the reporting techniques should be flexible enough to incorporate these changes without having to undergo extensive redevelopment.

1. *Reducing the Usage Data for Services.* When designing the techniques to reduce the usage accounting data for services, the most important points that the Charging Team will need to know are:

The amount, type, and format of the data that will be collected and stored.

The type of data that will be needed for preparing the reports on usage, for maintaining the user accounts, and for historical purposes.

The frequency with which the data will need to be reduced due to storage limitations or reporting needs.

2. *Calculate Charges.* When designing the techniques to calculate the charges, the Charging Team will need to know:

The number of different billing rates to be used.

The content and format of the reports.

3. *Preparing and Distributing Charges.* When designing the techniques to prepare and distribute the utilization reports, the Charging Team will need to determine three things.

The content and format of the reports should be determined. These will depend upon the information reported and the reports' recipients. It is likely that several different report formats will be needed, one for each type of recipient. The reports should at least contain information about what services have been used during the reporting period and the charges that are associated with each. Any type of information that provides suggestions on reducing costs (e.g., the cost estimate if users allocated only the memory that they actually used) will be valuable to the users. *The Charging Team should design some mechanism, for example, reports, to inform users how they can reduce their DP costs.* The mechanism could be anything from highlighting specific portions of end-of-work cost reports to providing a periodic newsletter of cost saving ideas.

Name: Project MCAS
Account No.: UX 5793
Billing Period: 1 Aug. 82–31 Aug. 82

Service	Usage	Rate	Charge
Processing A			
Prime			
High	10,000 sec	.0402	$ 402.00
Normal	162,000 sec	.0201	$ 3,256.20
NonPrime			
High	1,000 sec	.012	$ 12.00
Normal	50,000 sec	.01	$ 500.00
Applications Programming			
Senior Analyst	100 hrs	23.64	$ 2,364.00
Analyst	40 hrs	19.70	$ 788.00
Apprentice Analyst	150 hrs	9.85	$ 1,477.50
Reporting			
Microfiche	1,000	1.25	$ 1,250.00
Printing (1,000 lines)	10	3.75	$ 37.50
Payroll	500 checks	1.61	$ 805.00
	Total Charges =		$10,892.20
	Account Balance =		$62,792.50

Figure A-30. Sample billing report.

The recipients of the reports should be determined. If the Charging Team can identify the distinct types of user that will be utilizing the DP facility, this will help in determining the type, frequency, and content of the reports to be prepared. Various users will usually need or want different types of report information. Additionally, if the Charging Team tries to allocate scarce resources, a knowledge of the type of user will help determine the kind of information needed to encourage or discourage use of particular resources.

The frequency of preparing and distributing the reports should be determined. The correct frequency will be a function of the design and the objectives of the charging system. If all the usage accounting and reporting techniques for services are manual, it will be difficult to report usage and charges more frequently than once a week or month. If, on the other hand, the usage accounting and reporting techniques are automated, then reporting more frequently will be feasible. Some DP facilities provide reports of utilization and an estimate of the charges at the end of each computer run or interactive session. This information can be extremely valuable, and the Charging Team should consider providing it whenever possible. The main point that the Charging Team must remember is that the reports are the major source of information for the users on their use of the services, how much of their DP budget they have expended, and possible ways of reducing charges. *It is recommended that the Charging Team attempt to build into the reporting procedure, whenever feasible, the ability to provide users end-of-work cost estimates.*

C. Develop and Implement the Reporting Procedure

The second task of Step 13 is to develop and implement the reporting procedure. The Charging Team should follow standard systems development methodology when developing and implementing the reporting procedure. The major decision that the Charging Team will have to make in this task is whether to purchase automated reporting packages or develop them in-house.

If at all possible, the Charging Team should purchase these packages instead of developing them in-house. Automated reporting packages should be developed in-house only if the requirements are so unique that the vendor-supplied packages cannot be adapted to satisfy them or the requirements are so simple that it would not be cost-effective to purchase an expensive package.

Step 14. Recover Charges

The Charging Team should develop and implement the cost recovery procedure of the billing subsystem in this step. The Charging Team must decide:

Whether to recover charges.
From whom to recover charges.
How to recover the charges.
How to develop and implement the cost recovery plan.

This step assumes that the organization has predefined regulations and procedures for the transfer and handling of funds. This step consists of one task: designing, developing, and implementing the recovery procedure.

A. Fundamental Concepts

Before designing, developing, and implementing the recovery procedure, it is important for the Charging Team to understand the following concepts concerning the users of the DP facility.

There are two types of users of a DP facility, internal and external. The Charging Team must decide whether or not to recover charges from internal users. There are a number of factors that the Charging Team should consider prior to determining if charges should be recovered from the internal users.

Recovering charges by the actual transfer of funds can have the same effects (e.g., limiting DP utilization) as employing user DP budgets made up of "pseudo funds," but only if both approaches are enforced rigorously.

Recovering charges encourages more efficient use of the DP facility in order to conserve user funds.

Recovering charges will augment and emphasize the particular cost-based features designed into the charging system to allocate scarce services.

Recovering charges will improve the quality of the charging system data that will be sent to senior management, because users are forced to be more accountable for their DP usage.

Recovering charges will necessitate an increase in recordkeeping and in the overall cost of the charging system.

It is recommended that, whenever possible, the Charging Team choose to recover charges from its internal users.

B. Design, Develop, and Implement the Recovery Procedure

The only task of Step 14 is to design, develop, and implement the recovery procedure. When doing this, the Charging Team must remember that the major objective of the recovery procedure is to recover the charges reported to the user by transferring funds from the user's account to the DP facility's account. There are two techniques that the Charging Team can use to accomplish this objective.

The first technique involves recovering the charges after reporting them. Users in this situation would be required to transfer funds to the DP facility only when billed.

The second technique is for users to open accounts with the DP facility and transfer a prescribed amount of funds into that account. Each time a service is utilized, the user's account would be debited. Under this technique, users are never actually billed but merely receive reports of the charges.

The Charging Team will need to determine which of the two techniques is best for its own environment. Each organization should have existing regulations and policies governing funds transfer. If the Charging Team has decided to recover the charges from internal users, it should follow the organization's procedures for transferring funds.

The completion of this step should be used as the last major checkpoint by senior management to determine the progress of the Charging Team. At this time, a comprehensive review of the work completed by the Charging Team should be undertaken by senior management.

Glossary

This glossary contains accounting terms presented in the book as well as accounting terms used by accountants in the practice of accounting. The inclusion of terms not used in the book is to assist the data processing manager in understanding accounting terms that might appear in discussions with users, senior management, and accountants.

ACCOUNT. Record of day-to-day changes in items that appear on the balance sheet or income statement. (See also *T-account*)

ACCOUNT RECEIVABLE. An amount owed to the business, usually by a customer, as a result of the ordinary extension of credit.

ACCOUNTING, COST. The process of collecting material, labor, and overhead costs and attaching them to products.

ACCOUNTING CYCLE. The accounting process for each accounting period is a recurring accounting cycle, beginning with transactions recorded in a journal and ending with the preparation of financial statements.

ACCOUNTING PERIOD. The period of time over which an income statement summarizes the changes in the owner's equity.

ACCOUNT PAYABLE. An obligation to pay an amount to a creditor.

ACCRUAL CONCEPT. Net income is measured as the difference between revenues and expenses rather than between cash receipts and expenditures.

ACCRUED EXPENSES. Expenses incurred but not yet paid for.

ACCRUED INCOME. Income earned but not yet received.

ADJUSTING ENTRY. An accounting transaction recording the correction of an error, accruals, writeoffs, provision for bad debts or depreciation, etc., expressed in the form of a simple journal entry.

AMORTIZE. To write off a portion or all of the cost of an *intangible* asset.

ASSET. Property or property right owned by the business which is valuable either because it will be converted into cash or because it is expected to benefit future operations and which was acquired at a measurable cost.

ASSET, CURRENT. An asset that is either currently in the form of cash or is expected to be converted into cash within a short period, usually one year.

ASSET, FIXED. Tangible property of relatively long life that generally is used in the production of goods and services.

AUDIT. An examination made by independent accountants or internal auditors in order to express an opinion as to the fairness of financial statements, operations, and the adequacy of control.

BAD DEBTS. Accounts that are considered to be uncollectible.

BALANCE, BEGINNING. The amount in an account at the start of the accounting period.

BALANCE, NEW. The amount in an account at the end of the accounting period; the difference between the beginning balance plus increases minus the decreases. The amount reported on the next balance sheet.

BALANCE SHEET. A financial statement that reports the assets and equities of a company as of a specified time.

BALANCE SHEET, CONSOLIDATED. Aggregate accounts for the various categories of assets and liabilities of a corporate family (more than one corporation).

BANK RECONCILIATION. A comparison of the customer's records with the records of the bank, listing differences to bring balances into agreement.

BANK STATEMENT. A document rendered by the bank to the depositor, usually monthly, which reflects deposits and checks that have cleared the bank. These items are listed in chronological order of receipt by the bank.

BILLING PERIOD. The billing period is the period of time for which the charges for service usage are calculated. This time period varies widely between, and even within, DP facilities, from as short as a per job basis to as long as a fiscal year.

BILLING RATE. The billing rate is the amount that is charged to the users for utilizing each unit of a service.

CASH BASIS. A basis of keeping accounts whereby income and expenses are recorded on the books of accounts when *received* and *paid* without regard to the period to which they apply.

CASH DISCOUNTS. Discounts granted for early payment.

CASH FLOW. The cash flow calculation attempts to measure the actual cash expenses of a firm. Noncash expenses are not included, the principal noncash expense being depreciation. Noncash expenses do not cost money immediately but help to reduce the income figure (personal income in the case of proprietorships and partnerships) on which the corporation income tax is based. Most business owners put the noncash expense figures as high as the law allows, and a few even higher. To get the cash flow figure from an income statement, take the net income after tax figure and add the depreciation expense and any other noncash expense items on the income statement.

CHART OF ACCOUNT. A listing of accounts in balance sheet order, each with a designated number.

COLLATERAL. Something of value pledged as security for a loan.

CONTINGENCY. A possible future event or condition arising from causes unknown or at present undeterminable.

CONTRA ACCOUNT. One of two or more accounts that partially or wholly offset each other: on financial statements they may either be merged or appear together.

Example: an account receivable from and payable to the same individual.

CORPORATION. An artificial being, or business entity, which is legally separate from the persons who own it, which is created under state or federal law, in which ownership is in the form of stock, with power to make contracts and do business in its own name, and with liability of owners limited to the amount of their investment in the company.

COSTS. Costs are the funded and unfunded expenses incurred by the DP facility for the resources needed to provide DP services to the users. Examples of the costs that could be incurred for a CPU resource are lease or purchase expenses, maintenance, depreciation, delivery, and installation.

CR. Abbreviation of credit.

CREDIT ENTRY. An entry on the right-hand side of an account. The record of a decrease in any asset account. The record of an increase in an equity account.

CREDITOR. One who lends money.

CURRENT ASSETS. Cash and other assets that can be readily converted into cash.

CURRENT LIABILITIES. Obligations that will become due and payable within the current accounting period.

DEBIT ENTRY. A left-hand entry. The record of an increase in any asset account. The record of a decrease in an equity account.

DEBIT. Current and noncurrent liabilities; that is, equities of creditors that represent money, goods or services owed to another by virtue of an agreement, express or implied, giving rise to a legal obligation to pay.

DEFALCATION. The embezzlement of money.

DEPRECIATION. Portions of the cost of an asset charged off to expenses according to a predetermined plan; includes obsolescence. It also refers to the decline in value of an asset, such as machinery or buildings, over a period of years resulting from use. (This is reflected in the real accounts as "allowance for depreciation.")

DEPLETION. The exhaustion of a natural resource applied to a mineral deposit, standing timber, etc.

DIRECT LABOR. The cost of labor that is chargeable directly to the product.

DIRECT MATERIALS. Materials that are chargeable directly to and become a part of the product or products manufactured.

DIRECT RESOURCE. Direct resources are resources that can be associated with one or more work areas (i.e., subfunctions) because there is a distinct logical and measurable relationship between them. Computer equipment and application programmers are typically categorized as direct resources.

DISCOUNTS. Amount by which the face value of a financial instrument exceeds the sales price.

DISTRIBUTION MATRICES. The distribution matrices, which can be viewed as the nuclei of the rate-setting subsystem, are the mechanisms by which the costs of the resources are proportioned to the services and a billing rate is calculated for each of the services. The use of a series of matrices, instead of some other allocating mechanism, is recommended, because matrices provide the clearest, easiest technique for tracking the large volume of information required to calculate the billing rates.

DIVIDEND. Portion of profits distributed to stockholders.

DIVIDEND, STOCK. Dividend paid in the form of shares of stock in the issuing corporation.

DOUBLE-ENTRY ACCOUNTING. The type of accounting in which the two aspects of each event are recorded (debit and credit).

DP FACILITY. A DP facility is the organizational entity that obtains and utilizes resources to provide DP services to a user or group of users.

DR. Abbreviation for debit.

DRAFT. An order in writing directing the payment of money by one party (the drawee) to another party (the payee). A bank check is an example of a draft.

ENTRY, CLOSING. One step in transferring the balance of an account to another account; an entry reducing one account to zero and offset by an entry increasing another account by the same amount.

ENTRY, LEFT-HAND. See *Debit Entry.*

ENTRY, RIGHT-HAND. See *Credit Entry.*

EQUITIES, OWNER'S. Claims against assets by owners.

EXPENDITURES. Payment for acquiring an asset or service.

EXPENSE. A decrease in owners' equity resulting from the operation of the business. Also, a class term for expenditures recognized as operating costs of a current or past period.

EXPENSE, ACCRUED. A liability account arising from expenses that are incurred prior to the related expenditure; for example, accrued wages.

EXPENSE, PREPAID. An expense recognized after a relevant expenditure; an expense for future benefits.

FINANCIAL CONDITION. The results conveyed by presenting the assets, liabilities, and capital of an enterprise in the form of a balance sheet. Sometimes called financial position.

FIRST-IN, FIRST-OUT (FIFO). Applied in pricing an inventory where the cost of the last items received are assigned to the ending inventory.

FISCAL YEAR. An accounting period of 12 successive calendar months not starting on January 1 and ending December 31.

FIXED ASSET. An asset with a life longer than a single accounting period.

F.O.B. DESTINATION. Transportation terms in which the seller is responsible for the transportation charge.

F.O.B. SHIPPING POINT. Transportation terms in which the buyer is responsible for the transportation charges.

GENERAL LEDGER. A book containing accounts in which are classified, usually in summary form, all transactions of a business enterprise using the double-entry method.

GOODWILL. An intangible asset representing the difference between the purchase price and the value of the tangible assets purchased.

INCOME STATEMENT. An accounting report of the extent to which the owners' equity has increased or decreased during a given period of time, and the specific factors responsible for the change; a statement of revenues and expenses for a given period.

INCOME, NET. Excess of total revenues over total expenses in a given period. (See also *Accrual Concept.*)

INDIRECT RESOURCES. Indirect resources are resources that can be associated with one or more work areas (i.e., subfunctions) because there is only a logical and not readily measurable relationship between them. Space is typically categorized as an indirect resource.

INTANGIBLE ASSET. Any nonphysical asset, such as goodwill or patent that has no physical existence. Its value is dependent on the rights that posession confers upon the owner.
Example: Franchise.

INTERNAL CONTROLS. The methods and procedures adopted within a business to safeguard assets and control its operations.

INTEREST. Charge for the use of money.

INVENTORY. Goods being held for sale, and material and partly finished products that upon completion will be sold.

INVOICE. An itemized statement of goods bought or sold, delivered, or services rendered.

JOURNAL. A book of original entry where transactions are initially recorded in chronological order.

LAPPING. The substitution of checks for cash received. A term used in embezzlement schemes.

LAST-IN, FIRST-OUT (LIFO). A method of inventory pricing where the costs of the last goods received are used to value inventory used in operations.

LEDGER. A group of accounts where transactions are recorded from the journal.

LEDGER ACCOUNT. An account that records the changes in value of a particular asset, liability, or ownership.

LESSEE. The person or company possessing and using a leased item.

LESSOR. The person or company holding legal title to a leased item.

LETTER OF CREDIT. A document issued by a bank authorizing designated banks to make payments on demand to a specified individual up to a stated total amount.

LIABILITY. The equity of a creditor or that which is owed to another.

LIABILITY, CURRENT. Obligation that becomes due within a short time, usually one year.

LINE OF CREDIT. A commitment (after careful investigation) by a bank to a borrower to lend money at a stated interest rate for a stated period in the future.

LIQUIDITY. Ability to meet current obligations.

LOSS, NET. Excess of total expenses over total revenues in a given period.

MATURITY OF LOAN. The due date of a loan.

NET WORTH. The excess of asset value over creditor claims; assets − liabilities = net worth (equity).

NET WORTH METHOD. An indirect method of proving unknown or illegal sources of funds by comparing net worth at the beginning and end of a specified period of time.

NOTE. A written promise to repay a loan.

NOTE RECEIVABLE. A debt that is evidenced by a note or other written acknowledgment.

OVERHEAD RESOURCES. Overhead resources are resources that can be associated with one or more work areas (i.e., subfunctions) because there is only a logical and not readily measurable relationship betwen them. Space is typically categorized as an indirect resource.

PAR VALUE. A specified amount printed on the face of a stock certificate; not to be confused with market value.

PETTY CASH FUND. Established for a small payment (e.g., postage) to avoid writing checks for small amounts; fund should contain cash and receipts for money spent (cash paid out slips).

PHYSICAL INVENTORY, TAKING OF. Counting all merchandise on hand, usually at the end of an accounting period.

POSTING. Transfer of an entry from the journal to a ledger account.

PROFIT AND LOSS ACCOUNT. A temporary account to which are transferred revenue and expense accounts at the end of an accounting period.

PROFIT, GROSS. Sales minus cost of goods sold.

PROFIT, NET. The excess of revenues over expenses.

PROSPECTUS. A summary of a corporation registration statement designed to inform prospective purchaser of securities. It must contain a fairly extensive disclosure statement of essential facts pertinent to the security.

PURCHASE ORDER. Used by the purchasing department in placing an order with a supplier.

REGISTRATION STATEMENT. A statement describing in detail the financial condition of a corporation, its business, and the reasons it proposes to offer an issue of stocks or bonds to the public.

RESOURCE UNIT. A resource unit is the metric used to measure or determine the amount of a resource used to provide a particular subfunction. Only one resource unit should be associated with each resource. Examples of resource units are CPU seconds, for a CPU; number of hours, for operations staff; and square footage, for space occupancy. The resource unit selected should be an accurate metric of the dominant type of work performed by the resource. Resource units may or may not be the same as some of the service units.

REVENUE. An increase in owner's equity arising from operations. Measured by an inflow of assets received in exchange for goods or services.

SALES. An account that records the sale of merchandise.

SERVICE. A service is any work done by the DP facility for a user or group of users. In order to be formally classified as a service, the DP facility's work must be measured by a single metric (called a service unit) that has billing rate associated with it. A service can be as simple as a CPU service, for which a service unit is a CPU second, or as complex as a payroll service, for which a service unit is a printed check.

SERVICE UNIT. A service unit is the metric used to measure the amount of service received by the users. Only one service unit can be associated with each service. Examples of service units are CPU seconds, for a CPU service; lines printed for a printing service; and checks processed, for a payroll service. The service unit selected should be an accurate metric of the dominant type of work performed by the service. If a single unit cannot be determined, then the possibility of dividing the work into two services should be considered.

SHELL CORPORATION. One that has no assets or liabilities, simply a charter to do business.

SINGLE ENTRY. A system of accounting for financial transactions that make no effort to balance accounts.

SOURCE AND APPLICATION OF FUNDS. An indirect method of determining unknown or illegal sources of funds by comparison of all known expenditures with all known receipts during a particular period of time.

STATED VALUE. A specified amount usually set near the amount the corporation actually receives from the sale of stock; the amount at which stock is recorded on the balance sheet.

STOCK, AUTHORIZED. The number of shares authorized by directors, for issuance to investors.

STOCK, CERTIFICATE. A document evidencing ownership in a corporation.

STOCKHOLDERS. An owner of an incorporated business, the ownership being evidenced by stock certificates.

STOCK, ISSUED. The number of shares of stock actually sold or distributed by a corporation.

STOCK, PREFERRED. The class of stock entitled to preferential treatment with regard to dividends or with regard to the distribution of assets in the event of liquidation.

STOCK, OUTSTANDING. Issued stock less treasury stock (stock purchased back by the company and not yet resold).

STOCK SPLIT. An exchange of the shares outstanding for two or more times their number.

SUBFUNCTION. A subfunction is a discrete work area for which costs can be accumulated and work measurements made. A group of similar machines whose use is measured by a common unit can be considered a subfunction. A work function is usually made up of one or more subfunctions, and a subfunction is always contained within one work function. Costs are accumulated by subfunction in order to obtain a more detailed understanding of the costs of operating the DP facility and to distribute the costs to the service centers. Examples of subfunctions for a computer operation work function are central processing unit, core memory, storage devices, channels, and spooling functions.

SURPLUS, CAPITAL. An increase in owner's equity not generated through the company's earnings.

T-ACCOUNT. Form for recording increases and decreases on either side of vertical line, with account title on the top. (See also *Account*.) It is used for demonstrating the effect of transactions on various accounts.

TRANSACTIONS. Each business event that is recorded in the accounting records.

TRIAL BALANCE (WORKING TRIAL BALANCE). A list of the account balances arranged in "balance sheet order" by debits and credits with adjustment columns for entries. It is used as a basis summary for financial statements.

UNDERWRITER. A person or firm guaranteeing (and usually participating in) the marketing of securities to the public. The guarantee states the dollar amount that the underwriter guarantees that the corporation will receive from the sale.

UNDERWRITING SYNDICATE. A group of underwriters formed for the purpose of guaranteeing the successful sale of a particular issue of securities.

USER. A user is an organizational or programmatic entity (whether a single person or an entire company) that receives DP service. A user may also be either internal or external to the department responsible for the DP facility.

VOUCHER SYSTEM. A control system within a company for cash payment.

WORK UNIT. A work unit is the metric used to measure or determine the amount of a subfunction used to provide the services of a given service center. Only one work unit should be associated with each subfunction. Examples of work units are CPU second, for a CPU subfunction; number of hours, for an applications software development subfunction; and number of lines, for a printing subfunction. The work units selected for a subfunction should be an accurate metric of the dominant type of work performed by the subfunction. Work units may or may not be the same as some of the resource or service units.

WORKSHEET. Prepared by an accountant as a way of organizing accounting data.

Index